Talking Consent

16 Workshops on Relationship and Sex Education for Schools and Other Youth Settings

Thalia Wallis and Pete Wallis

Jessica Kingsley Publishers
London and Philadelphia

First published in Great Britain in 2021 by Jessica Kingsley Publishers
An Hachette Company

1

Copyright © Thalia Wallis and Pete Wallis 2021

Safestories is used with kind permission from SAFE!
Protective Behaviours exercises are used with kind permission and guidance from the Protective Behaviours Consortium
Exercise on eliciting ground rules is used with kind permission from Belinda Hopkins
The Wheel of Consent is used with kind permission from Betty Martin
Illustrations from *What Does Consent Really Mean?* have been reproduced with kind permission from Joseph Wilkins
Joseph Wilkins's website: www.josephwilkins.co.uk
The PSHE Curriculum themes are reproduced with kind permission of the PSHE Association
The FRIES image is reproduced with kind permission from Planned Parenthood

Front cover image source: Joseph Wilkins.

Content warning: Contains strong language and references to sex and sexual violence.

A CIP catalogue record for this title is available from the British Library and the Library of Congress

ISBN 978 1 78775 081 4
eISBN 978 1 78775 082 1

Printed and bound by CPI Group (UK) Ltd, Croydon, CR0 4YY

Jessica Kingsley Publishers' policy is to use papers that are natural, renewable and recyclable products
and made from wood grown in sustainable forests. The logging and manufacturing processes
are expected to conform to the environmental regulations of the country of origin.

Jessica Kingsley Publishers
73 Collier Street
London N1 9BE, UK

www.jkp.com

Contents

Introduction

As a result of campaigns such as #MeToo, issues of risk, safety, sexual abuse and harassment have increasingly been on the public radar. There is a growing understanding of the damaging impact of sexual abuse, and an increasing number of services and resources aimed at supporting individuals affected by sexual violence, to help them in processing those traumatic experiences. Although a holistic and supportive response to sexual violence is essential, the best way to address sexual trauma is through prevention. By equipping children and young people with the values, knowledge and skills that they need to navigate consent, we build more resilient, communicative and trusting communities which are protective factors against sexual violence occurring.

Consent is a challenging aspect of life for young people and can also be a tricky topic for us grown-ups. As adults, we may have our own problems around sexuality and relationships to contend with, and we inevitably bring our personal experience and beliefs into the mix. Initiating a discussion with teenagers about relationships – particularly in the context of the rising number of sexual assaults, sexist 'banter' and issues such as 'sexting', pornography, revenge porn, child sexual exploitation and sexual bullying – can feel daunting. We may feel ill-equipped to have these conversations with young people, and educational settings can fall short when integrating relationships education into the curriculum. And yet it is crucial. We need to listen to our young people (and their families) and hear what is important to them. We then need to give young people the opportunity to learn, explore and develop the values, skills and knowledge they are asking for with trusted adults in a safe environment, as they find their way into adulthood.

Talking Consent offers ideas for adults to structure exploratory conversations with young people around consent, dispel some common myths and misconceptions, and encourage discussion between peers. It includes plans full of activities and exercises for use in PSHE lessons, groupwork, assemblies, workshops or with individuals, as well as providing guidance for the adult and suggestions for how to respond to questions frequently asked by young people. Consent is relevant to everyone, and this book aims to be inclusive of young people from every background, ethnicity, faith, gender, the LGBTQI+ community and those with disabilities and special needs.

LGBTQI+ is an acronym for lesbian, gay, bisexual, transgender, queer or questioning and intersex, with a plus sign meant to cover anyone else who's not included. Stonewall has a useful glossary with a definition of each of these words on its website.[1] Although LGBTQI+ is used here, the language around sexual orientation and gender identity changes as times and attitudes change, and there isn't complete agreement on the most inclusive terminology. If in doubt, check with a reputable organization (such as Stonewall) for advice.

As well as providing a general resource, *Talking Consent* is tailored to the requirement for schools to deliver lessons on consent under current legislation. Relationships, sex and health education (RSE) classes are compulsory in all schools under the Children and Social Work Act 2017, and all 'pupils of compulsory school age' must learn about the relationship aspect of RSE.[2] Parents can't withdraw their children from this element, and the authors welcome making the teaching of consent compulsory. Most secondary schools already run assemblies, workshops and PSHE classes on consent. Ofsted is increasingly focussing on the behaviour and attitudes of students, and the benefits of helping young people feel equipped to make wise and informed choices and manage intimate relationships will reach far beyond the school gates.

This book is designed to accompany *What Does Consent Really Mean?*[3] – a graphic novel on consent for teenagers aimed at initiating discussions around healthy relationships and positive exploration of sexuality and consent. *Talking Consent* can be used alongside *What Does Consent Really Mean?* or as a stand-alone resource for use in schools, colleges and other youth settings, family centres, counselling services, children's social care, youth justice and victim services, and sexual health services, as well as by parents. There are additional PowerPoint presentations, resources and handouts that can be downloaded from https://libraryjkp.papertrell.com using the voucher code PAAZOKE. Although the book is primarily aimed at a younger audience, most higher education institutions and universities now run workshops and other events on consent, and the themes and exercises here are as relevant for young adults as they are for teenagers.

Disclaimer

Although learning about consent is an important life skill, these resources cannot replace the professional duty of care placed upon adults to protect children and young people from abuse.

These resources and exercises are offered as possible activities for use by adults

---

1   Stonewall (n.d.) 'Glossary of terms.' Accessed on 5/2/2020 at www.stonewall.org.uk/help-advice/glossary-terms
2   DfE (2019) *Relationships Education, Relationships and Sex Education (RSE) and Health Education: Statutory guidance for governing bodies, proprietors, head teachers, principals, senior leadership teams, teachers.* Accessed on 27/1/2020 at https://assets.publishing.service.gov.uk/government/uploads/system/uploads/attachment_data/file/805781/Relationships_Education__Relationships_and_Sex_Education__RSE__and_Health_Education.pdf
3   Wallis, P. and Wallis, T. (2018) *What Does Consent Really Mean?* London: Jessica Kingsley Publishers.

working with young people on the basis that they will be carefully assessed and selected as part of a planned approach to teaching about consent. Before using them, please give due consideration to ensure that they are relevant to the context, age, maturity and any special requirements or needs of the young people in your care. In addition to being appropriate for your audience, please bear in mind the wider community, which includes parents, staff, management and governors, making sure that you are bringing them along with you in your decisions. Follow the advice below, particularly on safeguarding, and ensure that support is available for both the young people and yourself. The authors are unable to take responsibility for any offence or harm caused. Seek advice from the PSHE Association or the Sex Education Forum if you are unsure.

The conversation about consent is rapidly evolving. If you try any of these materials, please share your experience of what works and what needs changing.

Why Is This Important?

Following a number of high-profile cases, concern about sexual violence and the culture surrounding it has risen up the agenda, sparking international campaigns such as #MeToo and Time's Up. The statistics for younger people are shocking. Estimates vary, but it is thought that between one in 20 and one in five children and young people will experience sexual abuse before they are 18,[5] and studies have found that one in three girls between the ages of 16 and 18 experience unwanted sexual touching/'groping' at school.[6] One in three girls and 16% of boys report that they have experienced sexual violence from a partner,[7] and one school had reports of intimate partner violence and sexual abuse in children as young as 12.[8] In a study commissioned by the British Board of Film Classification in 2019, more than half (51%) of 11–13-year-olds reported that they had seen

> 'I think SRE should be taken seriously as it helps children and young people be safe and understand what is happening to them.'
>
> – Boy, 13
>
> 'I trust my parents to talk to me about values. At school what I need in sex and relationships education is to understand about sex and relationships, and to understand what different people think.'
>
> – Girl, 16[4]

---

4   Quotations from Brook/PSHE Association/Sex Education Forum (2014) *Sex and Relationships Education (SRE) for the 21st Century: Supplementary advice to the Sex and Relationship Education Guidance DfEE (0116/2000).* Accessed on 27/1/2020 at www.pshe-association.org.uk/curriculum-and-resources/resources/sex-and-relationship-education-sre-21st-century

5   NSPCC (2019) 'Statistics briefing: Child sexual abuse.' Accessed on 23/2/2020 https://learning.nspcc.org.uk/media/1710/statistics-briefing-child-sexual-abuse.pdf. The Crime Survey for England and Wales (CSEW) estimated that 7.5% of adults aged 18–74 years experienced sexual abuse before the age of 16 years (3.1 million people); this includes both adult and child perpetrators: Office for National Statistics (2019) 'Child sexual abuse in England and Wales: year ending March 2019.' Accessed on 23/2/2020 at www.ons.gov.uk/peoplepopulationandcommunity/crimeandjustice/articles/childsexualabuseinenglandandwales/yearendingmarch2019

6   End Violence Against Women (2010) 'YouGov poll exposes high levels sexual harassment in schools.' Accessed on 23/2/2020 at www.endviolenceagainstwomen.org.uk/yougov-poll-exposes-high-levels-sexual-harassment-in-schools

7   A landmark report on teenage partner violence conducted by the University of Bristol and the NSPCC involved a confidential survey completed by 1,353 young people, between 13 and 17 years old, from eight schools in England, Scotland and Wales: Baxter, C., McCarry, M., Berridge, D. and Evans, K. (2009) 'Partner exploitation and violence in teenage intimate relationships.' Accessed on 23/2/2020 at www.womenssupportproject.co.uk/userfiles/file/partner_exploitation_and_violence_summary_wdf68093.pdf

8   Lights, Camera and Action Against Dating Violence (Lights4Violence), www.lights4violence.eu

pornography at some point, rising to 66% of 14–15-year-olds.[9] A Childline survey of 13–18-year-olds conducted in 2013 found that 60% had been asked for a sexually explicit image or video of themselves, 40% had created an image or video of themselves, and a quarter had sent this to someone else. A majority report being 'coerced' to do so.[10] Young people spend large amounts of time in an online world, and while the internet brings huge benefits and opportunities, for some it can be a scary and unsafe place.

What we know about the adolescent brain is that at the point at which young people are starting to develop an interest in sex, their decision-making skills are still a work in progress. The prefrontal cortex, the rational part of the brain that gives us good judgement and awareness of consequences, isn't fully developed, and teenagers may rely on the amygdala, the emotional part, to process information and make decisions. If they start experimenting with sexual behaviour without the knowledge, understanding and skills to keep themselves and others safe, young people may be at particular risk of either perpetrating or becoming a victim of abuse.

It is difficult to disentangle the statistics to establish whether the apparent rise in sexual offending is a result of an increasing number of incidents or greater awareness and reporting of these issues. What we do know is that sexual abuse in any form has a detrimental impact on the lives and futures of young people.

A Sex Education Forum survey of young people in 2013 found that although most know the basic legal facts about sexual consent, they are less sure about how consent works in real-life relationship situations, and don't know where to go for help if they need it.[11] A report by London Metropolitan University found that young people don't always recognize non-consensual situations including rape, and that victims are blamed for their abuse and rape by both girls and boys.[12] The study found that young people interpret consent as a simple yes-or-no issue, and may not grasp the contextual factors that can impede someone's ability to give or withhold consent.

As adults, we have a responsibility to teach young people about consent, develop their relationship skills and help them to recognize and challenge abusive behaviour. Young people want to learn about consent. When asked about their experience of sex and relationships education, older teenagers typically say that it was 'too little, too late and too biological'.[13] Talking about sex and relationships does not encourage young people to go out and have sex. In fact, consent skills are important in every aspect of life.

9   2344 parents and young people participated in the research, which was carried out by Revealing Reality. BBFC (2019) 'Children see pornography as young as seven, new report finds.' Accessed on 23/2/2020 at https://bbfc.co.uk/about-bbfc/media-centre/children-see-pornography-young-seven-new-report-finds

10   Childline (2014) 'Under Pressure – What's affected children in April 2013–March 2014', p.44. Accessed on 23/2/2020 at www.nspcc.org.uk/globalassets/blocks/testing/cl_report_under-pressure_final_online.pdf

11   Brook/PSHE Association/Sex Education Forum (2014) *Sex and Relationships Education (SRE) for the 21st Century: Supplementary advice to the Sex and Relationship Education Guidance DfEE (0116/2000).* Accessed on 27/1/2020 at www.pshe-association.org.uk/curriculum-and-resources/resources/sex-and-relationship-education-sre-21st-century

12   Coy, M., Kelly, L., Elvines, F., Garner, M. and Kanyeredzi, A. (2014) *Sex Without Consent: New Research on Young People's Understandings of Sexual Consent.* London: CWASU.

13   Brook/PSHE Association/Sex Education Forum (2014) *Sex and Relationships Education (SRE) for the 21st Century: Supplementary advice to the Sex and Relationship Education Guidance DfEE (0116/2000),* p.13. Accessed on 27/1/2020 at www.pshe-association.org.uk/curriculum-and-resources/resources/sex-and-relationship-education-sre-21st-century

However, they are essential when it comes to sexual interactions, where the consequence of getting it wrong is the difference between sharing a beautiful and intimate experience and abuse. We want conversations about consent between young people to become as ordinary as putting on a seat belt.

We can also open up a discussion with young people about the more pernicious aspects of the society they are growing up in when it reinforces stereotypes, normalizes and excuses sexual violence against women in the media and popular culture, and blames the people harmed for the abuse they suffer. We have found that young people are acutely aware of the pressures they are under to conform to gender expectations, which they know to be unrealistic and unfair, and of the consequences if they choose not to buy into that pressure. Part of the conversation is to build young people's confidence and self-esteem to enable them to challenge these prevailing attitudes and to change the conversation.

Well-taught sex and relationship education provides essential tools for life, strengthening young people's ability to make conscious, satisfying, healthy and respectful choices in their relationships and to stay safe both on- and offline. It is no surprise that research finds that when young people are healthy and happy and feel safe and secure in school, they do better.[14]

The Aims of *Talking Consent*

Talking Consent provides space and time for young people:

- to understand consent and how it works in every type of relationship
- to be confident in seeking and gaining consent
- to practise safe, respectful language and behaviour and reduce harmful behaviours
- to learn about safety and risk in relationships, recognizing exploitation and abuse
- to embrace diversity and be inclusive of difference
- to challenge stereotypes, prejudice and discrimination
- to counterbalance distortions in popular culture and the media and the impact of pornography
- to safeguard young people and support those who disclose abuse, including online
- to foster a healthy culture and sense of belonging with all members of the community
- to identify and strengthen networks of support and access to help
- to develop self-understanding and grow in confidence, empathy and resilience.

---

14 University of Hertfordshire and PSHE Association (2016) *Evidence Briefing: PSHE Education, Pupil Wellbeing and Safety at School.* London: PSHE Association.

What Is High-Quality Sex and Relationships Education?

The PSHE Association outlines the principles of high-quality RSE in all schools – including those with a religious character.

Sex and relationships education:

- is a partnership between home and school
- starts early and is relevant to pupils at each stage in their development and maturity
- is taught by people who are trained and confident in talking about issues such as healthy and unhealthy relationships, equality, pleasure, respect, abuse, sexuality, gender identity, sex and consent
- includes the acquisition of knowledge, the development of life skills and respectful attitudes and values
- has sufficient time to cover a wide range of topics, with a strong emphasis on relationships, consent, rights, responsibilities to others, negotiation and communication skills, and accessing services
- helps pupils understand on- and offline safety, consent, violence and exploitation
- is both medically and factually correct, and treats sex as a normal and pleasurable fact of life
- is inclusive of difference: gender identity, sexual orientation, disability, ethnicity, culture, age, faith or belief, or other life experience
- uses active learning methods and is rigorously planned, assessed and evaluated
- helps pupils understand a range of views and beliefs about relationships and sex in society including some of the mixed messages about gender, sex and sexuality from different sources, including the media
- teaches pupils about the law and their rights to confidentiality even if they are under 16, and is linked to school-based and community health services and organizations
- promotes equality in relationships, recognizes and challenges gender inequality, and reflects girls' and boys' different experiences and needs.[15]

Requirements for RSE Delivery in School

Schools have a statutory responsibility under Section 78 of the Education Act 2002 to support pupils' 'spiritual, moral, cultural, mental and physical development' and prepare

---

15 Brook/PSHE Association/Sex Education Forum (2014) *Sex and Relationships Education (SRE) for the 21st Century: Supplementary advice to the Sex and Relationship Education Guidance DfEE (0116/2000).* Accessed on 27/1/2020 at www.pshe-association.org.uk/curriculum-and-resources/resources/sex-and-relationship-education-sre-21st-century

them 'for the opportunities, responsibilities and experiences of later life'.[16] To help achieve this the National Curriculum stipulates that 'all schools should make provision for personal, social, health and economic education (PSHE)'. The PSHE Association provides guidance and resources on all aspects of PSHE, including 10 principles for effective PSHE education.[17]

PSHE is organized around three core themes: Core Theme 1 – Health and Wellbeing; Core Theme 2 – Relationships; and Core Theme 3 – Living in the Wider World. Although there is some overlap and flexibility between the core themes, consent largely falls under the second core theme, Relationships.

The Relationships Education, Relationships and Sex Education and Health Education (England) Regulations 2019[18] make relationships education compulsory for all pupils receiving primary education, and relationships and sex education (RSE) compulsory for all pupils receiving secondary education. The guidance sets out the content to cover in RSE, while giving schools the freedom to decide how this will be delivered, stating that '[e]ffective teaching in these subjects will ensure that core knowledge is broken down into units of manageable size and communicated clearly to pupils, in a carefully sequenced way, within a planned programme or lessons'.[19]

From Key Stage 1, primary schools lay the foundations for RSE by introducing the core themes and principles of healthy relationships, with topics and content appropriate to the children's age and stage. Year 1 children learn about their bodies and their relationships. Year 2 explores the differences between boys and girls, and teaches about personal hygiene and looking after other people. Year 3 looks at relationships and friendships, including bullying behaviours, conflict resolution and developing and maintaining support networks. Year 4 RSE is about puberty. In Year 5 children learn about adult relationships and consent. Year 6 RSE starts to cover sex and conception.

Secondary RSE revisits, reinforces and expands on these themes, further developing the young people's knowledge, understanding and skills. The Department for Education (DfE) provides a summary of what is expected when teaching about healthy relationships, sexual consent, exploitation and abuse, which forms the content of the workshops offered in *Talking Consent*:

> The importance of teaching young people about consent is central to learning about healthy, equal and safe relationships and choices... Pupils should be taught about all aspects of the law and sexual consent – notably that, in the law on

16 DfE (2014) 'Statutory guidance. National curriculum in England: framework for key stages 1 to 4', para 2.1. Accessed on 27/1/2020 at www.gov.uk/government/publications/national-curriculum-in-england-framework-for-key-stages-1-to-4/the-national-curriculum-in-england-framework-for-key-stages-1-to-4

17 PSHE Association (2014) 'Ten principles of effective PSHE education.' Accessed on 27/1/2020 at www.pshe-association.org.uk/curriculum-and-resources/resources/ten-principles-effective-pshe-education

18 Under sections 34 and 35 of the Children and Social Work Act 2017.

19 Department for Education (2019) *Relationships Education, Relationships and Sex Education (RSE) and Health Education: Statutory guidance for governing bodies, proprietors, head teachers, principals, senior leadership teams, teachers*, p.8. Accessed on 27/1/2020 at https://assets.publishing.service.gov.uk/government/uploads/system/uploads/attachment_data/file/805781/Relationships_Education__Relationships_and_Sex_Education__RSE__and_Health_Education.pdf

sexual offences, the onus is on getting rather than giving consent. As a principle, RSE should promote equality in relationships and emphasise the importance of seeking and gaining mutual consent through positive and active communication, and go beyond teaching how to say 'no'. Pupils should be taught how to identify behaviour in a relationship which is positive and supportive and that which is exploitative and controlling. Pupils should understand the impact of a pernicious culture that reinforces stereotyped and gendered expectations for both boys and girls, including blaming victims for the abuse they experience and other cultural norms and negative stereotypes that they experience and observe. Pupils should also develop the skills for negotiating consent and managing the feelings associated with their experiences, and how to seek help and support if they need it. Crucially, learning should open up discussion about real-life situations.[20]

The guidance is clear about RSE being inclusive of all relationships:

At the point at which schools consider it appropriate to teach their pupils about LGBT, they should ensure that this content is fully integrated into their programmes of study for this area of the curriculum rather than delivered as a standalone unit or lesson. Schools are free to determine how they do this, and we expect all pupils to have been taught LGBT content at a timely point as part of this area of the curriculum.[21]

Mapping an RSE Programme to Statutory Guidance with the PSHE Association Programme of Study

The PSHE Association publishes a programme of study for each age group, with suggested learning opportunities and detailed guidance on the topics to be covered in RSE. The PSHE Association also provides guidance on mapping programmes to statutory guidance on RSE.[22]

This book outlines which PSHE Association curriculum theme is covered in each of the 16 workshop plans. We have used the PSHE Association curriculum for Key Stage 3 and Key Stage 4, but it is for you to use your discretion in choosing which age group you teach this material to.

Talking Consent has been written in the UK, references UK laws and is oriented to the

---

20 Brook/PSHE Association/Sex Education Forum (2014) *Sex and Relationships Education (SRE) for the 21st Century: Supplementary advice to the Sex and Relationship Education Guidance DfEE (0116/2000)*, p.9. Accessed on 27/1/2020 at www.pshe-association.org.uk/curriculum-and-resources/resources/sex-and-relationship-education-sre-21st-century. Please note that this document was published in 2014, in line with the previous Sex and Relationship Education Guidance (2000). Schools may still find it useful to consult this document but should also ensure they meet the criteria of the new updated statutory guidance (2019).

21 Department for Education (2019) 'Relationships education, relationships and sex education (RSE) and health education: Statutory guidance for governing bodies, proprietors, head teachers, principals, senior leadership teams, teachers.' Accessed on 23/2/2020 at www.gov.uk/government/publications/relationships-education-relationships-and-sex-education-rse-and-health-education

22 PSHE Association (2019) *We've got it covered... Mapping the PSHE Association Programme of Study to the new statutory guidance on health education and relationships education/RSE.* Accessed on 27/1/2020 at www.pshe-association.org.uk/system/files/Mapping%20PoS%20to%20Statutory%20guidance%20July%202019%20update.pdf

UK PSHE Association curriculum, but any of the content can be applied and adapted to consent work with young people in other settings and locations.

Spiral Curriculum

Assemblies, workshops and lessons on consent work best when they form part of a 'spiral curriculum' approach to PSHE, reinforcing previous learning rather than being presented as random topics which come out of the blue. The UNESCO International Standards for Sexuality Education (2018)[23] suggest that RSE is developed through themes that are 'repeated multiple times with increasing complexity, building on previous learning using a spiral-curriculum approach'. When planning RSE, check out what has previously been covered. Although secondary RSE will be more complex and challenging than primary RSE, reflecting the young people's increasing independence, social awareness and experience, the principles of healthy relationships are the same, and RSE will be covering the core themes introduced at primary school.

Assessment of Need

To ensure that RSE is relevant and tailored to young people's needs, it is helpful to elicit their views when planning, delivering and evaluating a scheme of work. A range of activities can be used to give the children a voice, either as individuals, in a focus group or as a whole class. Post-it notes or online surveys can be used at the start as well as the end of a workshop or programme to establish a baseline against which any achievement of course objectives can be monitored. Circles, quizzes, debating, attitude or knowledge continuums, graffiti sheets, mind-maps and storyboards can help to assess current understanding, identify gaps in knowledge and skills, and highlight any misconceptions or harmful attitudes. Before introducing something new, you could ask the children to reflect on their previous experience of RSE. What have they found helpful? What might have been done better? What are their ideas for next steps? A flexible approach will ensure that RSE responds to the children's needs rather than being imposed as a standardised package.

Selecting the Topic and Considering the Audience

It is worth considering the timing and context of a programme or workshop session on sexuality and consent. Is it best to have a whole day on consent or several shorter sessions? Could it be integrated with sessions from the school nurse on sexual health? Consider what the young people will be doing immediately following the lesson, and where they can go if they have any lingering questions or concerns.

---

23 PSHE Association (2018) 'PSHE Association response to call for evidence on RSE and PSHE', p.1. Accessed on 23/2/2020 at www. pshe-association.org.uk/system/files/PSHE%20Association%20call%20for%20evidence%20response_0.pdf

The exercises here can be used individually or delivered to groups of young people in class, workshops or assemblies. You can choose one topic, pull out an individual exercise, adapt the workshops into shorter sessions or go through the whole scheme from start to finish. Some students report that they feel safer and more able to engage when sessions are delivered separately to those who identify as male or as female. Others report that they get more out of the discussion and benefit from hearing other perspectives when sessions are delivered in mixed-sex groups. This can also provide experience of conversations with peers from the opposite sex and empowerment to continue these conversations. Consulting and involving young people will help to inform staff of the best way to provide sessions where all can feel sufficiently safe and comfortable to engage.

The problem with delivering RSE through assemblies:

> 'You don't really learn, people don't listen in assembly.'

> 'You can't ask questions in assembly, you feel judged...'

With workshops on consent, it is not 'one size fits all'. What works with one group doesn't necessarily work with another. When creating a scheme of work, consider the age, maturity and ability of the young people. Sometimes large group conversations work well, and at other times smaller groups or one-to-one sessions are more likely to be successful. Assemblies can be a powerful way to engage a whole year group, but always need to be followed up with smaller classes or workshops. Select the exercises and adjust the language accordingly, while keeping it real and relevant.

Listening to the views of the children will focus your teaching on the needs of the audience. When designing a programme, consider the context of your school and its neighbourhood, and research any issues that are topical locally as well as nationally. RSE is all about relationships, and the school behaviour record may indicate the kinds of behaviour and incidents of concern that could be helpfully addressed through RSE, providing a baseline for evaluating the impact of PSHE programmes. It can be good to hear the views of colleagues, through staff meetings or inset days, and it is important to let the team know what is being planned so that they can support the young people and reinforce their learning.

A Holistic Approach

Attending a few sessions on consent in isolation will not equip young people with the knowledge, values and skills to develop healthy, consensual relationships. A holistic approach is required. In a school setting, relationships education can be embedded in the ethos of the organization, creating a whole-school approach where time and care is given to building respectful relationships between all members of the school community. Ideally, details of this holistic approach will be shared through publicly available policies. One small step is to put posters about consent and healthy relationships in the classroom and around school; there are plenty available.[24] Another step is for all professionals to have the confidence to encourage a conversation about consent outside PSHE lessons, and capitalise on those spontaneous teachable moments as they arise.

A holistic approach is also about creating a culture where difference is celebrated, all types of relationships are equally valued, and education is LGBTQI+ inclusive throughout the curriculum. The PSHE curriculum should include the LGBTQI+ community not as an add-on but threaded throughout the programme, with sex education that is inclusive – for example, offering safe-sex advice that relates to all relationships.

The Views of Parents/Carers

Most parents/carers welcome the teaching of RSE. A 2013 NAHT[25] survey found that 88% of the parents of school-aged pupils want RSE to be taught in all schools, and a YouGov Poll (2013) found that 86% of UK adults believe RSE that addresses sexual consent and respectful relationships should be taught in all secondary schools.[26] Parents/carers have the right to withdraw pupils from sex education (but not relationships or health education), and the process that head teachers should follow in considering a request from a parent is set out in the latest DfE guidance.[27] More details can also be found on the PSHE Association website.[28]

When planning a programme on consent in any setting, it is important to give adequate warning to both the young people and their parents/carers that this will be happening. Considering some of the content on the RSE curriculum, some parents/carers will naturally be anxious, and it is important to provide information on what is being taught to their child, and take their views, wishes and concerns into account. Parents/carers may have thoughts about the content and age-appropriateness of the programme. For example, pictures where body parts are on show (including in cartoons) are considered offensive in some religions. Some may fear that conversations about

Comments from LGBTQI+ young people whose experience of RSE was not inclusive:

▷ 'At the end they said, "If you want to talk about LGBT sex afterwards, raise your hand" so nobody did.'

▷ 'LGBT was briefly mentioned but nothing about what's involved in safe sex.'

▷ 'We didn't learn anything about non-binary – it wasn't until I found that out that I was able to understand who I am.'

---

24   For example, www.consentiseverything.com

25   National Association of Head Teachers (NAHT) (2013) 'Press release: Survey data on parents' views on the teaching of issues surrounding pornography in schools 2013.' Copy on file with author.

26   End Violence Against Women (n.d.) 'Government announces compulsory Relationships & Sex Education in all schools.' Accessed on 23/2/2020 at www.endviolenceagainstwomen.org.uk/451-2

27   Department for Education (2019) *Relationships Education, Relationships and Sex Education (RSE) and Health Education: Statutory guidance for governing bodies, proprietors, head teachers, principals, senior leadership teams, teachers.* Accessed on 27/1/2020 at https://assets.publishing.service.gov.uk/government/uploads/system/uploads/attachment_data/file/805781/Relationships_Education__Relationships_and_Sex_Education__RSE__and_Health_Education.pdf

28   www.pshe-association.org.uk/content/what-status-relationships-and-sex-education-rse

consent will expose their child to harmful material or make it more likely that they will engage in sexual activity (although this is not supported in any of the research on sex education).

Although young people say that they prefer to learn about RSE in school,[29] it may be worth reminding parents/carers that a few sessions on consent in school form just part of their child's learning. The Sex Education Forum has found that, for boys, the source of sex education while growing up is through school (39%), followed by friends (24%), with fathers accounting for 3% and mothers 4%.[30] By keeping them informed, parents/carers can be encouraged to have more conversations about consent with their children and to reinforce key messages from PSHE classes when they get home.

There is a range of ways of communicating with parents/carers, from a letter or newsletter to more active consultation via a survey or parents' forum. Government guidance on delivering RSE includes information about how to engage parents and carers (including comments on delivering material related to the LGBTQI+ community).[31] The DfE has provided a guide for parents on the RSE requirements, and the PSHE Association has provided a guide to parental engagement (which includes an overview of statutory requirements regarding withdrawal of pupils from sex education).[32] Websites that give advice for parents/carers about how to talk to their children about sex and consent can be found in Appendix 4.

Links to the Wider School Curriculum

When designing an RSE programme, it is often possible to relate workshops on consent to other subjects on the curriculum. English language texts or topics covered in history, geography or religious education may illustrate the range of attitudes to relationships, sexuality and consent across different times and places. Relationships and sexuality can have resonance with aspects of biology and psychology. Concern about the pressures on young people from advertising could be integrated with media studies, and the safe use of social media will be an important element of computer studies. Conversations about consent can also be creatively explored with art, drama and music, and voice recording and film can be additional tools for learning. Take a look at safestories created by the

29 Sex Education Forum (2019) 'New RSE guidance – the details.' Accessed on 27/1/2020 at www.sexeducationforum.org.uk/news/news/new-rse-guidance-details

30 Sex Education Forum (2019) 'New RSE guidance – the details.' Accessed on 27/1/2020 at www.sexeducationforum.org.uk/news/news/new-rse-guidance-details

31 Department for Education (2019) *Relationships Education, Relationships and Sex Education (RSE) and Health Education: Statutory guidance for governing bodies, proprietors, head teachers, principals, senior leadership teams, teachers.* Accessed on 27/1/2020 at https://assets.publishing.service.gov.uk/government/uploads/system/uploads/attachment_data/file/805781/Relationships_Education__Relationships_and_Sex_Education__RSE__and_Health_Education.pdf

32 'Understanding Relationships, Sex and Health Education at your child's secondary school: A guide for parents', https://assets.publishing.service.gov.uk/government/uploads/system/uploads/attachment_data/file/812594/RSE_secondary_schools_guide_for_parents.pdf; 'Relationships education: Supporting parental engagement', www.pshe-association.org.uk/system/files/Relationships%20Education%20-%20supporting%20parental%20engagement%20Primary.pdf; both accessed on 23/2/2020. See also Associated Press (2019) 'In #MeToo era, states debate teaching consent in schools.' *New York Post.* Accessed on 23/2/2020 at https://nypost.com/2019/05/20/in-metoo-era-states-debate-teaching-consent-in-schools

charity SAFE!,[33] in which small groups of young people created short cartoon animations exploring mobile and internet technologies. The young people developed the characters and script and were involved in the filming and editing.

Who Should Deliver?

Every school or other youth setting will have a different arrangement for delivering workshops on consent. It is important when designing a programme that staff involved are adequately prepared and willing, rather than simply being given the materials and directed to get on with it.

If resources allow, workshops on consent are ideally co-facilitated by a male worker and a female worker. They can be a challenging and potentially exhausting programme to manage. The group may become excitable, or a conversation might trigger a reaction which leads to someone becoming distressed. Two adults will allow one to follow a child out of the room if they need time out or to manage a disclosure. Having another adult in the room, even if they aren't involved in delivery, feels supportive and allows for reflection at the end of the session. Consider whether specific topics might be best introduced by either a male or a female worker – for example, is it important for a man to lead a discussion about toxic masculinity and seek LGBTQI+ speakers as role models?

The conversation can be led by internal staff, but there may be benefit in inviting in a guest speaker to augment an RSE programme; children may feel less inhibited and may talk more openly with a stranger. Schools using an external speaker may wish to consider:

- asking guests to provide information about their background and qualifications, including references and testimonials
- including confidentiality and safeguarding within the contract, and sharing information in advance about any special requirements or needs within the group
- describing the context of the school and its ethos, along with advance notice of particular issues that are topical to ensure that the input is appropriate to the audience
- providing the name of a contact person within the school who will take a lead on planning and follow-up as well as establishing clear lines of communication between the guest facilitator and the designated safeguarding lead.

Working collaboratively with both a guest and staff member from the school can work well. This arrangement allows the staff member to keep the conversation going in subsequent sessions, reinforce any messages and offer ongoing support to individuals.

The Sex Education Forum offers guidance on safe use of external visitors.[34]

---

33   www.safestories.org
34   Sex Education Forum (2010) 'External visitors and RSE.' Accessed on 27/1/2020 at www.sexeducationforum.org.uk/media/3458/external_visitors_and_SRE_10.pdf

Preparation

Launching into a workshop with a group of young people on sexuality, rape culture or pornography can feel daunting. Conversations about consent raise delicate issues that can be challenging for us adults as well as for young people, and it is important to consider your knowledge and skills, resilience, resources and support. Ask yourself: Am I prepared for this?

Before starting a topic, take time to understand the issues, your professional duties and the resources available. Have a copy of the legal definition of consent available and take time to explore what is known in this area, including in popular culture. You need to feel comfortable and confident talking about sex and consent, consent and the law, same-sex relationships, healthy and unhealthy relationships, equality, positive sexuality, porn, abuse, sexting, gender identity, etc. The start of each workshop plan has a brief knowledge section, drawing on research and signposting suitable websites and other resources, but it will be important to read around each topic and keep your knowledge current.

Involve colleagues in your planning and build in sufficient time for preparation, practice and reflection, drawing on them for support. This is not easy stuff to teach, and the material or reactions of the young people may trigger something in you. Check to see what training is available – for example, through the PSHE Association (in one survey 80% of parents thought that teachers should receive training in teaching RSE).[35] Take account of your own wellbeing, ensuring that you have sufficient personal resources, support and supervision. In the context of your wider team, consider individual and collective responsibilities – who needs to be involved in doing what?

If you are a visitor, liaise in advance with staff who can tell you who are the more confident, louder children and which pupils are quieter and more passive. Aim high. An assembly, lesson or workshop that is relevant, active, creative, inspiring and engages everyone's interest will be more enjoyable to teach and have a greater impact.

It is important to know, own and take into account your own core beliefs, opinions and values. Where do they come from? You may hold strong views about a particular topic – for example, pornography or gender double standards – and you are in a powerful position as the adult in the room. However, you're not there to impose your values on others and should be cautious about expressing your own views. Your role is to facilitate conversations about consent, helping young people to develop their knowledge, understanding, skills and moral compass. RSE is all about giving young people a voice, providing factual information and an understanding of consent, and giving them a sense of agency in their lives. If a safe environment is created and you have a good grasp of the material, you won't have to make pronouncements about what is right or wrong, or even challenge misconceptions because the young people will be enabled and empowered to

---

35   Independent poll of 1000 parents cited in Sex Education Forum (2019) 'Relationships and Sex Education: Briefing for Parliamentarians.' Accessed on 23/2/2020 at www.sexeducationforum.org.uk/sites/default/files/field/attachment/Briefing%20 on%20RSE%20for%20Parliamentarians%20-%2025%20Feb%202019%20debate.pdf

do this for each other. Many schools and other youth settings are adopting restorative practice, which is an excellent and empowering approach for managing conversations and developing healthy relationships.[36]

Diversity

Consideration of diversity issues is essential when planning and delivering a session or programme on consent to ensure that the conversation is inclusive and relevant for everyone involved, in line with the Equalities Act 2010. Culture, beliefs and ethnicity play a huge role in people's viewpoints on what is considered 'acceptable' sexual behaviour at different ages. Regardless of their background or ability, every young person needs to understand about healthy relationships, develop confidence in seeking and gaining consent and know where to go for support.

'While we did get taught about sex education, not any of it was sex education for lesbian, gay and bisexual people. Because I was not out at the time, I couldn't ask.'[37]

– Noah, 16, secondary school

Consent is not limited to heterosexual relationships, and RSE can help to foster LGBTQI+ and gender equality. Some adults are shy about talking to young people about same-sex relationships for fear of offending someone or getting it wrong. Young people who are LGBTQI+ are more likely to seek information on the internet for fear of having to come out to get advice,[38] which emphasizes the importance of all sessions being LGBTQI+ inclusive as a matter of course, and for this to be modelled in all the workshops. RSE is an ideal time to speak openly about people who are LGBTQI+ – for example, by making the point that consent is the same for same-sex relationships.

Young people with special educational needs and disability (SEND) are significantly more likely to have experienced and be at risk of abuse,[39] and are also known to have poorer access to sex education.[40] Be sensitive to your audience – for example, by considering the specific learning needs of young people with autistic spectrum disorder in relation to the topics covered in RSE such as communication skills, interpreting cues and boundaries, and managing strong emotions. In deciding which material is appropriate, it may be helpful to talk to your school SEND department for guidance or consult a relevant website – for example, the National Autistic Society.[41]

RSE is also a great opportunity to expand awareness of diversity by exploring how

36   More information can be found at https://transformingconflict.org and https://restorativejustice.org.uk

37   Stonewall (n.d.) *Staying Safe Online*. Accessed on 27/1/2020 at www.youngstonewall.org.uk/system/files/staying_safe_online_guide.pdf

38   Stonewall (n.d.) *Staying Safe Online*. Accessed on 27/1/2020 at www.youngstonewall.org.uk/system/files/staying_safe_online_guide.pdf

39   'Disabled children are at significantly greater risk of physical, sexual and emotional abuse and neglect than non-disabled children.' NSPCC (2014) '"We have the right to be safe": Protecting disabled children from abuse', p.1. Accessed on 27/1/2020 at www.nspcc.org.uk/globalassets/documents/research-reports/right-safe-disabled-children-abuse-report.pdf

40   Sterland, E. (2013) 'Sex education: young people with learning disabilities are being left out.' *The Guardian*. Accessed on 27/1/2020 at www.theguardian.com/social-care-network/2013/sep/17/sex-education-young-people-learning-disabilities

41   National Autistic Society (n.d.) 'Expert top tips – sex and relationship education.' Accessed on 27/1/2020 at www.autism.org.uk/about/communication/sex-education/top-tips.aspx

people from a range of backgrounds both within school, in wider society and across the globe have different values, viewpoints and experiences when it comes to relationships, sexuality and consent. You don't have to know everything about all the different cultures out there, but reflecting on the diversity of culture, family make-up and religious beliefs can develop young people's understanding of and empathy for others. Take a systemic approach, considering the young people in the context of their home, peer group, school, neighbourhood and as global citizens. No one is an island, and consent works at all those different levels.

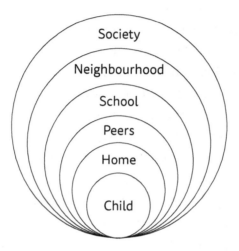

While you may be a respectful and inclusive role model, opening up a conversation about consent can expose harmful beliefs and opinions in your audience. It is fine for young people to express different views, and there may not always be a right or wrong answer on many of the issues discussed. However, be prepared to challenge derogatory comments, prejudices, stereotypes or discriminatory attitudes, particularly if they are directed towards people in the room. If this can be achieved without putting anyone down, gently bring the young people back to the group agreement, with a reminder about treating everyone with respect. It is worth considering in advance the most effective ways to steer or change the conversation when this happens.

It can be equally important to empower the group to challenge each other, so if you hear someone share a harmful belief, you can ask the rest of the group what they think about this and use it as a way of starting a discussion about the negative impact of certain opinions. Sexual violence is unacceptable, and the aim of RSE is to build healthy and respectful relationships.

Types of Stimulus

The workshops offered in *Talking Consent* are designed to help young people develop the knowledge, understanding and life skills to navigate the complexities of relationships and sex. The materials will get them thinking and talking about issues that relate to their own lives, challenge them to explore their attitudes and values, and provide an insight into the range of views and beliefs that exist in society. To get this discussion going, the materials offered here aim higher than completing worksheets or simply watching the 'cup of tea' video (excellent as it is). The sessions are designed to be as thought-provoking, interactive, fun and engaging as possible. Each workshop introduces stimuli to spark discussion, which include video clips, games, debates, cartoons, photos, quizzes and social media campaigns. As you plan your scheme of work, you could add in role plays, drama, lyrics, film projects, related coverage from the media and problem-solving circles. The stimulus materials can also be adapted or supplemented to reflect the context of the school and address issues that are current in the local community or wider society. Ensure that any material introduced into an RSE programme is inclusive of the diversity of beliefs about sex and relationships.

The workshops are accompanied by PowerPoint slides which can be downloaded from https://libraryjkp.papertrell.com using the voucher code PAAZOKE. Many of the slides are optional, and the content contained can be written on a flipchart or turned into handouts. The workshops are not intended to be dominated by slides, and to make the workshops as interactive as possible it is often better to build up ideas on a flipchart. Turn the projector off between slides when it is not in use; people tend to stare at the screen, which becomes the focus of their attention.

Timings and Pace

Schools organize RSE in any number of formats from assemblies and 20-minute slots in tutor groups to full-day events, and the plans and exercises here will need to be adapted as required. The actual time that each activity and session takes in practice will depend on the size and make-up of the group as well as how involved the young people get in the discussions. Delivery should be pacey, but flexible enough to allow for a longer discussion if a topic raises particular questions or concerns for the young people. It works well to have extra ideas for activities up your sleeve and be ready to drop an activity and move on if it isn't meeting the young people's needs. If a whole topic is not covered in one session, consider how to ensure that important elements will be picked up at a later stage.

We want the young people to engage because it is fun, relevant and interesting, not because they are forced to. Each plan has icebreakers and games; these are optional, but they can help to keep the energy up, release tension and regulate the young people so that they are ready to learn.

Delivery Style, Ensuring that the Group is Engaged

The workshops are most likely to run smoothly when they are well prepared and well paced, when you start the session exuding confidence (even if you don't feel it) and expecting full engagement, showing the group that you are really interested in the topic yourself and eager to hear their views. It will help enormously if you are able to learn and use everyone's names, and have eye contact with everyone in the room. When you are establishing the group agreement (see below) and at regular points during the workshop, check that everyone is following what is being discussed. Look for nods or verbal recognition that everyone is on the same page, and don't move on until you are satisfied that each individual is consenting to participate. A lively group is OK, providing the young people are on topic, and it is good practice during small groupwork to drift around the groups, listening and checking that they are doing the exercise.

There is often an element of performance in the role of the facilitator. When teaching about consent, you can include humour and fun, controversial comments or material and pejorative terms (such as 'slut') for generating a lively debate, although you may need to remind the group not to use them outside of class.[42] The aim is to get the young people thinking rather than adopting shock tactics or lecturing them on what they should or shouldn't do. Where possible, treat the young people as the experts, encouraging them to find their own ways through the moral maze that is sexuality and consent. We can offer information and guidance without feeding them pre-conceived advice.

Always make it real, using the young people's language where appropriate and referencing popular culture. If they come up with language that you don't understand, ask – it helps the young people to feel that you have an interest in their lives and allows them to educate you (e.g. they may refer to oral sex as 'Uck'). It is important for the group to know the 'real words' for things (e.g. blowjob/oral sex) to protect them as well. Draw on the latest research to guide you.

Facilitators are role models and a huge influence on the young people when learning about respectful and healthy relationships. Take care with your language and behaviour, being sure to avoid stereotypes, not to judge, shame or blame, or recreate the power dynamics that RSE is designed to challenge. Be aware of any nonverbal messages you may be sending – through frowning, for example. Even subtle body language can feel judgemental and send a negative message to the young people. People who experience harm often don't like to be given the label 'victim', which assigns them an identity based on something that happened without recognizing the many other aspects of them as a person. Rather than talking about 'victims of sexual assault' or 'rape victims', consider referring to 'people who experience sexual abuse' or 'a person who was raped'. Similarly, it may be best not to use labels such as 'rapist' or 'sex offenders', separating harmful words or actions from the person responsible and referring instead to people who commit rape or sexual offences.

Answering Tricky Questions

As far as possible, try to promote an inclusive culture in your group or class, allowing everyone a voice and encouraging respectful sharing and listening. As facilitator, you

---

42   You could note that it is easier to find pejorative terms for females than males. Remind the young people that although they may use the terms in discussing a specific topic (e.g. on victim blaming), they are not to direct them at each other.

can encourage this by using people's names, listening when someone speaks, avoiding filling in, and remaining curious and interested (rather than being interesting).

It is likely that the young people will raise some tricky questions, and it is helpful to be prepared for this. Ensure that you are fully familiar with the material you are using and have done some background research into the issues being discussed. If a young person asks an unexpected question, you may need a moment to decide whether it is helpful for the discussion. Always acknowledge the question and thank the young person for raising an interesting issue. Give an honest answer or, if appropriate and not too sensitive, throw the question back to the whole group, being aware of the impact of the question on the rest of the students: 'What does everyone think? Would anyone like to offer an answer to that question?'

A young person may try to embarrass you or target/trigger another group member, and if a question leaves you flustered, buy some time. It is fine to 'park' the question for discussion later or tell the group that it isn't one that will be discussed during this session, but that you would like to catch up with the young person about it afterwards. Be aware that a question may be an indication of an underlying safeguarding issue. Always follow up if you have any concerns.

Creating a Safe Environment

Conversations about consent work best when a safe enough space can be created for young people to explore new ideas, feel genuine feelings, try out skills and ask questions before meeting these complex and sensitive issues in the real world. It is recommended that every session starts with establishing or reminding the young people of the group agreement or expectations (example ground rules suggested by the PSHE Association can be found in Appendix 7). This helps to establish an atmosphere of respectful communication and provides a clear agreement that you can refer back to, if the group or an individual veers off track.

There are various ways to establish a group contract. It is best to make creating this a shared task rather than simply imposing a list of ready-made rules; at the very least, ensure that everyone nods when you read out the ground rules. Appendix 6 suggests a technique for creating a group agreement that you can try, and you may want to add in some rules of your own that are specific to the topic. For example, you could ask the young people not to point or call out other people if they know that something under discussion has happened to them (such as sexting), and you could agree in advance with the group how you will challenge things that are said that are discriminatory or harmful.

No matter how clear the agreement is, school is not a safe place for many young people, on account of its sheer size and dynamics. It is important to judge how safe you feel you can make the space, and choose the content of your workshop appropriate to that level of safety.

Confidentiality

A classroom can never be confidential space. It is often appropriate to ask the group to agree to keeping the discussion confidential, while recognizing that this is impossible to monitor or guarantee. Remind participants to only share what they would be happy being shared beyond the group, and ask them not to discuss personal issues or ask others to.

If you are a visitor to the school, ask to see the school's policy on confidentiality.

Support Network Signposting

The health of the school community and wellbeing of each child is dependent on the quality of relationships, and RSE relates closely to pastoral care and policy. Identifying and strengthening the children's support in school is essential, ensuring that any RSE programme is integrated with the support provided by form tutors, teaching assistants, the pastoral team, nurse, school counsellor, etc. Use this opportunity to invite staff responsible for safeguarding into the group to ensure that they are approachable. In addition to signposting children to these services, be clear at the end of each session when you are available if a young person needs a listening ear.

Developing support networks is integral to the Protective Behaviours approach, and the impact of RSE will be strengthened if it encourages young people to buddy up, develop peer support networks and mentor one another. RSE can skill young people up to be on the lookout for anyone who may be isolated or ostracized, and encourage them to be an 'Upstander' and not a 'Bystander'. Support networks will include links between home and school, and support locally and nationally (including Childline and online provision). Many young people know the Childline number off by heart; if not, they can be encouraged to memorize it.

You may wish to build in some reflection time, or alternatively add something light and grounding such as a game or the mindfulness exercise in Appendix 8 at the end of a workshop, before sending the children to their next lesson, particularly if the session has been intense.

Safeguarding

By enabling young people to learn about safety and risk in relationships, workshops about consent are a crucial element in meeting school safeguarding obligations, and Ofsted will expect to see quality teaching of RSE as part of a school's preventative programme.

One in three children who are sexually abused don't tell anyone at the time.[43] When you teach about consent, it is almost inevitable that some young people in your group will have experienced abuse or know someone who has. Some children may be particularly

---

43   Think U Know (n.d.) 'Why don't children tell their parents about sexual abuse?' Accessed on 27/1/2020 at www.thinkuknow.co.uk/parents/articles/Why-dont-children-tell-their-parents-about-sexual-abuse

vulnerable to abuse, including those with special educational needs and disability (SEND), young people from the LGBTQI+ community, young carers, gang affiliates and children who are new to the school. It is possible that the content of these sessions could make a young person aware that they have experienced sexual assault or violence and haven't acknowledged it as such. Where there is a safeguarding issue, procedures must be followed regardless of the culture and beliefs within different communities.

Always be mindful of safeguarding. Remain up to date with safeguarding training and be clear about your school's policy and your statutory duties. Know the signs of abuse, child protection procedures and how to handle a disclosure. Go to your designated safeguarding lead if you have any concern, need support or want further information or clarity, and make use of other sources of help from social services, CAMHS, the police, NSPCC and Childline. Act on your gut feeling – your body's early warning signs – and if you hear worrying stuff, escalate it.

One Step Removed: Being Mindful of Trauma

Talking Consent uses case studies and scenarios that are 'one step removed' to distance and de-personalize the discussion. Using third-person references feels safer for teachers and pupils, allowing a focus on 'them' instead of 'me' and 'us'. This enables the young people to express themselves openly and freely and explore their opinions safely without getting negative personal feedback. When talking about these issues, avoid real examples from school, and don't speak about your own experience. Personal disclosures during the session are discouraged to keep the environment safe. Plan in advance how to acknowledge that a pupil has something important to say and that a trusted adult will talk with them in a safer, more private environment where relevant. If a young person does talk about incidents that have happened to them or to others, refer them to the group agreement, taking care not to discount what is possibly important to them. Make a note in case there are wider safeguarding concerns to follow up (see Handling Disclosures below).

There is always the risk that initiating a conversation about consent could potentially be upsetting for a young person who has been abused or knows someone who has, although even neutral content can be a trigger. It is helpful to have some awareness of trauma, including how it presents in the body and in behaviour. While being mindful of the content you are sharing (e.g. avoiding films that depict sexual violence[44]) and sensitive to everyone's needs, it is important to hold on to the fact that whatever happens in your session is unlikely to be as bad as the abuse itself. It is better to have the conversation rather than feel paralysed by anxiety over what might happen if you talk about these issues. It might also be a relief for a young person who has been abused that a previously taboo

---

44 Eaton, J. (2018) *Can I tell you what it feels like? Exploring the harm caused by child sexual exploitation (CSE) films.* Accessed on 27/1/2020 at www.researchgate.net/publication/323150715_Can_I_tell_you_what_it_feels_like_Exploring_the_harm_caused_by_child_sexual_exploitation_CSE_films/citation/download

topic is finally being aired in a safe way. Abuse does happen, and we want young people to be prepared and confident when it comes to sexual consent, and to come forward if they have been harmed. You may never know the impact of a particular session, but even if only one young person is empowered, understood or helped, it will be worthwhile.

Handling Disclosures

There is a strong likelihood when opening up conversations on consent, particularly if young people are feeling heard and perceive that it is a safe environment, that individuals will choose to disclose harmful personal experiences. It is important to plan for this, by ensuring that there are processes and support mechanisms to handle this sensitively. Where possible, deliver classes or groups with a co-facilitator, so that one of you can focus on supporting an individual if they become upset or need to share privately. Discussion on this topic gives permission to young people to talk with someone about their concerns. Ensure that all the young people in the group are signposted to someone in the school (or whatever your setting is), to whom they can speak confidentially if anything comes up for them in the session that they wish to discuss (see Support Network Signposting above). Remind them of any anonymous reporting system that is available, as well as Childline (see Appendix 4).

Evaluation and Eliciting Feedback

After delivering an assembly, workshop or lesson, it is important to elicit feedback from the group to inform future planning. One very simple way of doing this is to give everyone a Post-it note and ask them to reflect on the session: what they have found useful, something they will take away, anything that could have made the session better. It is important for the facilitators to build in time for reflection, to review the learning that has taken place, and decide if a topic/area needs to be repeated or further explored.

In the longer term, consider what outcomes you are trying to achieve through the RSE programme, and how you might know if they are being met. Teaching RSE goes beyond fulfilling a directive from the DfE; getting consent right is crucial for healthy communities where young people feel safe and can develop positive, equal and supportive relationships.

Each workshop is accompanied by a PowerPoint presentation to aid facilitation. There is also an online folder of additional resources and handouts for each workshop. This can all be downloaded from https://libraryjkp.papertrell.com using the voucher code PAAZOKE.

What Does Consent Really Mean?

Informative and cleared up any confusion about consent

Session Overview

This workshop introduces consent, unpicks the concepts of freedom and capacity when making a choice, and explores the 'rules of consent' through the use of scenarios.

Info/Knowledge

RSE requires schools to teach young people the importance of consent, including on social media, and the skills for negotiating mutual consent through equal and respectful communication. Young people need to know about appropriate boundaries and acceptable behaviour, how to recognize risk and stay safe, and where to go for help. The #MeToo movement has raised the importance of consent and the potentially huge consequences of getting it wrong. Young people often know the basic legal facts about consent, but are less confident in real-life relationship situations, and there are some serious misconceptions; research by the sexual health charity FPA found that 37% of young people aged 14–17 learn about consent from TV and film, and 39% feel it's not OK to withdraw consent once you are naked.[1] Consent needs to be an enthusiastic 'Yes', not just an absence of 'No'.

---

1   FPA (n.d.) 'Less than half of people think it's OK to withdraw sexual consent if they're already naked.' Accessed on 27/1/2020 at www.fpa.org.uk/news/less-half-people-think-it%E2%80%99s-ok-withdraw-sexual-consent-if-theyre-already-naked

PSHE Association Curriculum Themes

▷ KS4 R8. About the concept of consent in relevant, age-appropriate contexts

▷ KS4 R15. How to seek consent and to respect others' right to give, not give or withdraw consent to engage in different degrees of sexual activity

▷ KS4 R18. To recognize the impact of drugs and alcohol on choices and sexual behaviour

Exercises

▷ Exercise 1: Introducing Consent
▷ Exercise 2: Exploring Values and Beliefs – Group Debate
▷ Exercise 3: Defining Consent
▷ Exercise 4: Exploring Freedom and Capacity
▷ Exercise 5: Free Choice and Forced 'Choice' Continuum
▷ Exercise 6: The Rules of Consent – Case Studies
▷ Exercise 7: Is Consent as Simple as a Cup of Tea?

Materials Needed

▷ 'Agree', 'Disagree' and 'Neither agree nor disagree' cards for Exercise 1 (Resources and Handouts 1.1)

▷ Handouts of the Rules of Consent for Exercise 6 if not using PowerPoint (Resources and Handouts 1.2)

▷ Scenarios for Exercise 6 (Resources and Handouts 1.3)

▷ Access to YouTube

Learning Outcomes

By the end of this session:

• I can discuss values and beliefs around consent and listen to and accept different perspectives

• I can define consent and explain it to others

• I can understand the factors that affect my, or someone else's, ability/capacity to give consent

• I can understand the factors that affect my, or someone else's, freedom to give consent

• I can apply this knowledge to case studies and understand different contexts where the rules of consent have been broken

If you have access to PowerPoint, you could show PowerPoint slide 1 as the young people are arriving for the session.

At the beginning of the session, inform the group of the topic – *What Does Consent Really Mean?* – and point out that it requires the group to approach the discussions with a certain amount of maturity and sensitivity. Remind the group of the agreed expectations, particularly emphasizing confidentiality and the importance of treating one another with respect. Check that everyone is in agreement, looking for nods or verbal recognition that they're on the same page. Remind the group that if something comes up in the session that upsets them or makes them feel uncomfortable, they have permission to leave the room or find some space, and remind them of where they can go or who they can approach for support. Creating a safe environment is covered in more detail in the Introduction. Before starting, briefly set out what will be covered in the workshop.

▲ **PowerPoint slide 1**

Exercise 1: Introducing Consent

Part 1

Show the young people the 'Disrespect NoBody' video to set the scene of the session:

www.disrespectnobody.co.uk/consent/what-is-consent (video length: 30 seconds).

▲ **PowerPoint slide 2**

Point out that the video says: 'It's only consent if you both actually want to have sex.' Then ask:

1) How can you tell if you're welcome or not?
2) What are the signs that the other person is keen/enthusiastic?

Part 2

Ask the group: Can you think of any examples the video gave of how to tell when you're *not* welcome? (Examples: if someone pushes you away, freezes or goes silent.)

Let the group know that:

- This is true whether you're in a relationship or not and if you've had consensual sex in the past or not.
- It's also true of touching other people in general, not just when it comes to sex.

Exercise 2: Exploring Values and Beliefs – Group Debate

Ask the group to imagine that there is a line across the room. Explain to the group that one side of the room is 'Agree' and the other side is 'Disagree' (you can put up signs to make this clear). Let them know that when you read out a statement, they are invited to stand where they feel they are on the line in relation to the statement. If it isn't possible for the young people to move about in the room, you can ask them to put up a hand or stand up if they agree, or give out the green, amber and red cards to each participant representing 'agree', 'neither agree nor disagree' and 'disagree' in Resources and Handouts 1.1. Reassure the group that there are no right or wrong answers, that they can stand in the middle if they are unsure, and that they are able to move at any time if their opinion has been swayed. Remind the group to remain respectful when listening to and debating views and opinions that differ from their own. If the group find it hard not to talk over each other, you can use an object to represent a 'talking piece' which gives the person holding it permission to speak, while everyone else listens until it is their turn with the talking piece (see Appendix 5).

When the young people have moved to where they want to stand, facilitate a debate between individuals or sides. Feel free to contribute to the debate (there are some facilitators' notes below that may be helpful discussion points).

You don't need to go through all of the statements; pick those that seem most relevant to the group.

Once you have used a few statements, ask the group if they have any other ideas that they want to debate. It might help if the young people talk briefly in pairs to give them time to come up with a statement.

- **If people say 'No', they are frigid.** (Facilitators' note: Being called 'frigid' is hurtful. People say 'No' for many different reasons and shouldn't be judged, bullied or threatened for any decision that they make which concerns their own body. Everybody has the right to decide and to be respected for their decision.)

- **Some people say 'No' when they really mean 'Yes'.** (Facilitators' note: Saying 'No' does not mean 'persuade me' and is not an indication that someone is playing hard to get. 'No' means 'No'. If someone seems unsure or in doubt, it's safer to interpret this as 'No' than to believe otherwise.)
- **Asking for consent ruins the mood.** (Facilitators' note: If you ask for consent in the right way, it can increase intimacy, and whether you believe it ruins the mood or not, it is always important to make sure that you are both enthusiastically consenting to any sexual contact.)
- **It's OK to change your mind.** (Facilitators' note: At the end of the discussion you can add that we will explore this further on in the workshop, but stress that it is always OK to change your mind and that any decisions you make about your body should be respected.)
- **Persuading someone to have sex with you is part of the fun.** (Facilitators' note: Although there are many magazine articles and blogs out there about 'playing hard to get' and 'making someone wait', if you have to persuade someone to have sex with you, then it isn't consent.)

Exercise 3: Defining Consent

Part 1

Begin by asking the group what words come to mind when they think of 'consent'. Record the words that the young people come up with as a list or a mind-map. Follow on from this by asking what words they associate with 'non-consent'.

After you have elicited and recorded their feedback, you could show them PowerPoint slide 3 or read out the ideas from the slide that they missed (if there is anything to add).

Words associated with consent	No consent words
Agreeing	Rape
Permission	Sexual assault
Asking	Harassment
Mutual	Grooming
No pressure	Force
Enthusiasm	Pressure
Yes!	Threats
Choice	Making someone feel guilty
Sex	Silence

▲ PowerPoint slide 3

Part 2

Ask the students to work in small groups to come up with a definition of consent based on the words you've recorded and those on the slide. Elicit feedback from each group and then ask the following questions:

1) Was this easy or hard?
2) Are there any new words that you identified as relevant to your definition that aren't covered on the board?

Part 3

At the end of this exploration, ask each group to try to rewrite the definition of consent so that a 6-year-old could understand it. Elicit feedback from any group that is happy to share their definition.

Part 4

Read out or show the slide with the following definition of consent from the Sexual Offences Act 2003. Let the group know that this is the legal definition that magistrates or judges use in court when deciding whether someone has consented or not:

A person consents if he or she agrees by choice, with the freedom and capacity to do so.
– Sexual Offences Act 2003

▲ **PowerPoint slide 4**

Part 5

Lead a group discussion about the definition using the following prompts:

1) What do you think about the definition?
2) Can consent be about anything? (Facilitators' note: You can point out that the definition doesn't explicitly relate to acts of a sexual nature.)

Part 6

Ask the group to discuss in pairs: What are the key words in this definition?

After eliciting some feedback, let the group know that the two key words are 'freedom' and 'capacity': without the freedom and the capacity (ability) to consent, there hasn't been a choice or an agreement.

Exercise 4: Exploring Freedom and Capacity

Part 1

Show the group PowerPoint slide 5, which defines freedom and capacity, or read out the following definitions:

▷ **Freedom:** Making a choice without restriction
▷ **Capacity:** Being fully able and capable to make a choice (physically, mentally and emotionally)
▷ **Physical capacity:** Being physically able
▷ **Mental capacity:** Being able to understand and process information, and effectively communicate your decisions to others
▷ **Emotional capacity:** Being able to understand and express feelings based on the available information

▲ **PowerPoint slide 5**

Part 2

Arrange the young people into small groups and ask them to think of as many things as possible that could get in the way of our freedom *and* capacity to make a choice.

When they have finished, elicit feedback from the groups before showing them PowerPoint slide 5 or reading out the following suggestions they might have missed in their discussions.

Freedom	Capacity
Threats	Drugs
Violence	Alcohol
Coercion	Mental ill health
Control	Trauma
Blackmail	Consciousness/unconsciousness
Willpower/control in relationships	Age
	Disability
	Learning difficulties
	Accurate information to make informed decision

▲ **PowerPoint slide 6**

Exercise 5: Free Choice and Forced 'Choice' Continuum

Part 1

Draw a horizontal line on the board with **FREE CHOICE** written at one end and **FORCED 'CHOICE'** written at the other.

Part 2

Elicit from the group some of the choices/decisions they have made between when they woke up and right now. Examples could include getting up, eating breakfast, putting on uniform, feeding the dog, going to school, etc. For each choice, ask a volunteer to come and make a mark on the line to indicate how freely this choice was made.

Part 3

After a young person has indicated where they would put this choice on the continuum, ask some follow-up questions such as:

1) Is this really a free choice or are we making this choice because there are consequences of not doing it?
2) Is this really a forced 'choice' or do we still have the ability to make a different decision?

Part 4

At the end of the activity, ask the young people whether we can ever make a totally free choice.

After you have received some feedback, show them PowerPoint slide 7 or let them know that:

YOUR BODY – YOUR DECISION
You are in **control** of your own bodies.

The **choice** to engage in any sexual activity should always be completely **free**.

Non-consensual 'sex' isn't sex – it's rape.

▲ **PowerPoint slide 7**

Exercise 6: The Rules of Consent – Case Studies

Part 1

You can either show PowerPoint slides 8 and 9 or provide each group with the 'Rules of Consent' handout (Resources and Handouts 1.2). Go through the Rules of Consent as a group, answering any questions that the students may have.

THE RULES OF CONSENT

- **Freely given:** Consenting is a choice you make without pressure, manipulation, sulking, persuasion, being under the influence of drugs or alcohol, or through someone withholding affection until they get what they want.
- **Reversible:** Anyone can change their mind or stop at any time. Even if you've done it before, and even if you're both naked in bed.
- **Informed:** You can only consent to something if you have the full story. For example, if someone says they'll use a condom and then they don't, there isn't full consent, and the same applies to if someone tells you they are older than they really are.
- **Enthusiastic:** When it comes to sex, you should only do stuff that everyone involved *wants*, not things that you feel you're expected to do, or things you're doing solely to please other people. Consent is mutual and everyone involved needs to agree; it is not a 'maybe' or an 'I'm not sure'.
- **Specific:** Saying yes to one thing (like going to the bedroom to make out) doesn't mean you've said yes to others (like having sex).

▲ **PowerPoint slides 8 and 9**

Part 2

You can either split the students into smaller groups and give each group a set of the scenarios (Resources and Handouts 1.3), or use the PowerPoint scenarios (slides 10–17) and go through each one as a whole group, referring back to the Rules of Consent as you go along. Point out that some of the scenarios are designed to be ambiguous about whether the characters are male or female, or heterosexual or LGBTQI+, because the content of the scenarios applies to everyone.

For each scenario, the group needs to decide whether consent was present or not, and which of the rules of consent were broken (if any). Some of the scenarios are similar and it can lead to an interesting discussion if you compare the responses to slightly altered situations. (See below for suggested answers for facilitators' reference.)

Scenario 1

Sandra is at a party where her friends are drinking alcohol. Charlotte passes her a bottle of vodka and Sandra passes it on without taking a sip, because she doesn't want to drink. Later in the evening, Charlotte pours some vodka into a soft drink and passes it to Sandra without telling her it contains alcohol. Sandra drinks it.

▲ **PowerPoint slide 10**

Scenario 2

Nathan is at a party where his friends are drinking alcohol. Jerome passes him a bottle and Nathan passes it on without taking a sip, because he doesn't want to drink. Later in the evening, Jerome pours out a shot of vodka and dares Nathan to down it. Nathan looks uncomfortable and says he doesn't want to, and Jerome starts chanting 'DOWN IT, DOWN IT' until other people in the room join in. Jerome downs the shot.

▲ **PowerPoint slide 11**

Scenario 3

Jess, Shannon and Seema (all 14) are on the way home from a party when they are approached by two men in a car who offer them a lift home because it's about to rain. The girls politely decline but stay chatting to the men who seem nice and friendly. When it starts to rain, the girls decide to accept the offer of a lift, and the men then suggest they take them to a drive-through to get a milkshake. The girls agree and stay chatting in the drive-through carpark with the men. Jess suggests they go home as it's getting late, and one of the men says that he'll drive them home once both of them have received oral sex, which the girls don't want to do.

▲ **PowerPoint slide 12**

Scenario 4

Jake and Layla have been talking online for three weeks when Jake sends Layla a nude photo and asks for one in return. Layla says that she doesn't feel comfortable sending one, and he replies, 'I thought you were into me?' Layla feels bad and sends Jake a photo of her breasts to show him that she's still keen. Two weeks later, Jake asks for another nude and Layla says no. Jake says he'll send the photo of her breasts to everyone at school if she doesn't do it.

▲ **PowerPoint slide 13**

Scenario 5

Christina and Mo have been thinking about having sex for the first time. Christina goes over to Mo's house after school when his parents are out, and they spend some time kissing on the bed and undressing each other. Christina asks Mo if he has a condom, and Mo replies that he does but he isn't sure if he's ready to use it and asks if they can 'just do other stuff instead'. Christina says this is OK and shows Mo how she likes to be touched.

▲ **PowerPoint slide 14**

Scenario 6

Aria and Jude have been thinking about having sex for the first time. Aria goes over to Jude's house after school when his parents are out, and they spend some time kissing on the bed and undressing each other. Aria asks Jude if he has a condom, and Jude replies that he does but he isn't sure if he's ready to use it and asks if they can 'just do other stuff instead'. Aria starts getting dressed and gets annoyed with Jude as they had agreed they were both ready. Jude feels worried about letting Aria down and agrees to give it a go.

▲ **PowerPoint slide 15**

Scenario 7

Alex and Charlie have been friends for years. One evening they are sharing a few drinks and watching films when Charlie comes on to Alex and they start kissing. Alex withdraws and says, 'I don't want to ruin our friendship.' Charlie responds saying that it won't and it's 'just a bit of fun'. Charlie continues kissing Alex and tries putting a hand down Alex's trousers. Alex asks Charlie to stop again and Charlie then slumps back, looking annoyed and sulky. Alex feels guilty and doesn't want to lose Charlie as a mate. Alex suggests they masturbate in front of each other instead.

▲ **PowerPoint slide 16**

Scenario 8

Jackie and Tafara have been friends for years. One evening they are sharing a few drinks and watching films when Tafara comes on to Jackie and they start kissing. Jackie withdraws and says, 'I don't want to ruin our friendship.' Tafara responds saying that it won't and it's 'just a bit of fun'. Tafara continues kissing Jackie and tries putting a hand between Jackie's legs. Jackie asks Tafara to stop again, which Tafara does. Jackie suggests they masturbate in front of each other instead.

▲ **PowerPoint slide 17**

Facilitators' Answers

Scenario	Rules of consent broken
1	Consent was not freely given, not enthusiastic and not informed, as Charlotte withheld the fact that the drink contained alcohol.
2	Consent was not freely given or enthusiastic as Nathan was pressured into drinking the shot.
3	Consent was not specific (the girls agreed to have a lift, but not to oral sex), not freely given, not enthusiastic and not informed (as the girls were not told before they got into the car that this was the price to pay for a lift).
4	Consent was not freely given as Layla was made to feel guilty and then threatened; it is not enthusiastic, not informed (she didn't know the full story that he'd threaten to distribute the image) and not specific (Layla didn't agree to continue sending photos).
5	No rules of consent have been broken – the choice was freely given, reversible (even though they had agreed to have sex, Mo decided not to and Christina respected this), informed (no one was hiding anything from the other), enthusiastic (they both still wanted to touch each other) and specific (Christina shows Mo what's OK and not OK by her).
6	Consent was not freely given, enthusiastic or reversible as Jude gave in because Aria was sulking and withdrawing affection.
7	Consent was not freely given as Charlie was trying to persuade Alex from the start; it is not specific (Alex agreed to kissing Charlie but didn't agree to go further) and it is not enthusiastic (as Alex suggests mutual masturbation as a response to Charlie becoming sulky).
8	Similar to scenario 7 but the difference is that there is no suggestion that Tafara acts in a way that causes Jackie to feel guilty. Before Jackie says to stop, this was not specific (Jackie consented to kissing Tafara but not to anything else). Jackie expressed feeling unsure, which means this was not enthusiastic or definite. Jackie was freely able to suggest mutual masturbation but we don't know whether this is to please Tafara or not.

Part 3

Open up a general discussion about how the group found this exercise, and whether they have any additional queries or reflections before you move on. Let the group know that when any of the rules of consent are broken, it is the person who broke the rules that is responsible: it is NEVER the fault of the person who is harmed. To reinforce this point you could go back through the scenarios and ask the group to identify which character is responsible for breaking the rules of consent/causing harm.

Exercise 7: Is Consent as Simple as a Cup of Tea?

Part 1

Show the group the 'Cup of Tea' video, which explains consent through the metaphor of making and receiving a cup of tea:

www.youtube.com/watch?v=lOS5_I3Yzog (video length: 3 minutes).

▲ **PowerPoint slide 18**

Part 2

Explore the video with the group, using the following prompts on the PowerPoint slide:

CUP OF TEA?

1. Is consent really as simple as a **cup of tea**?
2. Are there more ways to respond than **'Yes'**, **'No'**, **'Maybe'** or being unconscious? (Remember, if someone is unsure, or unresponsive, it means 'No'.)
3. If someone isn't saying **'No'**, does it mean they're saying **'Yes'**?
4. How would you know if someone was saying **'No'** but didn't say it out loud? What might their **body language** look like?
5. Is it easy to **change your mind**? If so, how come? If not, why not?

▲ **PowerPoint slide 19**

Part 3

Ask the group to put their hands up if they've ever drunk a cup of tea that they didn't enjoy or wasn't made the way they like it. If there are hands up in the group, ask them:

1) Was drinking this tea consensual?
2) Where would you put drinking a cup of tea that wasn't to your taste on the free–forced 'choice' continuum?
3) Did any of you say anything to the person who made it?
4) If so, what did you say and how did the person respond?
5) If not, why did you feel unable to say that you wanted it made differently?

(Facilitators' note: Bring up topics around guilt, disappointing people, taking the easiest route, fear of being rude or upsetting someone.)

This last question raises a hugely important point that is worth reflecting on and potentially discussing with the group. So many young people who experience sexual abuse end up feeling that what happened was their fault as they didn't want to seem rude or disappoint someone who had initially been kind to them. Here the metaphor with tea breaks down, as a lot of people would drink a cup of tea they didn't like to be kind and not to hurt someone's feelings – and that seems like an acceptable compromise to make. However, when it comes to consent, every individual's feelings and needs are as important as anybody else's, and we want to encourage young people to be enthusiastic, rather than compromising, when it comes to sexual experiences.

At the end of the discussion, read out or show the group PowerPoint slide 20:

Your needs are important!

If people feel guilty or worried about disappointing others when it comes to simple things like tea, imagine how much trickier it becomes when they're talking about sex.

If people are doing something sexual out of guilt or fear of hurting or disappointing others, IT IS NOT CONSENT.

ANOTHER PERSON'S NEEDS AND FEELINGS ARE **NEVER** MORE IMPORTANT THAN YOUR OWN.

▲ **PowerPoint slide 20**

Part 4

Let the group know that we will discuss the laws around consent in more detail in Workshop 4, but for now read out or show them PowerPoint slide 21:

WHAT THE LAW SAYS
The law is clear – there are no **grey areas** with consent.

Everyone must agree, have the capacity/ability to agree and be free to decide.

If it is not a DEFINITE and ENTHUSIASTIC **YES**, then it's a **NO**.

If someone is in doubt or seems unsure, then it's a **NO**.

▲ **PowerPoint slide 21**

Part 5

End the session with PowerPoint slide 22 and let the group know that there are many places they can go to get resources on this subject or seek support, and there are procedures in place for anonymous reporting. It is important for them to share any issues or concerns that they have about themselves or others related to this topic. Be mindful of the possible impacts and emotions that might be evoked for individuals from the discussion, and if a topic is emotive for someone, offer an opportunity to explore this outside the group, to ensure that they feel heard and safe.

Consider providing a handout on the Rules of Consent and leaflets about local support services, as well as displaying this information on the walls and around the classroom.

SIGNPOSTING AND RESOURCES

If anything in today's workshop has affected you, support is available.

▷ **Childline** can be contacted online or on the phone, any time, on 0800 1111. Check out the website: www.childline.org.uk

▷ **National Rape Crisis Helpline** offers a free, confidential helpline for young women aged over 14 who have experienced sexual violence or abuse. Open every day between 12 and 2.30pm and 7 and 9.30pm. Calls don't show up on phone bills. Phone: 0808 802 9999

▷ **The Survivor's Trust** has information about specialist support for women, men and children who have survived rape or sexual violence. For advice and support, phone 08088 010 818. https://thesurvivorstrust.eu.rit.org.uk/contact

▲ **PowerPoint slide 22**

Personal Space

I've learned to be happy with how I am

Session Overview

This workshop is about personal space. The young people are invited to explore their own personal boundaries and the feelings that arise when someone comes too close. It looks at different types of personal boundary and considers our rights and responsibilities to ourselves and others.

Info/Knowledge

We all know what it feels like when someone gets too close. Everyone has a personal space bubble, although its size varies from person to person. We begin to develop our individual sense of personal space at around the age of 3 or 4, and the sizes of our bubbles are thought to be fixed by the time we reach adolescence. Research indicates that the bubbles are created and monitored by the amygdala, the part of the brain responsible for survival instincts and, in situations involving personal space, the emotion of fear.[1] Adolescents are in the process of moving from parental influence to peer influence, making new acquaintances and developing existing relationships, sometimes including romantic or sexual partners. Who they allow into their intimate space, how that is negotiated and how they react to spatial invasions will be crucial for their wellbeing and safety, and that of those around them. Research shows that personal space varies between cultures,

---

1   Kennedy, D.P., Gläscher, J., Tyszka, J.M. and Adolphs, R. (2009) 'Personal space regulation by the human amygdala.' *Nature Neuroscience* 12, 10, 1226–1227. Accessed on 31/1/2020 at www.ncbi.nlm.nih.gov/pubmed/19718035

with someone from Argentina, for example, requiring less personal space than someone from Asia.[2]

PSHE Association Curriculum Themes

▷ KS4 R15. How to seek consent and to respect others' right to give, not give or withdraw consent to engage in different degrees of sexual activity
▷ KS4 R19. To manage unwanted attention in a variety of contexts (including harassment and stalking)
▷ KS4 R21. To assess readiness for sex (signs of feeling uncomfortable)

Exercises

▷ Exercise 1: Personal Space
▷ Exercise 2: Exploring My Boundaries
▷ Exercise 3: Personal Boundaries
▷ Exercise 4: Exploring Different Types of Personal Boundaries
▷ Exercise 5: Rights and Responsibilities

Materials Needed

▷ Space for people to walk around for the icebreaker
▷ Handouts with coloured cards with 'agree', 'neither agree nor disagree' and 'disagree' for Exercise 5 (Resources and Handouts 1.1)
▷ Handouts with the six boundary types cut out for Exercise 4 (Resources and Handouts 2.1)
▷ Handout of Rights and Responsibilities for Exercise 5 (Resources and Handouts 2.2)
▷ Internet access to watch video

Learning Outcomes

By the end of this session:

- I can understand that how much personal space I, or others, need is dependent on our relationship and the context we are in
- I can respect the boundaries of others and clearly identify my own needs when it comes to personal space
- I can think about different kinds of personal boundaries, how these might be intruded upon and what the impact of others violating these boundaries might be
- I can explain what rights I, and others, have, and what responsibilities we all have to respect each other's rights

---

2 Sorokowska, A., Sorokowski, P., Hilpert, P., Cantarero, K. *et al.* (2017) 'Preferred interpersonal distances: A global comparison.' *Journal of Cross-Cultural Psychology* 48, 4. Accessed on 31/1/2020 at https://journals.sagepub.com/doi/abs/10.1177/0022022117698039

At the beginning of the session, inform the group of the topic – *Personal Space* – and point out that it requires the group to approach the discussions with a certain amount of maturity and sensitivity. Remind the group of the agreed expectations, particularly emphasizing confidentiality and the importance of treating one another with respect. Check that everyone is in agreement, looking for nods or verbal recognition that they're on the same page. Remind the group that if something comes up in the session that upsets them or makes them feel uncomfortable, they have permission to leave the room or find some space, and remind them of where they can go or who they can approach for support. Creating a safe environment is covered in more detail in the Introduction. Before starting, briefly set out what will be covered in the workshop.

Exercise 1: Personal Space

Part 1

Show the group the BBC3 clip on personal space:

> www.bbc.co.uk/bbcthree/clip/ec61ba40-e155-47e7-b197-c96d435068cc
> (video length: 4 minutes).

▲ **PowerPoint slide 2**

Part 2

Ask the group if they can remember the four zones of personal space from the video. Once you've elicited feedback, show them PowerPoint slide 3 or read out the answers:

ZONES OF PERSONAL SPACE
▷ Public space
▷ Social space
▷ Personal space
▷ Intimate space

▲ **PowerPoint slide 3**

Part 3

Ask the group:

1) How were people responding in the video when the presenter Eline Van Der Velden was standing too close to them?
2) What were the signs that the public felt uncomfortable? (e.g. walking, backing away, moving their belongings away from her, etc.)

3) What sorts of things did people say to let her know she was too close to them? (e.g. 'What are you doing?', 'Why are you following me?', 'You're wayyyy too close – you're making me shy, bruv', 'This is really close, I'm going to go now', 'You're in my space, cheers!', 'You in my grill.')

Exercise 2: Exploring My Boundaries

Part 1

In this exercise the young people work in pairs to explore personal boundaries.

1) Ask the group to get into pairs and assign themselves A and B.
2) Ask the young people not to touch each other at all unless they have permission from their partner during the exercise, and stress that if the young people do not wish to be touched, then they can make that clear to you as well as their partner (be aware that interpersonal dynamics between peers might make it difficult for a young person to assert this boundary themselves).
3) Ask each pair to stand as far away from each other as they can, while still facing each other.
4) When you say 'Go', A will start walking towards B until B indicates that they should stop. They can choose to indicate this verbally or nonverbally.
5) Now do this with B walking towards A.

Reflections

Ask the pairs:

1) When and how did you know when to stop approaching your partner?
2) Did you notice any changes in each other's faces or body language that let you know you were close enough?
3) Are verbal or nonverbal indicators easier to read?

Part 2

Repeat the exercise, asking the pairs to role-play different situations by inviting them to walk towards each other and indicate when to stop if...

- they have never met before (A towards B)
- they are old friends being reunited (B towards A)
- they are an enemy (A towards B)
- they are in a position of authority such as a teacher, boss or policeman (B towards A)
- they are an elderly relative who always gives you a sloppy kiss on your cheek (A towards B).

Reflections

Explore with the group what the signs are that someone is uncomfortable. You could say: 'As a guideline having people at arm's length is generally a comfortable distance, and anyone closer than that is in our "intimate space". Is this what the group experienced during the exercise?

Exercise 3: Personal Boundaries

Part 1

Read out or show the group PowerPoint slide 4:

PERSONAL BOUNDARIES

Personal space is one of our boundaries.

However, there are other personal boundaries that aren't just about space.

Personal boundaries are the guidelines that we create to identify appropriate, respectful, comfortable and safe ways for others to behave around us, and how we will respond if someone disrespects our boundaries.

Personal boundaries are informed and created by a combination of our attitudes, beliefs, cultures and past experiences.

▲ PowerPoint slide 4

Part 2

Ask the group: Why is it important to have personal boundaries in relationships? (e.g. to know our limits, to keep us safe, to communicate to other people what's OK and not OK)

After eliciting feedback from the group, read out or show them PowerPoint slide 5:

ONE SIZE DOESN'T FIT ALL

When it comes to boundaries...

- We all have different rules about what boundaries are appropriate and not appropriate for us.
- Our boundaries might change depending on the context (e.g. whether we're at school, with parents/carers or in romantic relationships).
- We might have different rules at different times depending on our mood...
- ...which is why it's so important to be clear about where our boundaries are, and to check with other people about their boundaries.

This is what consent is all about.

▲ PowerPoint slide 5

Exercise 4: Exploring Different Types of Personal Boundaries[3]

Part 1

Split the students into small groups and give each group the handout with the different types of personal boundaries (Resources and Handouts 2.1). Either assign a boundary for each group to look at, or ask the students to look at all the different types of boundaries. Give the group about ten minutes to answer the questions at the end of the handout (you can also have PowerPoint slide 6 up with the questions).

QUESTIONS ABOUT BOUNDARIES

1. What are your own personal rules about this boundary?
2. How could you let others know your rules around this boundary?
3. How would someone behave around you if they respected this rule?
4. How might someone violate this boundary?
5. Why might someone violate this boundary?
6. What might be the emotional impact of someone violating this boundary?
7. How could you respond if this happened?

▲ **PowerPoint slide 6**

Facilitators' Answers

1	2
Physical boundaries: Refers to personal space, privacy, physical touch and your body, including awareness of what's appropriate in various contexts and different types of relationships (e.g. touching you, how others treat your possessions, phone, passwords, personal space)	**Mental boundaries:** Refers to thoughts, values, ideas and opinions, including respecting each other's opinions, beliefs and perspectives (e.g. whether others respect your ideas or not, interrupt you and make you feel stupid or encourage you to achieve)
3	4
Emotional boundaries: Refers to your feelings, including limitations on when to share personal information and when not to, and how you react or respond to others (e.g. whether others validate your feelings or dismiss them, talk behind your back or keep things private, do things that make you feel good or purposefully upset you)	**Sexual boundaries:** Refers to your comfort zone around sexual activity, including consent, mutual understanding, respect, communication about wants and needs and who can touch you and where, how and when (e.g. respecting your body and boundaries, communicating who can touch you and where, how and when; also includes sexual reputation, sending nude photos, calling people words like 'slut', etc.)

---

3   There are many typologies of personal boundaries out there which use different categories. See e.g. Whitfield, C. (2010) *Boundaries and Relationships: Knowing, Protecting and Enjoying the Self.* Boca Raton, FL: HCI Books; Katherine, A. (1994) *Boundaries: Where You End and I Begin.* New York, NY: Fireside; Townsend, J. and Cloud, H. (1992) *Boundaries: When to Say Yes, How to Say No to Take Control of Your Life.* Grand Rapids, MI: HarperCollins.

5	6
Material boundaries: Refers to money and possessions, giving, lending and borrowing, including setting limits on what you will share and with whom (e.g. controlling vs respecting how you spend your money, not stealing or damaging your possessions or putting pressure on you to lend them things)	**Social boundaries:** Refers to how you spend your time and with whom (e.g. someone demanding too much of another person's time, controlling someone's time, getting jealous, consistently being late or early, or respecting that it's your choice how you spend your free time and with whom)
Questions: 1. What are your own personal rules about this boundary? 2. How could you let others know your rules around this boundary? (e.g. communication, body language) 3. How would someone behave around you if they respected this rule? 4. How might someone violate this boundary?	5. Why might someone violate this boundary? (e.g. they may not know, or may be purposefully or unconsciously trying to get a reaction out of others) 6. What might be the emotional impact of someone violating this boundary? (e.g. think about sense of safety, trust) 7. How could you respond if this happened? (e.g. think about how you would communicate that someone has violated your boundary, how you can assert your boundaries in the future)

Part 2

At the end of the exploration ask each group to introduce what type of boundary they discussed and elicit the answers to the questions they came up with. Allow time at the end of each presentation to allow feedback or other ideas from the rest of the group.

Part 3

Ask the group why it is important to have personal boundaries. Elicit feedback before showing them PowerPoint slide 7 or reading out anything they may have missed.

WHY ARE PERSONAL BOUNDARIES IMPORTANT?

▷ They create intimacy in a relationship.
▷ They help you put your own needs first.
▷ Knowing your boundaries can help you with assertiveness skills and saying 'No'.
▷ They can help you respect other people's boundaries.
▷ They help you know yourself and your limits.
▷ They can remind you that you have self-worth and that you are important.
▷ Why else are they important?

▲ **PowerPoint slide 7**

Exercise 5: Rights and Responsibilities

Part 1

Explain to the group that you are going to read out three statements. Ask the young people to stand up if they agree with the statement or stay seated if they disagree (or give them green, red and yellow cards to indicate 'agree', 'disagree' or 'neither agree nor disagree/not sure'). After you have read out each statement and the group has made their choice, allow a chance for anyone to share their decision-making process and thoughts.

1) We have the right to our own personal space.
2) We have a right to feel safe.
3) We have a responsibility to respect other people's boundaries.

Show the group PowerPoint slide 8 or read out the message. Emphasize that with every right we also have a responsibility to make sure we are respecting the rights of others around us.

RIGHTS AND RESPONSIBILITIES

Each of us has the **right** to be treated with safety and respect and the **responsibility** to act safely and respectfully towards ourselves and others.

▲ **PowerPoint slide 8**

Part 2

Keep the students in small groups or split them into pairs and give them the handout about rights and responsibilities (Resources and Handouts 2.2).

The left-hand column is about some rights young people may have and the right-hand column is about the corresponding responsibilities that the young people have to ensure they are respecting the rights of others. The task for the young people is to fill in the gaps – where there is a right, they write the equivalent responsibility, and vice versa. There a couple of examples to start them off (and a completed example table for facilitators to use as a reference below). Depending on the time available and the levels of ability and engagement in the group, you may choose to select a smaller number of rights and responsibilities for the group to work on.

Note: The rights outlined here aren't necessarily fundamental human rights as enshrined in international law. Some of the responses could have a range of answers and the young people could take the discussion in different directions. You can open up a discussion around protective behaviours, being appropriate in different situations and remaining safe. You can also link this exercise to the free choice and forced 'choice' continuum in Workshop 1, where a young person's privacy is curtailed, for example, by a parent/carer who is taking responsibility to keep them safe by checking on their online activity, when it's necessary to wear appropriate clothing in different contexts (e.g. school uniform, places of worship) or when a medical practitioner needs to make physical contact to examine them.

Facilitators' Answers

Right	Responsibility
You have the right to wear what you want	I have a responsibility avoid shaming or judging other people for their choice of clothing
You have the right to socialize and spend time with friends and family	I have a responsibility to accept how others choose to spend their time
You have the right to choose who you spend your free time with	I have a responsibility to have safe relationships and let other people choose who they hang out with
You have the right to privacy	I have a responsibility to respect others' privacy
You have the right to worship and choose whether to be religious and what religion to follow	I have a responsibility to respect the values and beliefs of other people, without prejudice
You have the right to be treated with respect	I have a responsibility to treat others as they would like to be treated
You have the right to education	I have a responsibility to participate in my own education and avoid disturbing or disrupting others' education
You have the right to refuse consent	I have a responsibility to accept other people saying no
You have the right to choose who touches you, where and when	I have a responsibility to respect other people's intimate space and not push people's boundaries
You have the right to choose who you want to be in a relationship with	I have a responsibility to respect other people's choice of partner
You have the right to live free from violence	I have a responsibility to avoid harming others through violence
You have the right to live free from inequality regardless of your race, sex, gender identity, sexual orientation	I have a responsibility to treat other people equally and not to discriminate against anyone
You have the right to end a relationship when you want to	I have a responsibility to let someone go when they want to end a relationship
You have the right to choose when you want to have sex and to say when you don't	I have a responsibility to accept when my partner doesn't want sex
You have the right to have your boundaries respected	I have a responsibility to respect other people's boundaries
You have the right to change your mind	I have a responsibility to let others change their mind without making them feel guilty

Part 3

Pick a few of the examples from the groups, perhaps focussing on any rights that the students found it hard to agree on a responsibility for, which might make for a good discussion. Ask the group:

1) What behaviours would you see when someone was demonstrating this responsibility?
2) What behaviours would you see if someone was not acting responsibly towards others?
3) What might be the impact of someone not acting on their responsibilities?
4) What rights and responsibilities do adults have, which might conflict with a young person's choice to decide what they want or need? (e.g. the responsibility to keep young people safe, ensure they have access to and attend education)

End the session with PowerPoint slide 9 and let the group know that there are many places they can go to get resources on this subject or seek support, and there are procedures in place for anonymous reporting. It is important for them to share any issues or concerns that they have about themselves or others related to this topic. Be mindful of the possible impacts and emotions that might be evoked for individuals from the discussion, and if a topic is emotive for someone, offer an opportunity to explore this outside the group, to ensure that they feel heard and safe.

SIGNPOSTING AND RESOURCES
Too much on your mind?

▷ **Childline** can be contacted online or on the phone, any time, on 0800 1111.
▷ In addition to the helpline, Childline offers information, advice and support on: bullying and abuse; safety and the law; you and your body; your feelings; friends, relationships and sex; home and family; and school, college and work.
▷ Check out the website: www.childline.org.uk

▲ **PowerPoint slide 9**

Protective Behaviours

It was good learning about how my body responds to things

Session Overview

This workshop uses the body map to explore how our bodies physiologically react to our environment to tell us we are feeling unsafe. It looks at the survival brain and the five Fs (fight, flight, freeze, flop and friend), and introduces the Safety Continuum from Protective Behaviours, as a tool for young people to make conscious choices when they are considering activities that involve risk.

Info/Knowledge

Article 3 of the United Nations Declaration of Human Rights ('Everyone has the right to life, liberty and security of person') proposes that it is a basic human right for people to feel safe all the time. This is the core principle of Protective Behaviours and is Theme 1 of the Protective Behaviours process. Feeling safe is fundamental for humans to thrive, have equality in relationships and achieve in life (consider Maslow's Hierarchy of Needs[1]).

Protective Behaviours provides a practical and down-to-earth approach to personal safety, which originated in the 1970s in response to an observation that many young people lacked the skills to identify when they felt unsafe, threatened or frightened, leaving them vulnerable to physical, sexual or emotional abuse.

---

1   Maslow states that people are motivated by getting their needs met. When one need is met, we can begin to fulfil our higher needs and move 'up' the hierarchy towards personal growth and self-actualization. The five basic needs are: (1) Physiological Needs (air, food, drink, sleep, warmth); (2) Safety Needs (shelter, resources, protection, security, law, boundaries, freedom from fear); (3) Social Needs (belonging, attention, affection and love); (4) Esteem Needs (independence, respect from self and others, achievement); (5) Self-Actualization Needs (realizing potential, self-fulfilment, personal growth). To see more on Maslow's Hierarchy of Needs, we recommend this video: www.youtube.com/watch?v=O-4ithG_07Q; or this blog on how Maslow's hierarchy can be used in education and motivating young people to learn: www.eln.io/blog/maslows-hierarchy-needs-learners

Protective Behaviours is a unique approach as it puts an understanding of 'feeling safe' as its central premise, since identifying and choosing those behaviours that are protective or preventative are based on how safe a person feels. In terms of consent, this feeling is the most intuitive response that a person has. Protective Behaviours describes the concept of safety along a continuum from feeling safe, when it is fun to feel scared, through risking for a purpose, to feeling unsafe. Exploring this continuum enables young people to have fun and be adventurous while retaining choice, control and a time limit, knowing all the time that they have the right to feel safe and a responsibility to protect the safety of others.

The Safety Continuum helps individuals to reference what feels safe for them and recognize when they are not feeling safe by identifying their 'early warning signs', which are their intuitive physical sensations in response to risk and danger. Teaching young people to recognize and understand the physical sensations that go with feeling unsafe provides them with a simple template/model to manage their own behaviour, especially when risk taking is involved. This workshop explores the Safety Continuum in different situations and scenarios, recognizing that a young person may feel differently about the same situation at different times. The Protective Behaviours approach has the benefit of being relatable to multiple situations and puts the responsibility for negotiating different situations into their own hands, unlike the 'scare tactics' or being 'told what to do' approaches. More information, including access to Protective Behaviours courses, can be found on the Protective Behaviours Consortium website: www.protectivebehavioursconsortium.co.uk

PSHE Association Curriculum Themes
▷ KS4 R21. To assess readiness for sex (e.g. signs of feeling uncomfortable)

Exercises
▷ Exercise 1: Exploring Values and Beliefs – Group Debate
▷ Exercise 2: Creative Group Exercise – Body Map
▷ Exercise 3: Survival Mode
▷ Exercise 4: Sense of Adventure
▷ Exercise 5: The Safety Continuum

Materials Needed
▷ Coloured pens and paper
▷ Flipchart paper
▷ Cards with: 'Feeling safe', 'Scared but fun', 'Risking for a reason' and 'Feeling unsafe' to put around the room for Exercise 5 (Resources and Handouts 3.1)
▷ Access to YouTube

Learning Outcomes

By the end of this session:

- I can identify physical sensations that go with feeling unsafe and feeling uncomfortable
- I can understand risk-taking behaviour and how it relates to the teenage brain
- I can identify and understand 'what happens next' when we feel unsafe, and why my body responds like this to help me feel safe and keep me safe
- I can understand the difference between excitement and fear, and recognize that even when I'm taking risks, there are things that I can choose to do to reduce the likelihood of harm

▲ **PowerPoint slide 1**

Have the first slide up as young people enter the room.

At the beginning of the session, inform the group of the topic – *Protective Behaviours* – and how awareness of the physical sensations in our bodies can help us navigate multiple situations that involve risk. Point out that it requires the group to approach the discussions with a certain amount of maturity and sensitivity. Remind the group of the agreed expectations, particularly emphasizing confidentiality and the importance of treating one another with respect. Check that everyone is in agreement, looking for nods or verbal recognition that they're on the same page. Remind the group that if something comes up in the session that they feel upset about or they feel uncomfortable with, they have permission to leave the room or find some space, and remind them of where they can go or who they can approach for support. Creating a safe environment is covered in more detail in the Introduction. Before starting, briefly set out what will be covered in the workshop.

Exercise 1: Exploring Values and Beliefs – Group Debate

Ask the group to imagine that there is a line across the room. Explain to the group that one side of the room is 'Agree' and the other side is 'Disagree' (you can put up signs to make this clear). Let them know that when you read out a statement, they are invited to stand where they feel they are on the line in relation to the statement. If it isn't possible for the young people to move about in the room, you can ask them to put up a hand or stand up if they agree, or give out the green, amber and red cards to each participant representing 'agree', 'neither agree nor disagree' and 'disagree' in Resources and Handouts 1.1. Reassure the group that there are no right or wrong answers, that they can stand in the middle if they are unsure and that they are able to move at any time if their opinion has been swayed. Remind the group to remain respectful when listening to and debating views and opinions that differ from their own. If the group find it hard not to talk over each other, you can use an object to represent a 'talking piece' which allows the person holding it permission to speak, while everyone else needs to listen until their turn with the talking piece (see Appendix 5).

When the young people have moved to where they want to stand, facilitate a debate between individuals or sides. Feel free to contribute to the debate (there are some facilitators' notes below that may be helpful discussion points).

You don't need to go through all of the statements; pick those that seem most relevant to the group.

Once you have used a few statements, ask the group if they have any other ideas that they want to debate. It might help if the young people talk briefly in pairs to help them to come up with a statement.

- **It's easy to tell when someone is feeling scared.** (Facilitators' note: People respond to fear in many different ways, so it's not always easy to tell if someone else is scared.)
- **Asking for help makes you weak.** (Facilitators' note: The myth that asking for help is shameful or makes you weak or a snitch is just that – a myth. It's important that young people get the message that asking for help is one of the most courageous, and most important, things you can do if you feel that something is not right.)
- **If there's no force, it's not rape.** (Facilitators' note: Rape doesn't always involve force or violence.)
- **You always need to say 'No' to show you don't consent.** (Facilitators' note: This is not true. For example, some people 'freeze' or become paralysed with fear, and even though they aren't saying 'No' verbally, their body language is clearly not showing enthusiasm for sexual activity.)

(Facilitators' note: All of these statements will be explored and challenged throughout this session plan.)

Exercise 2: Creative Group Exercise – Body Map

Part 1

In small groups, ask the young people to think about things that cause people to feel frightened or unsafe – this could be anything from spiders to walking home alone at night. Stress that this is a 'one step removed' approach (see the section One Step Removed: Being Mindful of Trauma in the Introduction), as it could be difficult for some young people if they have to draw on their own experiences of what feels unsafe or frightening, given the overall context of the programme.

Following this, explore as a whole group some of the common themes around people's fears and record any responses on the board (e.g. powerlessness, being out of control, humiliation, being judged, death, uncertainty, violence).

Ask the group: Why is it important to recognize what is happening in our bodies when we feel unsafe/scared/frightened? (e.g. to protect us, to keep us alive, to let us know if we are in danger)

Part 2

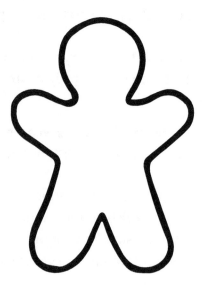

Give each group some flipchart paper and coloured pens and ask the young people in each group to draw the outline of a gingerbread person (without filling anything in like buttons or a smile; you can show them PowerPoint slide 2 as a template).

▲ **PowerPoint slide 2**

Part 3

Ask the young people to draw on the body map as many physical sensations as they can think of that happen in people's bodies when they feel unsafe (e.g. goose bumps, heart pumping faster, tears, holding breath, shallow breathing, fast breathing, clenching fists, grinding teeth, knots or butterflies in the stomach, shouting, sweating, sweaty palms).

Remind the group that there are no right or wrong answers.

Note: This is designed to be a fun activity that gets across the significance of the body's intuitive response to danger or 'early warning signs'. This is one of the most important Protective Behaviour activities to deliver as a 'one step removed' approach. It would not be safe or appropriate to ask the young people to reflect on times when they have felt unsafe and how that felt for them, as this could potentially be retraumatizing.

Part 4

After about ten minutes, ask each group to share their body map with the rest of the students, going through each of the physical sensations they identified. After they've given feedback, ask the whole group:

1) What did the body maps have in common?
2) Were there any differences? (It is worth recognizing that there are apparently hundreds of different physical bodily responses to feeling unsafe, so each person can experience a different range of feelings in response to a given situation and when compared with someone else.)

Following a discussion, show PowerPoint slide 3 or let the group know:

EARLY WARNING SIGNS

These physical sensations are called our **early warning signs**.

They are the clues that our body gives us to let us know that something doesn't feel right – whether it's that we feel frightened, scared, unsafe or out of our comfort zone.

Early warning signs are our body's way of making sure that we have the best chance of navigating risks and surviving.

▲ **PowerPoint slide 3**

Part 5

Explore the body maps further using the following questions:

1) Sometimes people's bodies respond in this way when there are no obvious threats. Why might this happen? (e.g. sometimes feelings just arise such as anxiety, stress or fear)
2) What physical signs might other people notice if a person is experiencing some early warning signs? (Facilitators' note: We might not be able to see if other people are feeling afraid, unsafe or outside their comfort zone, or we might misinterpret some of these physical signs as, for example, being out of breath, excited, embarrassed, cold/hot or sad.)
3) What could you do if you notice these early warning signs in yourself?
4) What could you do if you notice them in someone else?

At the end of the discussion, read out or show the group PowerPoint slide 4:

It can be hard and scary to accept that we need help or support.

But we can talk with someone about anything, even if it feels small or awful.

Think for 30 seconds about the people in your life whom you can trust, including friends, adults at home, adults at school and services.

And remember, you might be on someone else's list of people they can trust to go to for support.

▲ **PowerPoint slide 4**

Exercise 3: Survival Mode

Part 1

Read out or show the group PowerPoint slide 5:

SURVIVAL MODE

It's important to be aware of when we feel unsafe, threatened or frightened. It helps us to take action to help us to feel (and be) safer!

When we are faced with fear, our brain goes into 'survival' mode and it shuts down all the other parts of our brain that are involved in making decisions, problem solving or being rational.

When we are functioning from our survival brain, we can only REACT instead of RESPOND to the things around us.

▲ **PowerPoint slide 5**

Part 2

Ask the group to imagine that they are all terrified of or allergic to wasps. Ask them to imagine that a wasp has just flown into the room. Elicit some feedback about how they would respond to this situation (e.g. try to kill the wasp, run away, hide under a table, coax the wasp into a cup, scream).

Part 3

Read out or show the group PowerPoint slides 6, 7 and 8:

SURVIVAL

When our survival brain is triggered, our body responds with one of five reactions.

We don't have control over which one, as our brain makes the decision automatically to give us the best chance of surviving.

This can happen even when we are not in actual danger.

The five survival reactions are: **Fight**, **Flight**, **Freeze**, **Flop/Faint** and **Friend**.

▲ **PowerPoint slide 6**

THE 5 FS

▷ **Fight**: Aggression (physical or otherwise), or resistance such as saying 'No' or screaming – e.g. trying to bat the wasp away or kill it or stamp on it.

▷ **Flight**: Running or getting as much distance as possible from whatever is threatening us – e.g. running away from the wasp.

▷ **Freeze**: Becoming immobile. In the animal kingdom, this helps us survive by tricking the predator, and if we have already been harmed, it can prevent further injury by giving us time to recover. We might freeze when we have no chance of fighting off the threat or of escaping a situation – e.g. tensing up and staying really still until the wasp flies away.

▷ **Flop/Faint**: Our body shuts off and goes floppy. This is like 'playing dead' in the animal kingdom to make the predator less interested in you.

▷ **Friend**: 'If you can't beat them, join them' and 'Keep your friends close but your enemies closer!' are examples of this. If our brain assesses that we can't use the other survival responses, we might try to make friends with whoever is threatening us to try to reduce the amount of harm they may cause us. This can be seen when people befriend bullies or others who scare them. An extreme example of this is 'Stockholm syndrome' when people are known to fall in love with their captors.

▲ **PowerPoint slides 7 and 8**

Ask the group if they have any questions about the survival reactions and whether they make us safe. You can point out that these reactions are the same whether we are faced with a *real threat* or *perceived threat*, and whether the threat is small or big (e.g. being told off in class or being faced with a dragon).

Part 4

If you have access to YouTube, show the group the videos in PowerPoint slide 9 and ask them to identify which survival response is being used. (Facilitators' note: You may want to show just a section of the second and third videos.)

• www.youtube.com/watch?v=1hYDYrdiYX8 (video length: 12 seconds) (Answer: Fight).
• www.youtube.com/watch?v=YI4hzzepEcI (video length: 2 minutes) (Answer: Faint/Flop).
• www.youtube.com/watch?v=11x7nW2ywNA (video length: 2 minutes) (Answer: Flight).

▲ **PowerPoint slide 9**

Part 5

Lead a discussion with the group about how this all relates to consent. You could remind them of the four agree/disagree statements that we explored at the beginning of this session:

- It's easy to tell when someone is feeling scared.
- Asking for help makes you weak.
- If there's no force, it's not rape.
- You always need to say 'No' to show you don't consent.

Part 6

At the end of the discussion, show the group PowerPoint slide 10, and let them know that our body doesn't always respond in the way we expect it to. For example, our body can react as if it is turned on (e.g. getting wet or having an erection) even when we're not. This means that our body can respond physically – or even orgasm during a sexual experience – even when it is non-consensual. This is called 'arousal non-concordance'. Be aware that even physical signs that someone is turned on aren't always a reliable indication of enthusiastic consent. Ask the group if they have any questions about arousal non-concordance.

▲ **PowerPoint slide 10**

Part 7

Read out or show the group PowerPoint slide 11:

NO MEANS NO – BUT SO DO OTHER THINGS

You don't always need to say **'No'** to show you don't consent.

There are many reasons why people don't or can't say 'No' and it doesn't automatically mean they are saying 'Yes'.

There is a common myth that if someone didn't **'FIGHT BACK'**, then they **'LET IT HAPPEN'** – however, they may have automatically 'frozen' or become paralysed with fear. Most people 'freeze' and it is a perfectly natural response.

In the eyes of the law, being silent or being immobile (e.g. if someone is unconscious or has fainted or frozen) does not count as consent – because there needs to be 'reasonable belief' that the other person was consenting.

Rape is still rape, and sexual assault is still sexual assault, even if there was no force, violence or visible injuries involved.

▲ **PowerPoint slide 11**

Exercise 4: Sense of Adventure

Part 1

Say to the group: As we've explored, it's really important to recognize when we feel unsafe and listen to our bodies. However, it's also important to recognize that we can't feel safe all of the time – and nor would we want to! Instead, we need the skills to manage risks when they arise.

Part 2

Read out or show the group PowerPoint slide 12:

RISK AWARE

Risk is an important part of everyday life and it is even more important to take risks and be adventurous when we are teenagers. Teenage brains need to experiment, try new things, be adventurous and be outside their comfort zone in order to develop healthily and set them up for adult life.

This is why teenagers often have a reputation for being risky, impulsive, spontaneous and not thinking about the consequences of their actions – it's all true!

This is why adults in your life might be horrified at some of the things you do – they see the risk and danger, and you see the thrill and reward.

It's important to listen to your body and your early warning signs to assess which risks are worth taking and which risks are likely to be harmful.

▲ **PowerPoint slide 12**

Ask the group if they have any questions about the slide.

Part 3

Ask the group:

1) How many of the sensations you identified in your body maps would also occur if you were excited? (Facilitators' note: There isn't really a 'right answer' for this as it will depend on the individual; however, many of the physical responses for fear are also associated with excitement – e.g. knots in your stomach, goose bumps, changes in breathing.)

2) Have you ever taken a risk just to feel the thrill?

3) Are there times when it's important to take a risk?

4) How do we know the difference between excitement and fear? (Facilitators' note: This is often about how you feel about and interpret the physical responses in the body map – e.g. are they accompanied by curiosity or the potential for a positive outcome, or not?)

Exercise 5: The Safety Continuum

Part 1

Show the group PowerPoint slide 13 or read it out. If you are reading it out, it may be worth writing the three questions on the board to reinforce the message:

RISK TAKING

When we are faced with risks, there are three key things that can determine whether the risk is worth taking or not.

If we ask ourselves the following three questions, we are more likely to have positive experiences of risk taking rather than damaging or hurtful ones:

1. **CHOICE:** Have I chosen this?
2. **CONTROL:** Do I have some element of control?
3. **TIME LIMIT:** Do I know when it will come to an end?

▲ **PowerPoint slide 13**

Part 2

Place the 'Feeling safe', 'Scared but fun', 'Risking for a reason' and 'Feeling unsafe' labels around the room (Resources and Handouts 3.1) and either put up PowerPoint slide 14 or explain what each label means:

THE SAFETY CONTINUUM
- ▷ **Feeling safe:** When something has no risk and no fear involved
- ▷ **Scared but fun:** When something is both scary and exhilarating – e.g. going on a rollercoaster or watching a scary film
- ▷ **Risking for a reason:** When something is risky but we can get something out of it – e.g. performing on stage, asking someone out, or doing something risky to 'fit in'
- ▷ **Feeling unsafe:** When something is just plain scary!

▲ **PowerPoint slide 14**

Part 3

Explain to the group that you are about to read out some scenarios. As you read them out, you will be asking the group to move and stand by the label that they would most relate to if they were faced with that situation. Point out that individuals can test their thinking about where they are on the continuum based on how they feel and whether they have choice, control and a time limit for the activity.

Before starting, remind the group that there are no right or wrong answers and that we all have different tolerances and relationships to risk – what feels unsafe for one person might not be for another – *and this is OK.*

Read out the scenarios one by one, eliciting feedback after each one about what helped the students make a decision about this risk. There may be students who can't decide where they would go because their answer depends on further information such as whether they are alone or with someone, whether other people are doing it – you can use this as an opportunity to explore each scenario further, as there are many variables that affect our behaviour in different situations. It is helpful to note that movement along the continuum is in both directions: a person can choose the best options to help them move to a point of feeling safe again.

Note: If you have limited space, you can ask them to vote after each scenario.

Cheating on someone	Going on a rollercoaster	Walking home alone
Walking home alone at night	Asking someone out	Meeting in person someone whom you met online
Telling someone a secret	Crying in front of someone	Stealing something from a shop
Performing in a show	Asking someone for help	Having unprotected sex
Punching someone in the face	Defending yourself in a fight	Telling someone you love them
Doing an exam	Lying to your parents/carers	Holding a tarantula
Sending a nude	Getting high	Getting drunk
Holding a bag when you don't know what's in it	Talking to a stranger online	Getting in a car with people you don't know

Part 4

Repeat the Body Map exercise, but this time invite the groups to come up with as many physical sensations as they can think of that happen in people's bodies when they feel *safe*, or as many words as possible that they associate with 'safety' (e.g. comfortable, balanced, the right temperature, loved, relaxed).

Remind the group that there are no right or wrong answers and that this is likely to be more challenging than the Early Warning Signs body map because we rarely consciously notice when we feel safe!

Part 5

Before ending the session, you could show the inspirational quote on PowerPoint slide 15:

Adventure isn't hanging off a rope on the side of a mountain.

Adventure is an attitude we must apply to the day-to-day obstacles of life.
– John Amat

▲ **PowerPoint slide 15**

End the session with PowerPoint slide 16 and let the group know that there are many places they can go to get resources on this subject or seek support, and there are procedures in place for anonymous reporting. It is important for them to share any issues or concerns that they have about themselves or others related to this topic. Be mindful of the possible impacts and emotions that might be evoked for individuals from the discussion, and if a topic is emotive for someone, offer an opportunity to explore this outside the group, to ensure that they feel heard and safe.

SIGNPOSTING AND RESOURCES

If anything in today's workshop has affected you, support is available.

▷ **I Just Froze:** Rape Crisis Scotland's new public awareness campaign, which aims to challenge the idea that there is a right or wrong way for people to react during or after a rape: www.rapecrisisscotland.org.uk/i-just-froze

▷ **National Rape Crisis Helpline** offers a free, confidential helpline for young women aged over 14 who have experienced sexual violence or abuse. Open every day between 12 and 2.30pm and 7 and 9.30pm. Calls don't show up on phone bills. Phone: 0808 802 9999

▷ **Survivors UK – Male Rape and Sexual Abuse Support** offers a chat service via WhatsApp and text, and will point you in the right direction for local support: www.survivorsuk.org

▲ **PowerPoint slide 16**

What the Law Says

I know what consent is now

Session Overview

This workshop introduces the legal context of consent through a quiz and scenarios. It explores the history of the laws around consent, why these laws are important to protect children and young people, how they vary across different countries, and what laws the young people would put in place if they were politicians. Finally, the session looks at disclosures, and how and where people can go to report an offence or concern.

Info/Knowledge

The DfE states: 'Key aspects of the law relating to sex which should be taught include the age of consent, what consent is and is not, the definitions and recognition of rape, sexual assault and harassment.'[1] In 2018, Childline reported a 29% increase in young people asking for counselling for peer-on-peer sexual abuse, with many callers not clear about what consent means.[2] The legal definition of consent is agreeing by choice with the freedom and capacity to make that choice. Those last two are the key points to emphasize in this workshop, because even if someone says yes (and is therefore making a choice), it may be that legally they are not able to give their consent. Estimates vary but it is thought that between 1 in 20 and 1 in 5 children and young people will experience sexual abuse

1   Department for Education (2019) *Relationships Education, Relationships and Sex Education (RSE) and Health Education: Statutory guidance for governing bodies, proprietors, head teachers, principals, senior leadership teams, teachers.* Accessed on 27/1/2020 at https://assets.publishing.service.gov.uk/government/uploads/system/uploads/attachment_data/file/805781/Relationships_Education__Relationships_and_Sex_Education__RSE__and_Health_Education.pdf

2   Weale, S. (2018) 'Rise in young people seeking help over peer-on-peer abuse.' *The Guardian.* Accessed on 31/1/2020 at www.theguardian.com/society/2018/sep/18/childline-rise-young-people-seeking-help-peer-on-peer-abuse-uk

before they are 18,[3] and the NSPCC estimates that 90% of children who have experienced sexual abuse receive no substantial support.[4] Ensure that at the end of the workshop young people are given information on where to go if they need to talk to someone, including Childline and local victim and rape crisis services.

PSHE Association Curriculum Themes

▷ KS4 R8. About the concept of consent in relevant, age-appropriate contexts
▷ KS4 R15. How to seek consent and to respect others' right to give, not give or withdraw consent to engage in different degrees of sexual activity

Exercises

▷ Exercise 1: Interactive Quiz
▷ Exercise 2: Exploring Values and Beliefs – Group Debate
▷ Exercise 3: Legal or Illegal?
▷ Exercise 4: The History of the Law
▷ Exercise 5: Consent Laws Across the Globe
▷ Exercise 6: If Something Happens, What Happens Next?

Materials Needed

▷ 'True' and 'False' cards per table (optional) for Exercise 1 (Resources and Handouts 4.1)
▷ Legal or Illegal scenarios cut out for Exercise 3 (Resources and Handouts 4.2)
▷ History of the Law cards for Exercise 4 (Resources and Handouts 4.3)

Learning Outcomes

By the end of this session:

• I can understand the laws around consent and why they are in place
• I can talk about the history of the law around consent
• I can compare the law in the UK with other places around the world
• I can understand the consequences of the law
• I can consider the options people have if they decide to disclose a sexual offence, and the reasons why people might not disclose

---

3   NSPCC (2019) 'Statistics briefing: Child sexual abuse.' Accessed on 31/1/2020 at https://learning.nspcc.org.uk/research-resources/statistics-briefings/child-sexual-abuse
4   NSPCC (2006) 'Treatment and Therapeutic Services', cited in Wallis, P. (2010) *Are You Okay? A Practical Guide to Helping Young Victims of Crime*. London: Jessica Kingsley Publishers.

At the beginning of the session, inform the group of the topic – *What the Law Says* – and point out that it requires the group to approach the discussions with a certain amount of maturity and sensitivity. Remind the group of the agreed expectations, particularly emphasizing confidentiality and the importance of treating one another with respect. Check that everyone is in agreement, looking for nods or verbal recognition that they're on the same page. Remind the group that if something comes up in the session that upsets them or makes them feel uncomfortable, they have permission to leave the room or find some space, and remind them of where they can go or who they can approach for support. Creating a safe environment is covered in more detail in the Introduction. Before starting, briefly set out what will be covered in the workshop.

Exercise 1: Interactive Quiz
Part 1

Start the session by exploring the knowledge in the room with an interactive quiz. A quiz can be a great way to capture the interest of the group.

There are many ways you can conduct this quiz in an interactive way:

1) By reading out the statements and asking the group to stand up if they think the statement is true and remain seated if they think it's false.

2) Allowing small groups or pairs to discuss each question before presenting their answers to allow for further exploration around each law. You can ask individual students in the group why they have decided true/false before revealing the answer and the additional information.

3) You can give out 'True' and 'False' cards (Resources and Handouts 4.1) to be held up.

4) You can have two or more groups competing against each other, with a prize to be won.

Note: Ensure that you have enough knowledge to field questions that may arise and use the quiz to explore some of the key themes around consent in the UK. If there are questions that you can't answer, make a note of them on the board and either ask the young people to research the answers and feed back in the following workshop, or take the questions away and let them know the answers in the next session.

Facilitators' Answers

Statement	True or false?
1. The age of consent is different for men and women.	**False:** The age of consent for sex is 16 for all genders in the UK, although in some countries the age of consent is different for males and females.
2. The age of consent is the same regardless of your sexual orientation or gender identity.	**True:** Consent applies to everyone regardless of their sexual orientation or how they identify.
3. If you're under 16 you can't get advice from a sexual health clinic.	**False:** It is not an offence to give people information, treatment or advice regardless of their age if it is in order to protect the young person's safety, emotional wellbeing or physical health, and is thought to be in the best interest of the young person.
4. Children who are 12 and under have the capacity to consent.	**False:** Under the Sexual Offences Act 2003, children aged 12 and under do not legally have the capacity to consent to any form of sexual activity. There is a maximum life sentence for offences involving children under 12. It is called 'statutory rape' if anyone has sex with someone who is a child, even if they believe the sexual activity was consensual.
5. Women cannot go to prison for rape.	**True:** Only a man can commit rape as the definition of rape involves 'penetration by a penis'. Women can be charged with other offences that can hold the same length of sentence for sexual assault, coercion or assault by penetration, if they involve others in sexual activity without consent.
6. If two 15-year-olds had consensual sex, they would be prosecuted (i.e. have legal action taken against them).	**False:** Even though having sex when you're under 16 is outside the law, the Home Office guidance states that it doesn't intend to prosecute teenagers under 16 if they both mutually agree/consent to any sexual activity and their ages are similar.
7. It is an offence for anyone over 18 to engage in sexual activity with someone under 18 if they have a position of trust (e.g. a teacher, youth worker, sports coach, etc.).	**True:** This would be an abuse of the position of trust. Even though the age of consent is 16, when it comes to sexual offences you are still considered a child until the age of 18.
8. It is not an offence if you touch someone with sexual intent if you 'reasonably believe' the other person consented.	**True:** This is an interesting law in England and Wales as 'reasonable belief' is very subjective and difficult to prove in court. Note that this makes things tricky for young people. This is why it is so important for everyone involved to mutually agree and be enthusiastic about sexual activity, as it reduces the chance that there are any grey areas, uncertainty or doubt during any sexual interaction.
9. It is an offence for someone to be naked in public.	**False:** Unless someone is exposing their genitals with the intention of causing 'alarm, distress or harassment' or they refuse to put their clothes back on when a member of the public or a police officer asks them to get dressed, they are not committing an offence.
10. If you are under 13, you can't be charged with a criminal offence.	**False:** The age of criminal responsibility in England, Wales and Northern Ireland is 10!

Part 2

Lead a discussion with the group about some of the laws explored in the quiz. You can ask questions such as:

1) Why is it important to have laws around sex and consent in place? (e.g. to protect children and young people)
2) Were there any laws that were new to the group or surprised them?

Exercise 2: Exploring Values and Beliefs – Group Debate

Ask the group to imagine that there is a line across the room. Explain to the group that one side of the room is 'Agree' and the other side is 'Disagree' (you can put up signs to make this clear). Let them know that when you read out a statement they are invited to stand where they feel they are on the line in relation to the statement. If it isn't possible for the young people to move about in the room, you can ask them to put up a hand or stand up if they agree, or give out the green, amber and red cards to each participant representing 'agree', 'neither agree nor disagree' and 'disagree' in Resources and Handouts 1.1. Reassure the group that there are no right or wrong answers, that they can stand in the middle if they are unsure and that they are able to move at any time if their opinion has been swayed. Remind the group to remain respectful when listening to and debating views and opinions that differ from their own. If the group find it hard not to talk over each other, you can use an object to represent a 'talking piece' which allows the person holding it permission to speak, while everyone else needs to listen until their turn with the talking piece (see Appendix 5).

When the young people have moved to where they want to stand, facilitate a debate between individuals or sides. Feel free to contribute to the debate (there are some facilitators' notes below that may be helpful discussion points).

You don't need to go through all of the statements; pick those that seem most relevant to the group.

Once you have used a few statements, ask the group if they have any other ideas that they want to debate. It might help if the young people talk briefly in pairs to help them to come up with a statement.

- **The legal age of consent should be reduced.** (Facilitators' note: While people mature at different times, our brains aren't fully developed until well into our 20s, and the age of consent reflects the fact that even at 16 our brains are still developing.)
- **Underage sex is normal.** (Facilitators' note: You may want to mention after this discussion that the average age in the UK for people having sex for the first time is 18.3 according to a study by Durex.[5])

---

5   Joe (2016) 'Here's the average age people lose their virginity around the world.' Accessed on 31/1/2020 at www.joe.ie/fitness-health/heres-the-average-age-people-lose-their-virginity-around-the-world-564505

- **People don't always know that they're committing an offence.** (Facilitators' note: This could be true – many people don't know the law around consent, which is why it's so important for it to be taught. There are other reasons people may not know they are committing an offence – they might not know the true age of other people involved, and there was a case in America involving a teenager with learning difficulties who was put on the sex offenders register for texting a girl he fancied quoting something he'd heard in porn.[6] Obviously, whether knowledge or intention are there or not, the impact on the victim is the same, and breaking the law is still breaking the law.)

Before moving on, show the group PowerPoint slide 2 or read out the John Oliver quote and invite any thoughts or comments on it:

Consent is like boxing. If both people do not agree to it, then one person is committing a crime.[7]
– John Oliver

▲ **PowerPoint slide 2**

Exercise 3: Legal or Illegal?

Part 1

Now that the groups have explored some of the laws relating to sex and consent, they can put their knowledge into practice. This exercise involves the young people deciding whether specific scenarios are legal or illegal. Have the definition of consent (from the Sexual Offences Act 2003) and the Rules of Consent on PowerPoint slide 3 (or written up on the board) so that the group can refer to this while they consider each scenario.

There are many different ways to conduct this exercise:

1) Give small groups or individuals a handout of the scenarios (Resources and Handouts 4.2) to mark their answers on.
2) Cut out the scenarios and ask small groups to sort them into legal and illegal.
3) Conduct the exercise in the same way as Exercise 2, with one end of the room representing 'legal' and the other representing 'illegal', reading out the scenarios one by one and eliciting a discussion (including the facilitators' answers) as you go along.

When you reveal the right answers to the group, you can discuss how, despite some of the examples being legal, they can still be immoral, unethical or harmful. Remember to stress the point that the laws concerning consent apply to all relationship types, regardless of sexual orientation.

---

6   Cited in Jon Ronson, *The Butterfly Effect* podcast series.
7   Source: 'Sex Education: Last Week Tonight with John Oliver.' *HBO*. August 2015. Available at https://www.youtube.com/watch?v=LOjQz6jqQS0&t=5s

A person consents if he or she agrees by choice with the freedom and capacity to do so.
– Sexual Offences Act 2003

▲ **PowerPoint slide 3**

Facilitators' Answers

Two 16-year-old males having consensual sex.	**Forcing someone to get married.**
This is legal as both parties are over the age of consent.	This is illegal – it is marriage without consent or against someone's will. There is now a specific criminal offence for forced marriage which can include a fine, a suspended sentence, time in prison and community sentences. There are also a range of other criminal offences covering acts which often occur when someone is forced into a marriage (e.g. rape, assault, theft, kidnapping, blackmail and harassment).
Two 16-year-olds having sex when they are both drunk at a party.	**An 18-year-old male having a sexual image of his 15-year-old girlfriend on his phone.**
If both people are consenting and have the capacity to consent, then this isn't illegal. It can be hard to know if someone has the capacity to consent if both people are drunk and you still need to have 'reasonable belief' that the other person is consenting.	This is illegal – possessing and viewing a sexual image of anyone under 18 is considered child pornography. This is not illegal when it involves consenting adults, but if there is someone under 18 involved, it can be seen as exploitation. If someone then sent or showed the photo to someone else, it would be distributing child pornography. Even sexting is illegal when it involves someone under 18 and can be punished by between 5 and 20 years in prison, and the possibility of being put on the sex offenders register. Workshops 5 and 6 explore this in more detail.

Having an abortion. In England, Scotland and Wales this is legal if: the pregnancy is less than 24 weeks, the termination is carried out by a medical practitioner and the pregnant person consents to having the pregnancy terminated. In terms of consent, this is important because it's about women having the choice of what happens to their body and the freedom and capacity to make the decision. In the US there are many states where abortions are illegal, even if the pregnancy is the result of incest or rape. Medical professionals who have carried out an abortion in Alabama, for example, can face up to 99 years in prison.	**A 17-year-old male taking off his condom during sex when he and his partner consented to protected sex.** This is illegal and is called 'stealthing'. Although there is no specific law about stealthing, technically if you have consented to protected sex and your partner removes the condom, then there is no longer consent and the unprotected intercourse is therefore rape. Remember the Rules of Consent being as simple as FRIES (Freely Given, Reversible, Informed, Enthusiastic and Specific). If someone takes off a condom during sex, then the rule of informed consent has been broken.
Someone uploading a video of themselves having sex with an ex-partner to shame them. This is illegal. If the people involved are over 18, this is called revenge porn and involves the distribution of private and personal explicit images or video footage of an individual without their consent, with the intention of causing them embarrassment and distress. Often revenge porn is used maliciously to shame ex-partners. It is against the law and carries a sentence of up to two years in prison, even if both parties were consenting adults and agreed to the video being made. Revenge porn is discussed further in Workshop 6. If the people are under 18, this is still illegal as it is distributing child pornography.	**A 14-year-old and a 12-year-old agreeing to have sex.** This is illegal because the 12-year-old does not have the capacity to consent to any sexual activity due to their age.
A 14-year-old having naked photos of themselves on their phone. This is illegal. Even if the photo is of yourself, it is against the law to have the image on your phone as it still counts as child pornography!	**Someone 'upskirting' a classmate in the playground and showing everyone the photo.** This is illegal. Upskirting is taking a photo or video under someone else's clothing for sexual gratification or to cause humiliation or distress. It is a criminal offence carrying a sentence of up to two years in prison and/or being included on the sex offenders register.

Not disclosing that you have an STI before having unprotected sex. This is illegal. It is illegal to expose someone else to an infection without telling them. Remember the Rules of Consent being as simple as FRIES (Freely Given, Reversible, Informed, Enthusiastic and Specific). If someone withholds information, then the rule of informed consent has been broken. There has been a case where someone was jailed for up to 14 months for knowingly exposing their partner to an STI without telling them first.[8] Even though this was seen as 'reckless rather than deliberate', it was prosecuted under Grievous Bodily Harm, which is normally a sentence for physical violence such as stabbings or beatings.	**Sending a dickpic.** This is a trick question as it depends on the circumstances. If sending a dickpic is done with the intention of causing harm, distress or anxiety to the recipient, then this is committing a crime. If both people are over 18, and both sending and receiving a dickpic is consensual, then this is not a crime.
Two 16-year-olds having consensual sex when one of them asks the other to stop because it hurts. Their partner does not stop because they know they are close to orgasm and carries on for a further minute after hearing the request to stop. Even though the sex started as consensual and is therefore legal, someone changed their mind and communicated this which means the remainder of the sexual activity is non-consensual and therefore illegal. Remember the Rules of Consent being as simple as FRIES (Freely Given, Reversible, Informed, Enthusiastic and Specific). If someone changes their mind and requests to stop during sex, then the rule of reversible and enthusiastic consent has been broken.	**Someone cheating on their partner without their partner's knowledge.** This is legal. Even though this is unethical, it is not outside of the law to cheat or have an affair. Some relationships are non-monogamous and have a 'don't ask, don't tell' agreement where people can explore relationships outside of their partnership, without having to disclose this to their partner (we will look at different types of relationships in Workshop 7).
Two 17-year-olds kissing at a party and one of them takes it further and puts their hand down the other's underwear. The other partner tenses up but says nothing and so they carry on. This is illegal – sexual activity with someone who is not voluntarily participating, being passive, freezing or not demonstrating that they are enthusiastic is non-consensual. Remember the Rules of Consent being as simple as FRIES (Freely Given, Reversible, Informed, Enthusiastic and Specific). If someone tenses up, then the rule of enthusiastic consent has been broken. Remember – people are not always able to say 'No', and this does not mean that they are at fault or to blame for what happened – the responsibility is with the other person who was acting without consent.	**Forcing or pressuring your husband or wife into having sex.** This is now illegal, although in the past forced sex within a marriage wasn't illegal as a husband could legally 'enforce his conjugal rights' (expect sex from his partner) without committing an offence. Staying married was seen as the consent. Now, even within a marriage, non-consensual 'sex' is rape.

8   Bernard, E.J. (2014) 'UK: Court of Appeal upholds man's conviction for recklessly passing on genital herpes during sex with ex-girlfriend.' HIV Justice Network. Accessed on 23/2/2020 at www.hivjustice.net/news/uk-court-of-appeal-upholds-mans-conviction-for-recklessly-passing-on-genital-herpes-during-sex-with-ex-girlfriend

Part 2

Answer any questions the group have on the quiz and then remind the group that, regardless of the intention of the person, they need to be confident that they have consent. Even if someone is not intending to cause harm, it doesn't always mean that harm hasn't been caused.

Part 3

Read out or show PowerPoint slide 4 to the group:

Remember – however old you are, sex should always be consensual.

You are **allowed** to say NO, you are allowed to **change your mind** and you should never feel pressured or exposed to something that you didn't **choose** for yourself.

Make sure everybody involved is not only up for it, but **enthusiastically** up for it!

▲ **PowerPoint slide 4**

Exercise 4: The History of the Law

Keep the students in small groups and give each group one of the cards (Resources and Handouts 4.3) with a different UK law.

Ask a representative from each group to come up to the front (holding the card) and read out the text on the card.

Once all the cards have been read out, the task is to try to sort the laws in the order of when they were passed, with one end of the room being the most recent law and the other being the oldest law. You can do this by getting the rest of the group to vote 'earlier' or 'later' while the representatives at the front move around until they are in the correct order.

Facilitators' Answers

2019	Upskirting (taking a photo or video under a person's clothing without their permission for sexual gratification or to cause humiliation or distress). Before this became a specific law, you could still prosecute someone for 'upskirting' using the laws for outraging public decency or as a crime of voyeurism under the Sexual Offences Act.
2015	Revenge porn (sharing private sexual images of someone on the internet without their consent to cause distress or embarrassment). If you are accused of revenge porn and found guilty of the offence, you could face up to two years in prison if the person distributing the image is over 18.
2013	Legalization of same-sex marriage. Before 2013 it was against the law for people to marry someone of the same sex or gender as them. It took a year for this law to come into full effect, although it was possible for same-sex couples to be in a civil partnership from 2004.
2007	Discrimination on the basis of sexual orientation was banned for the first time in 2007.
2001	The age of consent in the UK was equalized for homosexual people. Before 2001, the age of consent was 16 for heterosexual (straight) people and 21 for homosexual (gay and lesbian) people.
2000	Being openly homosexual or transgender and being allowed to serve in the armed forces, free from discrimination, was illegal before 2000.
1992	Marital rape (forced sexual activity within a marriage). Before 1992, rape within a marriage wasn't illegal as a husband could legally 'enforce his conjugal rights' (expect sex from his partner) without committing an offence. Staying married was seen as the consent.
1974	Contraceptive advice for under-16s. Before 1974, medical professionals could not provide contraceptive advice for under-16s without speaking to their parents first.
1968	Having an abortion in England, Scotland and Wales was illegal until 1968. Abortion is now legal if: the pregnant person consents to having the pregnancy terminated, the pregnancy is less than 24 weeks, and a medical practitioner carries out the abortion. In Northern Ireland, access to abortion is still limited.

Once the group have got into the timeline, check whether they are correct by revealing the answers on PowerPoint slide 5 or by rearranging the representatives from each group using the facilitators' answers above.

Timeline

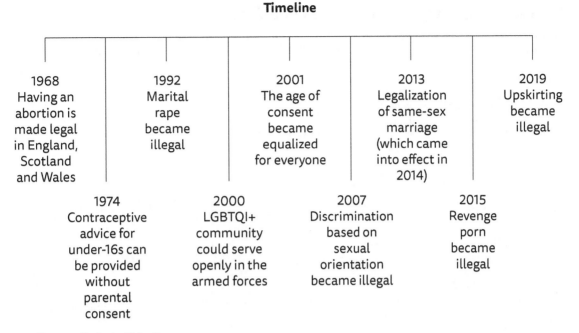

1968
Having an
abortion is
made legal
in England,
Scotland
and Wales

1974
Contraceptive
advice for
under-16s can
be provided
without
parental
consent

1992
Marital
rape
became
illegal

2000
LGBTQI+
community
could serve
openly in the
armed forces

2001
The age of
consent
became
equalized
for everyone

2007
Discrimination
based on
sexual
orientation
became illegal

2013
Legalization
of same-sex
marriage
(which came
into effect in
2014)

2015
Revenge
porn
became
illegal

2019
Upskirting
became
illegal

▲ **PowerPoint slide 5**

1) Once the students are all in their seats, you can ask the group: Why is it important for laws to be updated? (e.g. they keep up with changing times – revenge porn wouldn't have been a common problem before mobile phones)

2) If you were the leader of the UK, what laws would you change or add?

3) Does society change the law? Or does the law change society? (Facilitators' note: Show the group PowerPoint slide 6 following this discussion.)

DOES SOCIETY CHANGE THE LAW? OR DOES THE LAW CHANGE SOCIETY?

Social approval of same-sex couples has changed drastically in the last 30 years. Young people are at least five times more likely than those aged over 65 to identify as gay, lesbian or bisexual (Office for National Statistics).

Until 1967 (in England and Wales) it was illegal to be homosexual. Now, the LGBTQI+ community is protected and it is illegal to discriminate or commit hate crimes against them.

Think about smoking in public, charging for plastic bags and wearing a seatbelt...

What do you think?

Does society change, and then the law is updated as a result?

OR

Does the law change, and then society's perceptions change as a result?

▲ **PowerPoint slide 6**

Exercise 5: Consent Laws Across the Globe[9]

There are 70 countries that criminalize same-sex relations and several that impose the death penalty for same-sex relationships (according to the International Lesbian, Gay, Bisexual, Trans and Intersex Association (ILGA)).

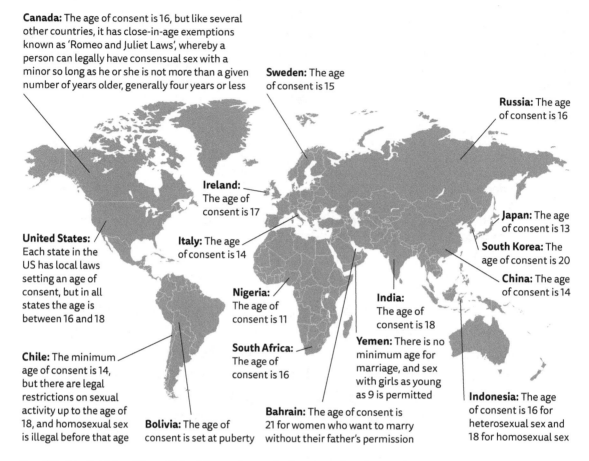

Canada: The age of consent is 16, but like several other countries, it has close-in-age exemptions known as 'Romeo and Juliet Laws', whereby a person can legally have consensual sex with a minor so long as he or she is not more than a given number of years older, generally four years or less

Sweden: The age of consent is 15

Russia: The age of consent is 16

Ireland: The age of consent is 17

Japan: The age of consent is 13

United States: Each state in the US has local laws setting an age of consent, but in all states the age is between 16 and 18

Italy: The age of consent is 14

South Korea: The age of consent is 20

China: The age of consent is 14

Nigeria: The age of consent is 11

India: The age of consent is 18

Chile: The minimum age of consent is 14, but there are legal restrictions on sexual activity up to the age of 18, and homosexual sex is illegal before that age

South Africa: The age of consent is 16

Yemen: There is no minimum age for marriage, and sex with girls as young as 9 is permitted

Bolivia: The age of consent is set at puberty

Bahrain: The age of consent is 21 for women who want to marry without their father's permission

Indonesia: The age of consent is 16 for heterosexual sex and 18 for homosexual sex

Saudi Arabia, Pakistan, Libya, Afghanistan and several other countries: The age of consent is not specified, but marriage is required

▲ PowerPoint slide 7

Show the group the map, either printed out, one per table, or on PowerPoint slide 7, and read out some of the facts relating to sexual consent around the globe. Ask the young people to put on their lawyer hats and discuss the following questions (either in small groups or all together):

1) Are there any laws that particularly surprise you?
2) What do you think about laws where the age of consent is different for people who are heterosexual and people who are homosexual? Why do you think there is a difference? Do you think this is fair?
3) What would it be like to be a child or young person growing up in some of the places highlighted on the map?

---

9   Sources: www.theweek.co.uk/92121/ages-of-consent-around-the-world; https://www.ageofconsent.net/world; http://worldpopulationreview.com/countries/age-of-consent-by-country; https://ilga.org/maps-sexual-orientation-laws

4) Are there any laws on the map that you would like to change if you could? Which ones?

5) If you were the leader of a country, what laws would you put in place around the age of consent? (This question could be expanded into a small group discussion or a piece of written work.)

Exercise 6: If Something Happens, What Happens Next?

Part 1

Read out or show the group PowerPoint slide 8, which has statistics about sexual violence:

1. Only **15%** of rape survivors report it to the police.[10]
2. **79%** of male victims/survivors of sexual harassment didn't report it to anyone.[11]
3. In the US, nearly **1 in 10** women have experienced rape by an *intimate partner* in their lifetime.[12]
4. Only **2–8%** of rapes are falsely reported, the same percentage as for other crimes.[13]
5. Studies suggest that around **half** of transgender people and bisexual women will experience sexual violence at some point in their lifetimes.[14]

▲ **PowerPoint slide 8**

Ask the group: Why might people, including men and people from the LGBTQI+ community, not report sexual harassment or sexual violence?

After you have elicited ideas from the group about why people are reluctant to report sexual violence following an offence, show them PowerPoint slide 9 or read out any ideas that the group haven't come up with from the list:

WHY DO PEOPLE CHOOSE NOT TO DISCLOSE?
- Not realizing that what happened was wrong/illegal
- Fear of consequences or repercussions
- Fear of discrimination (particularly people who experience stigma due to their sexual orientation or gender identity)
- Fear of having to give details of what happened
- Feeling to blame

10 Ministry of Justice, Home Office, Office for National Statistics (2013) *An Overview of Sexual Offending in England and Wales: Statistics Bulletin.* Accessed on 23/2/2020 at https://webarchive.nationalarchives.gov.uk/20160106113426/http://www.ons.gov.uk/ons/rel/crime-stats/an-overview-of-sexual-offending-in-england---wales/december-2012/index.html

11 Price, H. (2019) 'What is sexual harassment at work? How to tell when lines are crossed in the workplace.' BBC Three. Accessed on 31/1/2020 at www.bbc.co.uk/bbcthree/article/931fb95e-039c-44db-a8f0-67bbd61fa30e

12 Centers for Disease Control and Prevention (2014) 'National Intimate Partner and Sexual Violence Survey, United States, 2011.' Accessed on 31/1/2020 at www.ncbi.nlm.nih.gov/pmc/articles/PMC4692457

13 Lonsway, K., Archambault, J. and Lisak, D. (2009) 'False reports: Moving beyond the issue to successfully investigate and prosecute nonstranger sexual assault.' *The Voice* 3, 1. Accessed on 31/1/2020 at www.nsvrc.org/sites/default/files/publications/2018-10/Lisak-False-Reports-Moving-beyond.pdf

14 Human Rights Campaign (n.d.) 'Sexual assault and the LGBTQ community.' Accessed on 31/1/2020 at www.hrc.org/resources/sexual-assault-and-the-lgbt-community

- Embarrassment, shame
- Low self-esteem
- Lack of self-worth
- Threats by the people who have harmed them
- Not knowing who to disclose to
- People from the LGBTQI+ community may be reluctant to disclose if it would mean they would have to come out

▲ **PowerPoint slide 9**

Part 2

Ask the group to raise their hands if they believe that you can only report rape to the police. Then read out or show them PowerPoint slide 10:

FAKE NEWS

Myth: You can only report rape to the police.

Fact: There are non-legal approaches people can take to get support without having to speak to the police. SARCs (Sexual Assault Referral Centres) can offer advice and support and take evidence. If in the future someone changes their mind and does want to report the crime, they can use the evidence collected by the SARC. People can also seek advice and support from Rape Crisis Centres, Childline and the Samaritans.

If someone does go to the police, what next?

- They will ask for the details of the situation – who, what, where, when, how.
- They will complete a 'Victim Impact Statement' to find out how the crime has affected the victim/survivor.
- They will collect information and decide whether there is enough evidence to take to court.

▲ **PowerPoint slide 10**

Part 3

Wrap up the session by reminding the group why it is so important for people to have awareness of consent and the law. Read out or show them PowerPoint slide 11:

Being aware of the law around sex and consent is important for many reasons...

It means people are more likely to:

- have healthy, communicative sexual relationships that make them feel good
- check that they have consent (and therefore be less likely to commit a sexual crime)

- know what their options are if they are concerned that they have been a victim of sexual violence (including rape and sexual assault).

▲ **PowerPoint slide 11**

End the session with PowerPoint slide 12 and let the group know that there are many places they can go to get resources on this subject or seek support, and there are procedures in place for anonymous reporting. It is important for them to share any issues or concerns that they have about themselves or others related to this topic. Be mindful of the possible impacts and emotions that might be evoked for individuals from the discussion, and if a topic is emotive for someone, offer an opportunity to explore this outside the group, to ensure that they feel heard and safe.

SIGNPOSTING AND RESOURCES

If anything in today's workshop has affected you, support is available.

▷ **Childline** can be contacted online or on the phone, any time, on 0800 1111. Check out the website: www.childline.org.uk

If you've been sexually assaulted, there are services out there to help. You don't have to report to the police if you don't want to. Consider getting medical help quickly as you may be at risk of sexually transmitted infections or pregnancy.

▷ **Rape Crisis England and Wales** is the umbrella body for a network of independent Rape Crisis Centres which provide specialist support and services for victims and survivors of sexual violence. The freephone helpline is 0808 802 9999 (between 12 and 2.30pm and 7 and 9.30pm every day of the year. Calls don't show up on phone bills).

▲ **PowerPoint slide 12**

Social and Antisocial Media

> It's a necessary class and should be taught more

Session Overview

This workshop starts by looking at different social media platforms and campaigns. It uses scenarios to explore online risks including catfishing and cyberbullying behaviours. The young people are then asked to consider how to respond to something hurtful or distressing they see online, and explore the difference between being a 'Bystander' and an 'Upstander'.

Info/Knowledge

Young people are increasingly growing up engaging in two separate but interconnected worlds – the online world and IRL (in real life). Bullying behaviours exist in both worlds. Cyberbullying behaviours can have a devastating impact on young people, leading to anxiety, depression and even self-harm and suicide. A survey by Public Health England of young people aged 11–15 years old found that 17.9% reported being on the receiving end of cyberbullying behaviour in the two months prior to being surveyed.[1] Cyberbullying behaviour is usually committed by someone known to the young person, and while the person displaying this behaviour most likely knows whom they are targeting, they will often choose to remain anonymous or use a false name. This can be very frightening for their target. Technology and terminology change rapidly, but RSE should still cover issues such as privacy, online safety, the influence of peers and young people's own personal responsibilities, as well as what the law says. Ofsted

---

1   Public Health England (2014) 'Cyberbullying: An analysis of data from the Health Behaviour in School-aged Children (HBSC) survey for England, 2014.' Accessed on 6/2/2020 at https://assets.publishing.service.gov.uk/government/uploads/system/uploads/attachment_data/file/621070/Health_behaviour_in_school_age_children_cyberbullying.pdf

considers, among other things, 'children's and learners' understanding of healthy and unhealthy relationships and how they are supported to keep themselves safe from relevant risks including when using the internet and social media'.[2] Inspectors should include online safety in their discussions with children and learners (covering topics such as online bullying and safe use of the internet and social media). Inspectors should investigate what the school or further education and skills provider does to educate pupils in online safety and how the provider or school deals with issues when they arise. When planning a lesson about social media, be sure to communicate with your school's computing department who may be covering similar issues of online safety, to avoid any duplication or contradictory messages.

PSHE Association Curriculum Themes

▷ KS3 L4. Strategies for safely challenging stereotyping, prejudice, bigotry, bullying behaviour and discrimination when they witness or experience it in their daily lives

▷ KS4 R16. To recognize when others are using manipulation, persuasion or coercion and how to respond

Exercises

▷ Exercise 1: Exploring Values and Beliefs – Group Debate
▷ Exercise 2: Exploring Social Media Platforms
▷ Exercise 3: Exploring the #MeToo Movement
▷ Exercise 4: Exploring 'Catfishing'
▷ Exercise 5: Cyberbullying Behaviours
▷ Exercise 6: Exploring Our Online Behaviour
▷ Exercise 7: Bystanders and Upstanders
▷ Exercise 8: Prevention Is Better Than Cure

Materials Needed

▷ Printed pictures of the #MeToo movement if you don't have access to PowerPoint for Exercise 3 (Resources and Handouts 5.1)
▷ Case studies to cut out for Exercise 5 (Resources and Handouts 5.2)
▷ 'True' and 'False' cards per table (optional) for Exercise 1 (Resources and Handouts 5.3)
▷ 'Am I Cyber Sorted?' quiz handout one per student for Exercise 6 (Resources and Handouts 5.4)

---

2   Ofsted (2019) Inspecting safeguarding in early years, education and skills settings: Guidance for inspectors carrying out inspections under the education inspection framework from September 2019 . Accessed on 10/7/2020 at https://assets.publishing.service.gov.uk/government/uploads/system/uploads/attachment_data/file/828763/Inspecting_safeguarding_in_early_years__education_and_skills.pdf

Learning Outcomes
By the end of this session:

- I can understand and express the pros and cons of social media
- I can understand the unique challenge of online abuse including abusive relationships online, cyberbullying behaviours, catfishing, sexting and revenge porn
- I can reflect on my own online behaviour and whether this causes harm to others
- I know what to do if someone is affected, both practically and in terms of providing emotional support
- I can confidently talk about online safety, including privacy, peer influence and personal responsibility
- I have an awareness of my digital/online footprint and reputation

At the beginning of the session, inform the group of the topic – *Social and Antisocial Media* – and point out that it requires the group to approach the discussions with a certain amount of maturity and sensitivity. Remind the group of the agreed expectations, particularly emphasizing confidentiality and the importance of treating one another with respect. Check that everyone is in agreement, looking for nods or verbal recognition that they're on the same page. Remind the group that if something comes up in the session that upsets them or makes them feel uncomfortable, they have permission to leave the room or find some space, and remind them of where they can go or who they can approach for support. Creating a safe environment is covered in more detail in the Introduction. Before starting, briefly set out what will be covered in the workshop.

Exercise 1: Exploring Values and Beliefs – Group Debate

Ask the group to imagine that there is a line across the room. Explain to the group that one side of the room is 'Agree' and the other side is 'Disagree' (you can put up signs to make this clear). Let them know that when you read out a statement they are invited to stand where they feel they are on the line in relation to the statement. If it isn't possible for the young people to move about in the room, you can ask them to put up a hand or stand up if they agree, or give out the green, amber and red cards to each participant representing 'agree', 'neither agree nor disagree' and 'disagree' in Resources and Handouts 1.1. Reassure the group that there are no right or wrong answers, that they can stand in the middle if they are unsure and that they are able to move at any time if their opinion has been swayed. Remind the group to remain respectful when listening to and debating views and opinions that differ from their own. If the group find it hard not to talk over each other, you can use an object to represent a 'talking piece' which allows the person holding it permission to speak, while everyone else needs to listen until their turn with the talking piece (see Appendix 5).

When the young people have moved to where they want to stand, facilitate a debate between individuals or sides. Feel free to contribute to the debate (there are some facilitators' notes below that may be helpful discussion points).

You don't need to go through all of the statements; pick those that seem most relevant to the group.

Once you have used a few statements, ask the group if they have any other ideas that they want to debate. It might help if the young people talk briefly in pairs to help them to come up with a statement.

- **People do and say things online that they wouldn't in real life.** (Facilitators' note: If you wouldn't say it to someone's face, don't say it online either – behind every account is a real person.)
- **Social media is dangerous.** (Facilitators' note: The way that people use social media can be dangerous and most social media platforms are designed in a way that encourages people to use them as much as possible.)
- **Sending a nude means you're looking for someone to have sex with.** (Facilitators' note: This can be a harmful myth. People send nudes for multiple reasons and doing so doesn't reflect someone's sexual availability or experience.)
- **Parents/carers should monitor what their children do online.** (Facilitators' note: All social media platforms have age restrictions for a reason – to protect children and young people from being exposed to shocking or damaging things online, or to protect them from other online users who may have harmful intentions.)
- **Social media is addictive.** (Facilitators' note: Research shows that not only is social media addictive, but it is designed and developed to keep people using it so the industry makes more money. On average, teenagers spend around 18 hours a week on their phones and most of this is on social media.[3])
- **You can trust what you read online.** (Facilitators' note: There is a lot of 'fake news' online and it is important to do your own research, use sites with reliable sources and see everything online with a critical eye, when reading the news but especially when seeing gossip.)

Exercise 2: Exploring Social Media Platforms

Facilitators' note: If you have access to computers for the young people to use for research on Exercise 2, we recommend using the website:

www.childnet.com/young-people/secondary/hot-topics

---

3   Andersson, H. (2018) 'Social media apps are "deliberately" addictive to users.' BBC News. Accessed on 31/1/2020 at www.bbc.co.uk/news/technology-44640959

Part 1

Ask the group what they most enjoy doing online, and what it is about these things that makes them fun.

Part 2

Get the young people into approximately six groups and ask each group to choose a social media platform that they want to research and represent (e.g. Instagram, Snapchat, WhatsApp). It doesn't matter if more than one group chooses the same platform, but try to ensure there are multiple platforms explored. Note that the popularity of social media platforms is constantly changing, so encourage the group to think of which platforms are most relevant to them.

Part 3

Give each group a piece of flipchart paper, some pens and 15 minutes to discuss and explore the following questions (on PowerPoint slide 2 or write them on the board) relating to the platform they have:

SOCIAL MEDIA PLATFORMS
1. Why do people like this platform?
2. What are the negatives?
3. Are there any risks associated with using this platform?
4. What are the age restrictions/recommended age? Does this stop younger people from using it?
5. Does this platform have any content of a sexual nature?
6. Does this platform promote violence or bullying?
7. Does this platform have any content relating to self-harm and suicide?
8. Does this platform have any content relating to alcohol, drugs and crime?
9. Does this platform have a 'Block' or 'Report' button?

▲ **PowerPoint slide 2**

Part 4

Ask each group to feedback their answers and reflections to the rest of the group. Then ask the group as a whole whether they believe that parents/carers should be worried about young people's access to social media and why.

Exercise 3: Exploring the #MeToo Movement

Part 1

Explain to the group that we are going to look at a powerful example of how social media has connected communities and brought important, and often hidden, information into public awareness – the #MeToo movement.

Show the group PowerPoint slide 3 (if you don't have access to PowerPoint, you can print out some images of the #MeToo movement and still ask the follow-up questions).

THE HISTORY OF #METOO[4]

The term 'MeToo' was coined in 2006 by Tarana Burke who wanted to promote 'empowerment through empathy' among women of colour who had been sexually abused. A 13-year-old girl confided in Tarana that she had been sexually assaulted, and Tarana later wished that she had simply replied, 'Me too.'

Tarana's Me Too movement was different from the Me Too movement of Alyssa Milano, which now involves women from all over the world connecting, speaking out and responding to each other's stories of sexual abuse.

▲ PowerPoint slide 3

---

4   Image courtesy of 123RF.

Part 2

Ask the young people the following questions:

1) How many of you have heard of the #MeToo campaign? (Facilitators' note: If some of the young people haven't heard of it, ask a student who has to describe it to them or let them know that in 2017 the #MeToo movement against harassment and sexual assault spread across the world as a reaction to a series of sexual harassment and assault allegations made against powerful men in Hollywood. Women and men came forward with #MeToo, sharing their experiences of harassment and violence.)

2) Why do you think #MeToo had such a big impact on the world? (Facilitators' note: It brought awareness to the scale of the problem of sexual violence, empowered people to speak out, made people feel less alone and more supported, caused less shame to be attached to being a victim/survivor and held people in the public eye accountable for their behaviour. Many industries adopted stricter sexual harassment policies in the workplace and people started challenging occurrences of sexual violence.)

3) Do you think movements like #MeToo are important? (Facilitators' note: This will be answered on PowerPoint slide 4.)

4) Do you think the reach of this movement would have been possible without social media?

Part 3

Show the group PowerPoint slide 4 or read out the facts about the #MeToo Movement:

DID YOU KNOW...?

▷ #MeToo has been Googled in every country in the world.

▷ #MeToo shockingly revealed that **81%** of women and **43%** of men have experienced some form of sexual harassment or assault in their lifetime. This was even higher for people with disabilities or gay or bisexual men[5].

▷ Since #MeToo people have felt more empowered to speak out and challenge sexual harassment – this is especially true of young people, which is a big step in working towards ending sexual violence altogether.[6]

▲ **PowerPoint slide 4**

Part 4

Finally, ask the group: Can you think of any negative impact the #MeToo movement

---

5   https://www.bbc.co.uk/news/world-44045291
6   https://www.independent.co.uk/life-style/women/young-people-metoo-sexual-harassment-fawcett-society-research-a8565011.
     html

might have had on the world? (e.g. some survivors felt that the campaign resurfaced pain attached to their past experiences)

Exercise 4: Exploring 'Catfishing'

Part 1

Explain that the next part of the workshop explores online risks including catfishing and cyberbullying behaviours.

Part 2

Explore the knowledge in the room by asking:

1) What is 'catfishing'? (Facilitators' note: This question will be answered on Power-Point slide 5.)

2) How common is catfishing? (Facilitators' note: Consumer group Which? ran a survey which suggested that around 60% of people had seen what they believed to be a fake profile online.[7])

At the end of the discussion, show the group PowerPoint slide 5 or read out the definition of catfishing:

WHAT IS CATFISHING?

'Catfishing' is the term used to describe someone using deception to hide their true identity online.

Catfishing is not a crime, but it is illegal under certain circumstances – e.g. when the motive is sexual, identity theft, etc.

Other forms of identity theft include 'fraping' and using people's passwords to access their accounts.

▲ **PowerPoint slide 5**

Part 3

Lead a discussion with the group around catfishing using the following questions:

1) What might motivate someone to catfish? (Facilitators' note: This could include loneliness, feeling dissatisfied with their physical appearance, a desire to escape, exploring their sexual orientation or gender identity and wanting to be anonymous, experimental reasons such as expressing desires and urges, an attempt to target someone in a specific way, or for practical reasons such as being too young for a website and creating a new identity to gain access.)

---

7   You can read more about this survey at www.which.co.uk/news/2016/02/fake-and-suspicious-profiles-rife-on-dating-sites-432850

2) Are all catfishers malicious?

3) What would you do if you found out you were being catfished online?

4) What would be the emotional impact of being catfished?

5) What can you do to avoid being catfished? (Facilitators' note: You could fact-check, protect yourself, suspect people who always avoid video calls, only connect with people you know, don't give away personal information, be suspicious if someone contacts you randomly, ask yourself: Does this sound too good to be true?)

Exercise 5: Cyberbullying Behaviours

Part 1

Explore the knowledge and experiences in the room by asking the group:

1) What is your definition of cyberbullying behaviour?

2) What does it look like? Can you give any examples?

3) How can cyberbullying behaviours differ from bullying behaviours offline? (e.g. people can change their profiles to send a message to others, there is the potential for a massive audience, people can remain anonymous, there is digital evidence of cyberbullying, cyberbullying behaviours can occur 24/7.[8])

Part 2

After eliciting feedback, show them the definition of cyberbullying behaviour on PowerPoint slide 6 or read out the text:

CYBERBULLYING

Cyberbullying, or online bullying, can be defined as the use of technologies by an individual or by a group of people to deliberately and repeatedly upset someone else.[9]

▲ **PowerPoint slide 6**

Part 3

Ask the group to raise their hands if they have ever heard of anyone who has (a) received a nasty, hurtful comment online or (b) sent a nasty or hurtful comment online. It is useful for the group to get a sense of how common the experience is, but in order to avoid the young people sharing their personal experiences of cyberbullying or talking about other people known to the group, move the conversation on quickly rather than opening up a debate at this point.

---

8   Childnet (n.d.) 'Executive Summary: Understanding, Preventing and Responding to Cyberbullying.' Accessed on 16/3/2020 at www.childnet.com/ufiles/Executive-Summary.pdf

9   This definition is from Childnet, a UK-based charity whose aim is to make the internet safe for children: 'Executive Summary: Understanding, Preventing and Responding to Cyberbullying.' Accessed on 16/3/2020 at www.childnet.com/ufiles/Executive-Summary.pdf

Part 4

Show the group PowerPoint slide 7 or read out the statistics on cyberbullying behaviours:

DID YOU KNOW...?

▷ Around **1 in 3** young people have been victims of cyberbullying behaviour.

▷ Cyberbullying makes young people more than **twice** as likely to self-harm or attempt suicide.

▷ People who engage in cyberbullying behaviour have often been victims themselves.

▷ People who are on the receiving end of bullying behaviours online are less likely to report and seek help than people who have been bullied offline.

▷ Cyberbullying behaviour is often linked to discrimination – for example, girls and people who identify as lesbian, gay, bisexual and transgender are more likely to experience cyberbullying.[10]

▲ **PowerPoint slide 7**

Part 5

Ask the group:

1) Why do people say things on screen that they wouldn't say to someone's face? (Facilitators' note: Being online can allow people to feel anonymous and believe they are protected from repercussions because they are communicating through a screen.)

2) Why are people less likely to report cyberbullying than bullying that occurs offline? (Facilitators' note: They may have been the one who started it off, and would have to admit to their part in it; they are worried the person they tell will restrict their online access; they are worried that they will expose dangerous ways they use social media and get into trouble for it; they feel ashamed or embarrassed; they feel that they should be able to solve it themselves; they're worried they won't be taken seriously by adults because 'it's only online'; the people displaying the bullying behaviour may be anonymous so they don't think anything can be done.)

Part 6

Ask the young people to explore the case studies (Resources and Handouts 5.2) in small groups or pairs. Each case study is followed by some questions which the groups need to answer. You can choose whether you want the small groups/pairs to have one case study

---

10 John, A., Glendenning, A.C., Marchant, A., Montgomery, P. *et al.* (2018) 'Self-harm, suicidal behaviours, and cyberbullying in children and young people: Systematic review.' *Journal of Medical Internet Research 20*, 4, e129; Childnet (n.d.) 'Executive Summary: Understanding, Preventing and Responding to Cyberbullying.' Accessed on 16/3/2020 at www.childnet.com/ufiles/Executive-Summary.pdf

each and present their answers to the questions, or whether all the groups go through all the case studies.

Trigger warning: Let the group know that the content of the case studies may be triggering or distressing, especially if they describe situations that are of personal significance to group members. Remind the group that anyone feeling personally affected by the content has permission to opt out of doing an exercise, leave the room or come and speak to you at the end of the session. Always allow the young people to swap for a different scenario if they request to do so.

Case Study 1: Amy's Story

Hi, I'm Amy. When I was 13, I started playing around on webcams with my friend. More and more guys started asking us to flash our breasts, but we kept on saying no and switching off the camera. About a year later this guy I had been talking to for a while asked me again and I took off my bra and flashed him. I didn't know that he'd screenshotted an image of me topless until a week later when he sent me the photo of my breasts and said he'd send it round school if I didn't send him a photo of me totally nude. I said I wouldn't, and then he messaged me with my address, the name of my school and a list of all my mates I hang out with, and said he was serious. I sent him a photo of me naked out of fear, but when I turned up to school, he had sent the photo around anyway. Literally everyone had seen it. I just couldn't look anyone in the eye. The police came to speak to me but I didn't want to tell them anything or press charges against the guy because now he had a photo of my whole body and I didn't want it to come out or for me to get into trouble for sending it. Once it's out there, you can't get it back! Boys at school started hassling me for sex, calling me a slut and trying to grope my breasts. Nobody tried to stop them or told them it wasn't OK. I was humiliated. I was devastated, I couldn't stop crying, I stopped going to school and hid away from my mates. I just felt anxious all the time. It was never ending – every time I thought it had gone away, someone from school would send me the picture with a nasty or sexual comment, or people would put it as their profiles just to taunt me.

Questions

- What happened to Amy?
- Has she been a victim of a crime?
- Who is responsible for what happened to Amy?
- At what point were the rules of consent broken?
- What was the impact on Amy's emotional health, sense of safety, peer relationships, self-esteem and reputation?
- What do you think of Amy's comment – 'once it's out there, you can't get it back'?
- Was Amy right not to speak to the police?

- How would you have supported her if you were a friend and you knew this was going on?
- What would you do next if you were Amy?

Case Study 2: Tom's Story

Hi, I'm Tom and I love online gaming. I'm 15, and after my parents split up, I noticed I felt like shit the whole time. I didn't really enjoy playing sport anymore, or even really seeing my mates much – I just didn't feel like the normal me. My teachers all commented on how my grades were slipping, and my mum, who used to let me game whenever I wanted, started going on and on at me about it. The truth is none of this bothered me. Online I could be all the things that I couldn't be in real life any more – confident, funny, competitive. It was the only thing that made me feel good, or at least that didn't make me feel worse. That's when I met Blake. Blake was a couple of years older than me, he was cool, smart, had good banter and had already left school because he had a wicked job working for Apple. He made me feel good, giving me compliments on my game and tips to complete it. He even offered to buy me add-ons to help me improve.

We started talking and gaming all through the night. I prioritized it over doing my homework or sleeping. We started talking on other messaging sites and Blake became the only person I trusted. Sometimes Blake sent me videos of porn that he liked and then asked me if they'd turned me on. Sometimes they did, sometimes they didn't. He was the only person who asked me how I really was, or who actually seemed to care about what I was into. My mum was getting more annoying and depressed, and my mates all started getting girlfriends so they didn't really invite me out any more.

One day Blake offered to buy me more add-ons and suggested we masturbate together on webcam. I wasn't really expecting it, but he said this is what real mates do and sent me a picture of himself naked to prove it. He asked how I was going to feel confident getting a girlfriend if I wasn't comfortable doing this with my best mate first. Blake's webcam was broken, but he said he'd keep the sound on and we could see who could last the longest. I did, and Blake said that was something to be proud of for a virgin.

One day the police came round to my house and sat me and mum down. They asked if I knew anyone called Will Barnet and I said I didn't recognize the name. I thought I was in trouble for something, but it turned out that the police had found the video of me masturbating on a porn site online and had tracked the owner to a guy called Will. They said it wasn't the first time this guy had put child pornography on to the internet, but they wanted it to be the last. Will, as I now knew him, was 36 and didn't work for Apple. Everything he said to me was a lie. I broke down. I couldn't believe Blake had done this to me, I told him all my secrets, thoughts, everything.

He'd even seen me naked. I felt so betrayed, lost and angry, but knowing that Blake did this to loads of other boys my age made me feel like speaking to the police because making him stop felt important.

Questions

- What happened to Tom?
- Has he been a victim of a crime?
- Who is responsible for what happened to Tom?
- At what point were the rules of consent broken?
- What was the impact on Tom's emotional health, sense of safety, peer relationships, self-esteem and reputation?
- Was Tom right to speak to the police?
- How would you have supported him if you were a friend and you knew this was going on?
- What would you do next if you were Tom?

Case Study 3: Liam's Story

My name's Liam and I realized I wasn't into girls when I was really young, like 8. It took me much longer before I started having sexual feelings towards other guys. Even when I did, I didn't know how to approach men, find out if they were gay too, or tell any of my mates about this. See, at my school there's loads of homophobia. People say 'gay' all the time as an insult. They don't seem to think the same about lesbians, maybe it's because they're sexualized in porn. Or maybe boys at school are just scared of someone coming on to them and they behave as a bully out of fear. Anyway, this all made me feel really uncomfortable and worried about being judged or people finding out.

I thought this all changed when I met Dontae at a party. He made it obvious he was into me and I couldn't have been more flattered. He told me he was bisexual and started kissing my neck, my shoulders, my mouth. I spent the whole week fantasizing about Dontae and hoping I'd see him again. The next week at school a photo went round of me and Dontae kissing. Someone had seen us at the party and I hadn't even realized. Immediately, people started writing horrible comments, sending me videos of gay porn and telling me I was disgusting. I didn't realize the photo had gone around Dontae's school too, and Dontae had told everyone that I had pushed him against the wall and forced my tongue into his mouth. This couldn't have been further from the truth, but people started sending me messages calling me a 'rapist' and saying 'stay away from me, gayboy'. It didn't matter what I said to defend myself – people just didn't believe me.

I didn't go to school for a week because I felt so scared and upset. I tried not to look at my phone, but every time I did, I had a new picture or comment sent to me, people superimposing my face on to the bodies of naked men and stuff, and everyone liking it.

My dad and stepmum found out I was gay because a teacher at school called them and told them I'd been seen forcing another man to kiss me. They were so ashamed – not that I was gay, but that I had done something like this. They wouldn't believe me when I said it was consensual. I was so full of hatred for myself that I started cutting my thighs with a razor. I'd just spend hours staring at myself in the mirror, feeling emptiness and black. The bullying was constant. I felt like I had nowhere to turn to. Comments like 'What you gonna do, cry?' made me feel ashamed and stupid for being hurt by it all, so I was too scared to speak out. I was angry at everyone, I stopped trusting people, and after I started receiving messages saying I should just throw myself off a bridge and die, I started considering it.

The school had got the police involved because Dontae had said I forced him. They came to take a statement and I told them about the bullying. I told them the kiss was consensual and Dontae had said that it wasn't to avoid everyone reacting like this to him. About a week later I got a message from Dontae saying 'I hadn't realized it had got so bad. Sorry I said you forced me.' When the police interviewed him again, he admitted it was consensual and said he'd lied to save face. The police stopped investigating it as sexual assault and started investigating the people sending me hate mail and bullying me online.

Questions

- What happened to Liam?
- Has he been a victim of a crime?
- Who is responsible for what happened to Liam?
- What was the impact on Liam's emotional health, sense of safety, peer relationships, self-esteem and reputation?
- How would you have supported him if you were a friend and you knew this was going on?

Part 7

Begin the case study feedback by showing PowerPoint slide 8 and/or having a discussion about the idea that 'anything online stays there forever'. Ensure the group know that although you can't get things back or control what happens when something is online, you can still get help.

Facilitators' Tip: When discussing the question 'who is responsible for what happened to X' in the case studies, remember to reinforce the fact that the person responsible for what happened is ALWAYS the person who caused the harm.

In Amy's case the person responsible is the guy who targeted Amy on a webcam, manipulated her, threatened her and then blackmailed her. Other people who caused harm included the boys at school harassing Amy and trying to touch her breasts without consent.

In Tom's case this is Blake, who targeted him online, exposed him to porn, groomed Tom by buying him things and manipulated him into masturbating on a webcam and then uploading the video to a porn site without Tom's awareness.

In Liam's case this involved many people: the people at school being homophobic in the first place, making Liam (and probably others) uncomfortable about their sexuality, the person who filmed and then distributed the video of Liam and Dontae kissing without their knowledge or consent, and all the people responding to the video in hurtful ways including telling Liam to commit suicide. Although Dontae behaved in a hurtful way towards Liam by lying and saying he was forced to kiss him, Dontae did this to protect himself, so is also a victim of homophobic abuse – sometimes people can be both the victim and the person who causes harm.

▲ **PowerPoint slide 8**

Now ask the groups for feedback on the rest of their questions and any thoughts they had about what happened, and the impact this had on Amy, Tom and Liam.

Part 8

When you are discussing the 'practical advice' that the groups would have given Amy, Tom and Liam, read out or show them PowerPoint slide 9 on how to deal with cyberbullying behaviours:

HOW TO DEAL WITH CYBERBULLYING BEHAVIOURS

- Don't keep it to yourself or deal with it alone. Tell someone you trust. It can help to talk.
- Don't reply to any nasty messages you receive. Keep the messages that you've been sent so you can show someone and use it as evidence (once you have done that, delete them and don't look at them again).
- Don't share, comment on or like any posts that involve bullying behaviour. Sharing or commenting could make things worse.
- Tell a responsible adult or the police if something is serious. Even if you have done something you're not proud of, they can still protect you from anything becoming worse.
- Block people who bully on all social media sites.
- Report people who bully to website administrators.
- Avoid sharing personal details online (e.g. photos in school uniform).
- Avoid speaking to people you don't know online.
- Don't send photos that may cause someone upset.
- Report it when you see things online that make you uncomfortable, even if it's not directly related to you.
- Remember that things can change. Get help to build your confidence.[11]

▲ **PowerPoint slide 9**

Exercise 6: Exploring Our Online Behaviour

Part 1

When we see things online that might cause someone to feel upset or distressed, we always have options of how to respond. Read out or show the group PowerPoint slide 10:

WE HAVE CHOICES...

When we see things online that might cause distress or upset, we always have choices of how to respond.

We can:

- behave as a **Bully** (initiate or join in with bullying behaviour)
- be a **Bystander** (do nothing and stay silent)

---

11   www.safestories.org.uk

- be an **Upstander** (be an ally and stand up against cyberbullying).

▲ **PowerPoint slide 10**

Part 2

Explain that we are going to look at each of these options in more detail. But first we are going to do the 'Am I Cyber Sorted?' quiz.

Explain to the group that they won't need to share their answers with anyone else and that this quiz is just to build awareness of their online behaviour and the possible impact it has on others.

Quiz

Take the following quiz to find out more about how you behave online, and whether you avoid being involved in bullying behaviour.

Statement	True	False
I would never hide my true identity when speaking to someone online		
I would stand up for someone online if they were being targeted by others		
I would decide not to press 'send' if I thought a comment might upset someone else		
I would never forward a private conversation without the permission of the other person		
I would block someone who was engaging in cyberbullying behaviour		
I would never block a friend just to upset them		
I would never give someone I don't know personal details about myself online		
I would never show someone inappropriate images just to shock them		
I would report something inappropriate or harmful online to the social media platform or a trusted adult		
I would never post personal things, rumours or lies about someone online		
I would do something positive if I saw negative comments about others online		
I would decline a friend request or follow from a stranger		
I would never insult someone in an interactive game room		
I would never take a purely online relationship offline (meet someone in person)		
I would never pass on a humiliating image of someone else		
I would apologize for something harmful I've said online		
I would never purposefully exclude someone from online conversations		
I would never do something online to purposefully upset or humiliate someone		

I would ask someone's permission before uploading a photo of them		
I would never send an 'indirect' message about someone else, without actually naming them		
I would never bait someone out/snitch on someone online		
I would never pressure someone to do something they didn't want to online		
I would never screenshot an image without the other person's knowledge		
I would never use someone else's password for any reason without their permission		
I would never say something online that I wouldn't say to someone's face		
I would never hide online accounts from adults at home		
I would never pretend to be a friend online with the intention of damaging their reputation/making them look bad		
I update my privacy settings regularly online		
Score: Total True: Total False:		

Add up all the answers you ticked 'true' for, and all the answers you ticked 'false'.

Now calculate your total score:

- If your score for 'true' is 22 or above you are: Cyber Sorted.
- If your score for 'true' is 14 or above you are: Cyber So-So.
- If your score for 'true' is under 14 you are: Cyber Risky.

Cyber Sorted

Well done! You are cyber sorted, you know how to keep yourself and others safe, happy and respected online, how to protect yourself and how to respond when things go wrong. Keep up the good work and don't forget to encourage others to be as cyber sorted as you!

Cyber So-So

Not bad! Your online behaviour is OK, with room for improvement. Remember to ask yourself: 'How would I feel if someone behaved like this towards me online?' and think before you post or comment. Try to be more on it when it comes to protecting and respecting yourself and others online.

Cyber Risky

Careful! Some of your online behaviour is risky, and could be harmful to yourself, and harmful, humiliating or upsetting for others. Start thinking before you post or comment online. Remember, you are responsible and in control of your own behaviour, which also means that you can change it.

Part 3

The quiz may have made some young people feel uncomfortable or exposed. Rather than exploring the quiz further, show the group PowerPoint slide 11 or read out the points made:

HOW TO BE CYBER SORTED

- Bullying is a *behaviour* that you have the power to stop. It is not who you are!
- **Think** before you post or comment – if you were on the receiving end of this, how would you feel?
- Is there something going on in your life which you are not happy about or which is making you feel sad, angry or out of control?
- **Talk** to someone about how you feel; don't bottle it up and take it out on someone else. Causing pain and hurt to someone else won't take your pain away.
- If you choose to be kind, you may feel better about yourself and have more positive responses from the people around you.
- Work on building your own **self-esteem** and **confidence**.
- If you realize you have engaged in bullying behaviour towards someone, you can approach this person and apologize.[12]

▲ **PowerPoint slide 11**

Exercise 7: Bystanders and Upstanders

Part 1

Explain to the group what is meant by being a Bystander.

Being a Bystander means either going along with what other people do without questioning it, challenging it or thinking about what you want, *or* doing nothing at all when you witness something that could be distressing to someone. Being a Bystander doesn't mean you are actively causing the harm yourself, but by doing nothing you send the message that you are OK with the harm being caused and allow the behaviour to continue.

Read out or show the group the quote from PowerPoint slide 12:

Can doing nothing be as bad as doing wrong?

▲ **PowerPoint slide 12**

---

12   Adapted with permission from www.safestories.org

Part 2

Explain to the group that we are going to explore what is meant by being an Upstander (e.g. being an ally, a friend, and standing up against behaviour that may be harmful and unethical).

Ask the group how an 'Upstander' would behave if they saw something that might be distressing online. Record their responses on the board and then read out or show them PowerPoint slides 13 and 14.

BEING AN UPSTANDER

You can be a **Passive** Upstander or a **Proactive** Upstander.

Passive Upstanders:

- respect and embrace differences
- don't laugh or join in with discriminatory behaviour towards others
- don't join in with negative comments
- try to think about how they would feel in a similar situation.

Don't be a Bystander – by doing nothing you are allowing the bullying behaviour and abuse to go on, therefore becoming a part of it.

Proactive Upstanders:
- focus on the person being targeted rather the person displaying the bullying behaviour
- don't pass on messages that could be upsetting to other people
- think about how they could support others – could they post a supportive comment online?
- ask their friend what they could do to help – encourage them to talk to a trusted adult
- talk to an adult to get advice about the best way to support their friend
- don't keep things to themselves if they are worried – they have a responsibility to make sure they are safe
- act as a role model and show others how to behave well online
- support their friend in reporting or blocking the person online.

The golden rule of Proactive Upstanding is to intervene only if it's safe for you to do so.

▲ **PowerPoint slides 13 and 14**

Part 3

Explain that it can be hard to be an Upstander, especially if the people you are standing up to are your peers. Let the group know that it's important to understand:

- If you suddenly start standing up for yourself, other people might be surprised or try to make you go back to the way you used to be.
- A good friend should respect you for standing up for yourself and others, and saying how you feel.

Part 4

Finish this section by showing PowerPoint slide 15 on being an Upstander or reading out the text:

If you know someone who has been the victim of any cyberbullying behaviour, whether it be having an image shared of them, being intimidated or threatened, or receiving horrible messages, they are probably going through a difficult time.

You can make a difference to that person.

BE AN UPSTANDER, NOT A BYSTANDER

▲ PowerPoint slide 15

Exercise 8: Prevention Is Better Than Cure

Let the group know that although there is always something that can be done when things go wrong online, preventing things from going wrong in the first place is the best approach.

Ask the young people to spend 10 minutes, in groups or pairs, to either:

1) create a poster advocating for online safety, or
2) write a list of online dos and don'ts aimed at an 8-year-old.
   (Facilitators' note: You can have PowerPoint slide 16, which is about online safety, up on the screen, or give the group some ideas and tips from it before they start the exercise.)

After 10 minutes, ask a representative from each group to share what they have come up with.

KEEPING SAFE ONLINE
- Be careful who you add as a friend online, especially if you don't know them in real life.
- If you meet someone over the internet, you don't know who they really are (they might be a lot older or a lot younger than you think they are).
- Never meet someone in person who you only know online – if you do, bring a friend and meet in a public place.
- Only share things online that you would be happy for your family and teachers to see.
- Check your privacy settings, have a strong password and keep it updated.
- Report or block whenever you see something that could cause distress or harm.
- Take time for yourself offline too – switch off and connect with people face to face.[13]

▲ PowerPoint slide 16

At the end of the session, read out or show the group PowerPoint slide 17 on what the law says:

---

13   Adapted with permission from www.safestories.org

WHAT THE LAW SAYS

There is not a criminal offence called 'cyberbullying', so cyberbullying behaviour itself is not a crime. However, behaviours linked to cyberbullying, such as stalking, threats, accessing computer systems without permission and circulating sexual images do break specific laws.[14]

For example:

▷ Protection from Harassment Act 1997
▷ Communications Act 2003
▷ Malicious Communications Act 1988
▷ Public Order Act 1986
▷ Computer Misuse Act 1990
▷ Protection of Children Act 1978 (Section 1)

Sometimes young people are prosecuted for engaging in cyberbullying behaviour. The first person to be prosecuted for posting abuse online was an 18-year-old girl who got three months in youth custody after pleading guilty to harassment.[15]

▲ PowerPoint slide 17

End the session with PowerPoint slide 18 and let the group know that there are many places they can go to get resources on this subject or seek support, and there are procedures in place for anonymous reporting. It is important for them to share any issues or concerns that they have about themselves or others related to this topic. Be mindful of the possible impacts and emotions that might be evoked for individuals from the discussion, and if a topic is emotive for someone, offer an opportunity to explore this outside the group, to ensure that they feel heard and safe.

SIGNPOSTING AND RESOURCES

If you are worried about online sexual abuse or the way someone has been communicating with you on the internet, you can report what is happening and get support.

▷ **Childnet Hub** contains tips, competitions and blogs to help you use the internet safely, responsibly and positively: www.childnet.com/young-people/secondary
▷ **CEOP:** If you have been a victim of online abuse or you're worried about somebody else, you can report securely to CEOP at: www.ceop.police.uk
▷ **Ditch the Label** is an international anti-bullying charity which offers support, help and advice to young people: www.ditchthelabel.org

▲ PowerPoint slide 18

---

14   Childnet (n.d.) 'Executive Summary: Understanding, Preventing and Responding to Cyberbullying.' Accessed on 16/3/2020 at www.childnet.com/ufiles/Executive-Summary.pdf
15   Adapted with permission from www.safestories.org.uk

Sexting and Nudes

It was good to see what everyone else in the room thought about the issues as well as my own opinion

Session Overview

This workshop looks at sexting and nudes. It outlines the legal situation, explores the impact and uses scenarios to consider the motivations for young people sending a 'nude'. The workshop finishes with funny responses the young people might make to a request for a nude.

Info/Knowledge

Section 88 of 'Keeping children safe in education: Statutory guidance for schools and colleges'[1] details a school's statutory safeguarding responsibilities, stating that they 'should ensure that children are taught about safeguarding, including online safety. Schools should consider this as part of providing a broad and balanced curriculum.' Social media has created new opportunities for sharing personal information, and young people should be encouraged to consider what they wish people to know and see about them. Sexting, nudes and revenge porn are a particular online safeguarding concern, with the Institute for Family Studies finding that nearly 15% of teenagers have sent a sext, while over 27% have received one.[2]

Young people appreciate clear information about the law to do with sexting and nudes. They should learn that it is illegal to make, possess or share an indecent image or pseudo-photograph of a person under the age of 18 – even if it's a picture of themselves. Make sure that you are confident about the law and

---

1   Published by the Department for Education in 2019. Accessed on 31/1/2020 at https://assets.publishing.service.gov.uk/government/uploads/system/uploads/attachment_data/file/835733/Keeping_children_safe_in_education_2019.pdf
2   IFS (2018) 'How many teens are sexting?' Accessed on 31/1/2020 at https://ifstudies.org/blog/how-many-teens-are-sexting

can field questions, such as 'Will you get jail time for it?' National guidance is provided by the UK Council for Internet Safety.[3] As well as providing schools and colleges with information on how to manage sexting, it also provides information about the law and links to further resources for education.

Young people may have their own terms for sexting and nudes, including 'selfies', 'dickpics' or 'fanpics'. Be ready for giggling, as initiating a discussion on these issues and using this terminology can cause embarrassment and nervousness.

PSHE Association Curriculum Themes

▷ KS4 R7. To develop an awareness of exploitation, bullying, harassment and control in relationships (including the unique challenges posed by online abuse and the unacceptability of physical, emotional, sexual abuse in all types of teenage relationships, including in group settings such as gangs) and the skills and strategies to respond appropriately or access support

▷ KS4 R16. To recognize when others are using manipulation, persuasion or coercion and how to respond

Exercises

▷ Exercise 1: Exploring Nude Photos and Sexting
▷ Exercise 2: Quiz – What the Law Says
▷ Exercise 3: The Impact of Sexting and Nudes
▷ Exercise 4: Pass the Pulse
▷ Exercise 5: In Control

Materials Needed

▷ Access to YouTube
▷ A coin for Pass the Pulse
▷ Scenarios for Exercise 1 (Resources and Handouts 6.1)

Learning Outcomes

By the end of this session:

- I can understand why young people sext or send nudes, including the influence of peer pressure
- I can understand the risks involved
- I will know the law around sexting, sending nudes and revenge porn
- I can understand the impact of sexting/nudes, and have some strategies for responding to requests
- I will know the importance of supporting someone
- I can reflect on how to stay in control online

3   www.gov.uk/government/publications/sexting-in-schools-and-colleges

At the beginning of the session, inform the group of the topic – *Sexting and Nudes* – and point out that it requires the group to approach the discussions with a certain amount of maturity and sensitivity. Remind the group of the agreed expectations, particularly emphasizing confidentiality and the importance of treating one another with respect. Check that everyone is in agreement, looking for nods or verbal recognition that they're on the same page. Remind the group that if something comes up in the session that upsets them or makes them feel uncomfortable, they have permission to leave the room or find some space, and remind them of where they can go or who they can approach for support. Creating a safe environment is covered in more detail in the Introduction. Before starting, briefly set out what will be covered in the workshop.

Exercise 1: Exploring Nude Photos and Sexting

Part 1

Show the video 'I saw your willy':

> www.youtube.com/watch?v=z1n9Jly3CQ8 (video length: 1 minute).

▲ **PowerPoint slide 2**

This short video from the NSPCC introduces the topic of sexting and nudes. Although it is aimed at a younger audience and parents, it can provide an amusing a way of introducing the topic and getting young people to start thinking about these issues. The message it contains tends to stick in people's minds.

Part 2

To explore the knowledge in the room, ask the group the following questions:

1) What does sexting mean?
2) What other words do you use for it?
3) Is there a difference between sexting and sending a nude photo or dickpic? (Facilitators' note: A nude usually refers to an image or video, and sexting may also include explicit text.)

Remind the group that sexting and nudes can happen in any relationship, including between people of the same sex.

Part 3

Divide the young people into small groups. Give each group one of the five scenarios. Explain to the young people that people may send nude photos for a number of reasons. In their groups, ask the young people to discuss the motivations of the people involved, and the advice that they would give them if they were a friend. You can ask each group to read out their scenario and share their responses to encourage a group discussion.

Trigger warning: These scenarios contain sexual language and describe behaviour that might be shocking or triggering to certain young people. Ensure that you read the scenarios before introducing them to the group to assess their suitability for the young people's age and the context of the session (see Disclaimer on page 12).

Scenario 1: Milo and Xante

Milo is single. He loves nothing more than looking through people's profiles on Snap, PMing girls when he thinks they're hot. He often sends photos of himself posing at the gym and sometimes sends dickpics to try to seduce 'the ladies'. He expects photos in return, and when he doesn't get them, he loses interest.

Xante has just gone through a horrible break-up with her girlfriend and feels all over the place. Her ex cheated on her with her best friend and she wants to take revenge. Milo PMs her, saying she's buff and asks for a nude. Xante knows that sending him a photo will make her ex insanely jealous.

- What are the motivations for Milo and for Xante sending nudes?
- What advice would you give Milo and Xante?

Scenario 2: Lila and Tom

Lila is very popular and attractive but doesn't want to be in a relationship or have sex before marriage. She makes this clear to anyone that comes on to her, but it sometimes makes other people try to persuade her into sexual activity; they see getting with her as a challenge.

Tom has never had sex but watches a lot of porn and sometimes masturbates to photos of his female friends posing on Insta. He's friends with and has been in love with Lila for the past two years. He spends a lot of time scrolling through her photos when he feels horny. At a party they start playing 'Truth or Dare' and Lila requests a dare. Tom dares her to go to the bathroom, take a photo of her breasts and send it to him, which she does.

- What is the motivation for Lila sending a nude?
- What advice would you give Tom and Lila?

Scenario 3: Rose and Luke

Rose and **Luke** have been together for a year and both had sex for the first time with each other. Over the summer Luke goes on holiday with his carers for two weeks, which is the longest time they've ever been apart. Rose asks Luke for a nude photo to remember him by because she knows she's going to miss him.

- What is the motivation for Luke sending a nude?
- What advice would you give Rose and Luke?

Scenario 4: Millie and Somaia

Millie is bubbly, confident and loves parties and taking selfies. She wants to own a club when she's older. She lives with her single dad who feels too awkward to discuss anything related to sex and relationships but is very protective of her. Her dad has a new girlfriend whom Millie hates, so she's started rebelling more, bunking off school and experimenting with drugs. Millie meets **Somaia** at a party and they exchange snaps and start messaging. The messages between them get increasingly sexual when Millie sends Somaia a topless photo of herself and asks Somaia to return the favour.

- What is the motivation for Millie sending a nude?
- What advice would you give Millie and Somaia?

Scenario 5: Sonny and Jack

Sonny is worried. He feels like everyone is having sex apart from him, and from what he's read in magazines and heard from his mates, he should definitely have had sex by now. Some of his mates tease him, while others patronize him and say, 'Don't worry, it'll happen.' Sonny feels the pressure and is ready to 'get it over with', but finds it hard to come on to people or know whether other men are interested in him. Sonny goes to a party, thinking, 'Tonight will be the night.' Sonny is quite drunk by the time he leads **Jack** upstairs to a bedroom. He has decided that he'll be the one (for now), and he knows that Jack has already had sex so will probably know what he's doing.

Without Sonny or Jack knowing, **Luke** is in the bathroom next door. He sees the two of them getting undressed and decides to start filming for a laugh.

- What is the motivation for Luke taking the film?
- What advice would you give Luke?
- What advice would you give Sonny and/or Jack?

Part 4

Ask the group the following question: Why do people send nudes or dickpics?

After eliciting feedback from the group, you can add additional thoughts, show them PowerPoint slide 3 or read out any suggestions that haven't arisen from the discussion:

WHY DO PEOPLE SEND NUDES OR DICKPICS?

- Pressure from the media
- It's normal/expected
- Under the influence of drugs or alcohol
- Individual pressure in a relationship, either:
  - **ACTIVE** e.g. because their partner is pressuring them and asking for a photo, saying they won't love/trust them if they don't send one, or
  - **PASSIVE** e.g. because they think it will make their relationship better or show that they like them
- Group pressure – they think all of their friends are doing it, when actually they probably aren't[4]
- They are trying to hook up with someone
- For blackmail or revenge at the end of a relationship
- Risking for a reason (e.g. scared of losing someone)
- Fun to feel scared (e.g. thrill and excitement)
- Some people find it fun or empowering, or they just want to

▲ **PowerPoint slide 3**

Part 5

After eliciting any feedback or questions on the slide, continue the discussion by asking: What are the risks involved? (Facilitators' note: Worst-case scenario is messages/photos get leaked online, screenshotted and sent to other people without your knowledge or consent, being prosecuted or being put on the sex offenders register. Sometimes the consequence that young people mention with greatest horror is the possibility of their family seeing what is sent. Young people may also suggest damage to reputation and risks to mental health and low self-esteem.)

---

4   In a recent study by the NSPCC of over 1000 young people aged 11–16, only 7% of them had shared a naked or semi-naked image of themselves.
     Martellozzo, E., Monaghan, A., Adler, J.R., Davidson, J., Leyva, R. and Horvath, M.A.H. (2016) 'I wasn't sure it was normal to watch it.' London: NSPCC. Available at https://learning.nspcc.org.uk/research-resources/2016/i-wasn-t-sure-it-was-normal-to-watch-it

Exercise 2: Quiz – What the Law Says

Part 1

The law around sexting, nudes and revenge porn can be explored with an interactive quiz. A quiz can be a great way to capture the interest of the group.

There are many ways you can conduct this quiz in an interactive way:

1) By reading out each statement and asking the group to stand up if they think the statement is true and remain seated if they think it's false.

2) Allowing small groups or pairs to discuss each question before presenting their answers to allow for further exploration around each law. You can ask individual students in the group why they have decided true/false before revealing the answer and the additional information.

3) You can give out 'True' and 'False' cards (Resources and Handouts 5.3) to be held up.

The questions and answers for the quiz are in PowerPoint slides 4–9. Here are some notes:

1) **It's true that as far as the law is concerned the age when you can share nudes (with the consent of the other person) is over the age of 18.** (Facilitators' note: The Sexual Offences Act 2003 (England and Wales) defines a child, for the purposes of indecent images, as anyone under the age of 18.)

2) **It's illegal to take and keep nude pictures of yourself on your phone even if you don't share them with other people.** (Facilitators' note: The law says that making, possessing and distributing any imagery of someone under 18 which is 'indecent' is illegal. This includes imagery of yourself if you are under 18.)

3) **Revenge porn laws apply if you are over 18.** (Facilitators' note: Revenge porn was criminalized in the UK in 2015 and carries a maximum prison sentence of two years if you are over 18 and found guilty.)

Part 2

Read out or show the group PowerPoint slide 10, which sums up the law:

WHAT THE LAW SAYS

Making, possessing and distributing any imagery of someone under 18 which is 'indecent' is illegal. This includes imagery of yourself if you are under 18.

The relevant legislation is contained in the Protection of Children Act 1978 (England and Wales) as amended in the Sexual Offences Act 2003 (England and Wales).

Specifically:

- It is an offence to possess, distribute, show and make indecent images of children.
- The Sexual Offences Act 2003 (England and Wales) defines a child, for the purposes of indecent images, as anyone under the age of 18.

Revenge porn laws apply to over-18s only. If you are under 18, it is the laws about indecent images of children (see above) that apply.

▲ **PowerPoint slide 10**

Use the PowerPoint slide to provide young people with the correct information about the law. Point out that the police don't aim to criminalize young people. The police[5] have made clear that incidents involving what they call 'youth produced sexual imagery' should primarily be treated as safeguarding issues. There may be occasions where the police will get involved, such as when young people are under 13, when there is coercion or exploitation involved or repeat offences. This could lead to a young person being put on the sex offenders register. Reassure the young people that these are not likely outcomes but a risk they should be aware of.

Lead a discussion and answer any questions that the young people have about these laws. You could ask:

1) Are you already aware of them?
2) Are there any laws that surprised you?
3) Do you think that these laws are effective?

Ask the group: So why do you think that people still send nudes?

You could explore with the group whether there are different reasons for boys and girls. (Facilitators' note: This can bring out a range of different responses, and may expose gender double standards, as young people may point out that sending nudes is typically a 'no win' situation for girls but may enhance rather than damage a boy's reputation.)

Exercise 3: The Impact of Sexting and Nudes

Ask the group: What would be the impact for someone of having a nude photo shared without their permission? (Facilitators' note: You can prompt the group by asking about the impact on people's emotional wellbeing, confidence, reputation, relationships, etc.) If the group haven't contributed the following, then add them into the discussion:

- shame
- feeling out of control
- feeling self-conscious
- feeling unsafe

---

5   The National Police Chiefs Council (NPCC). For more information, refer to UK Council for Internet Safety (2016) 'Sexting in Schools and Colleges.' Accessed on 6/2/2020 at www.gov.uk/government/publications/sexting-in-schools-and-colleges

- feeling betrayed
- humiliation/embarrassment
- worrying they're in trouble
- reputation
- being targeted by others
- changing relationships with peers, parents/carers, professionals
- finding it difficult to trust
- possible involvement with the police.

Exercise 4: Pass the Pulse

Note: This interactive game can only be played if there is sufficient space for all the young people to sit or stand in two rows, facing each other across the room.

Part 1

You need two teams of equal size, and someone to flip a coin multiple times.

Ask the teams to stand or sit facing each other and ask them to hold hands or wrists along each line, forming a human chain. At the end of the rows place a chair with a small object such as a ball or bottle, and at the other end is the person who is going to flip the coin.

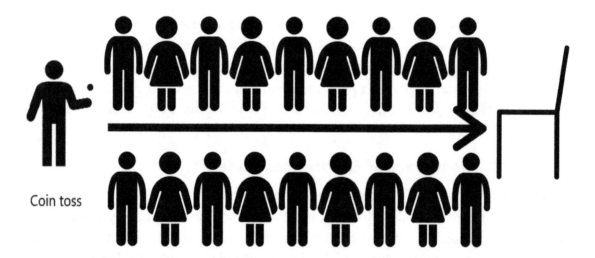

Coin toss

The two players closest to the coin flipper can keep their eyes open and face the person with the coin. Instruct everyone else to close their eyes or look in the direction of the object.

The coin flipper quietly flips the coin and shows it only to the first two people in the row (ensuring that everyone else either has their eyes shut or is facing away).

The purpose of the game is for the young people to pass a pulse or signal, in silence, down their row. The pulse can be passed *only* if the coin has landed on heads. If the coin lands on tails, the team does nothing. If someone's hand gets squeezed, they squeeze the hand of the next person so a pulse gets passed all the way down the line. The goal of the game is to be the first team to send a pulse all the way down the line and grab the object. The team with the fastest pulse grabs the object first and wins a point. If the coin lands on tails and the pulse is still passed, the opposite team is awarded a point.

When a team has been awarded a point, the person at the front of the row goes to the back and everyone else in the line moves up one space.

Let the group know that you will deduct points for people giving verbal instructions, shouting down the line or inappropriate squeezing.

Play the game as a competition for first to 5 or first to 10 depending on how much time you have.

Part 2

Ask the group:

1) Why do you think we played this game?
2) How does it relate to talking about nude images and sexting? (Facilitators' note: Once you've sent something, you can't get it back or control where it goes. Sometimes it can be hard to control our impulses. Actions have consequences that affect people other than ourselves.)

At the end of the discussion show the group PowerPoint slide 11 or remind them of the message:

If someone has had an image shared of them, they are probably going through a difficult time.

You can make a difference to that person.

Remember to be an Upstander.

▲ **PowerPoint slide 11**

Part 3

Ask the group:

1) What would a Bystander do if a friend had an intimate image of them shared?
2) What would an Upstander do if a friend had an intimate image of them shared?

At the end of this discussion, read out or show the young people PowerPoint slide 12:

IF IN DOUBT, DON'T SEND IT

Once it's out there, there's **no control** over where it goes. No one wants intimate pictures of them posted on the internet.

We all have a 'digital footprint' – everything we do or are tagged in online can be traceable, and we are not as anonymous as we think.

Instagram, Snapchat, Facebook and other platforms own every photo put up on their site.

▲ **PowerPoint slide 12**

Exercise 5: In Control

Part 1

Read out or show the group PowerPoint slide 13:

Sometimes people send nude photos or dickpics because they feel under pressure to do so, or they are worried about the consequences of not sending something – under these circumstances there is NO CONSENT.

If you are unsure or in doubt, **don't press send**.

Listen to your **early warning signs**.

Someone responding badly to you saying 'No' may not be somebody who has your best interests at heart.

There are many clever and funny ways to respond to someone requesting an explicit image.

▲ **PowerPoint slide 13**

Part 2

Ask the group whether they can think of any funny responses to a request for a nude or dickpic that they don't feel comfortable sharing. If you want to make this section more interactive, you can ask the young people to research their own funny responses, or set this task as homework so people can share their ideas in the next session.

Facilitators' note: Ideas of funny responses include:

- a picture of the loading sign
- a picture of a dark screen
- saying 'use your imagination'
- a picture of some chicken breasts/a cockerel
- a picture of something dirty (e.g. toilet, bin), saying 'Is this dirty enough for you?'

PowerPoint slide 14 has some examples that you could share.

Part 3

Ask the group: What other ways can we stay in control of images of ourselves online?

(Facilitators' note: If you send an explicit image, think about whether you want to include your face in it; don't sext/send images when under the influence of drugs or alcohol; trust the person you are sending them to; send it securely; use something like Photo Vault so any photos you keep are private and secure on your phone; be in control of all your privacy settings; report anything inappropriate; be aware of the risks and the law.)

At the end of the discussion show the young people PowerPoint slide 15, or let the group know about the 'ZIPIT' app:

DID YOU KNOW...?
Childline have an app called 'ZIPIT' which allows you to:

- save GIFS and images onto your device and share with friends and on apps like Insta and Snap
- get advice and ideas to help you flirt without sending nude images/sexts
- respond to unwanted chat using humour and GIFs
- call Childline or save a number to your phone if you receive an inappropriate request

▲ **PowerPoint slide 15**

End the session with PowerPoint slide 16 and let the group know that there are many places they can go to get resources on this subject or seek support, and there are procedures in place for anonymous reporting. It can be helpful to open the CEOP (Child Exploitation and Online Protection) website on the whiteboard to show them the reporting button. It is possible to go through the first few steps of making a report without it being submitted – it is not a case of one click and the police are instantly on their way!

It is important for the young people to share any issues or concerns that they have about themselves or others related to this topic. Be mindful of the possible impacts and emotions that might be evoked for individuals from this discussion, and if a topic is emotive for someone, offer an opportunity to explore this outside the group, to ensure that they feel heard and safe.

SIGNPOSTING AND RESOURCES
There is plenty of support available if you are worried about sexting and nudes. For example:

▷ You can get an intimate photo you've regretted posting removed... **CEOP** has a 'Report It' button which you can find on websites. It takes you to their website to make a report. When reporting to CEOP, 'the most important thing to remember is whatever happened it is not your fault and you have done nothing wrong'.
▷ If you are receiving unwanted pictures or requests, you can make a report to the police and to your mobile phone company.

Childline: If you are experiencing or are concerned about issues relating to sexting or nudes and you're not ready to report it, you can call Childline on 0800 1111.

▲ **PowerPoint slide 16**

Dating and Relationships

It was interesting hearing different people's perspectives

Session Overview

This workshop looks at the characteristics of a healthy relationship and the diversity of different relationships that people are in. It explores the range of strong emotions that people have, particularly around break-ups and endings. The group are asked to consider how they might help others through an agony aunt/uncle exercise.

Info/Knowledge

Our teenage years are when we develop skills for healthy relationships. Falling in love is an emotional rollercoaster at any age, but especially so for teenagers, with the rapid changes that come with adolescence. Some things are new to the mix, with teenagers now heavy consumers of online pornography, posting their romantic status and adventures on social media, sending and receiving sexts and dating via apps, but young people are still on a developmental journey and need support to guide them in their early relationships. It is rare for young people to be invited to talk about these issues, and RSE is an ideal opportunity to explore topics such as mutual respect, consent and how to spot the signs of emotional, physical and sexual abuse in an intimate relationship. Young people will tend to approach this topic from a heteronormative perspective, and this is an opportunity to remind the group that these issues are important for all types of relationships.

PSHE Association Curriculum Themes

▷ KS4 R2. The characteristics and benefits of positive, strong, supportive, equal relationships

▷ KS4 R5. To recognize when a relationship is unhealthy or abusive (including the unacceptability of both emotional and physical abuse or violence, and strategies to manage this or access support for self or others at risk)

▷ KS4 R6. Managing changes in personal relationships including the ending of relationships

▷ KS4 R9. About the impact of domestic abuse (including sources of help and support)

▷ KS4 R7. To develop an awareness of exploitation, bullying, harassment and control in relationships (including the unique challenges posed by online abuse and the unacceptability of physical, emotional, sexual abuse in all types of teenage relationships, including in group settings such as gangs) and the skills and strategies to respond appropriately or access support

▷ R16. To recognize when others are using manipulation, persuasion or coercion and how to respond

Exercises

▷ Exercise 1: Exploring Values and Beliefs – Group Debate
▷ Exercise 2: Exploring Healthy Relationships
▷ Exercise 3: One Size Doesn't Fit All
▷ Exercise 4: Managing Strong Emotions and Endings
▷ Exercise 5: Ending a Relationship
▷ Exercise 6: Speed Endings – Role Plays
▷ Exercise 7: Coping with Break-Ups
▷ Exercise 8: Agony Aunts and Uncles

Materials Needed

▷ Body map from Workshop 3
▷ Post-its
▷ Agony Aunt/Uncle letters for Exercise 8 (Resources and Handouts 7.1)

Learning Outcomes

By the end of this session:

• I can identify characteristics that make a relationship healthy
• I can define different kinds of relationships and attraction and be aware that healthy, consensual relationships come in different shapes and sizes
• I can recognize the signs of an unhealthy relationship
• I can think about ways to non-judgementally support others in difficult situations
• I can use my early warning signs to recognize signs of an unhealthy relationship
• I can understand the complexities of ending relationships and have communication skills to navigate break-ups

At the beginning of the session, inform the group of the topic – *Dating and Relationships* – and point out that it requires the group to approach the discussions with a certain amount of maturity and sensitivity. Remind the group of the agreed expectations, particularly emphasizing confidentiality and the importance of treating one another with respect. Check that everyone is in agreement, looking for nods or verbal recognition that they're on the same page. Remind the group that if something comes up in the session that upsets them or makes them feel uncomfortable, they have permission to leave the room or find some space, and remind them of where they can go or who they can approach for support. Creating a safe environment is covered in more detail in the Introduction. Before starting, briefly set out what will be covered in the workshop.

Although issues such as power, control and harassment are likely to come up during this session, Workshop 8 is specifically dedicated to exploring these features of unhealthy relationships.

Exercise 1: Exploring Values and Beliefs – Group Debate

Ask the group to imagine that there is a line across the room. Explain to the group that one side of the room is 'Agree' and the other side is 'Disagree' (you can put up signs to make this clear). Let them know that when you read out a statement they are invited to stand where they feel they are on the line in relation to the statement. If it isn't possible for the young people to move about in the room, you can ask them to put up a hand or stand up if they agree, or give out the green, amber and red cards to each participant representing 'agree', 'neither agree nor disagree' and 'disagree' in Resources and Handouts 1.1. Reassure the group that there are no right or wrong answers, that they can stand in the middle if they are unsure and that they are able to move at any time if their opinion has been swayed. Remind the group to remain respectful when listening to and debating views and opinions that differ from their own. If the group find it hard not to talk over each other, you can use an object to represent a 'talking piece' which allows the person holding it permission to speak, while everyone else needs to listen until it is their turn with the talking piece (see Appendix 5).

When the young people have moved to where they want to stand, facilitate a debate between individuals or sides. Feel free to contribute to the debate (there are some facilitators' notes below that may be helpful discussion points).

You don't need to go through all of the statements; pick those that seem most relevant to the group.

Once you have used a few statements, ask the group if they have any other ideas that they want to debate. It might help if the young people talk briefly in pairs to help them to come up with a statement.

- **If you love your partner, you should have sex with them.** (Facilitators' note: If your partner loved you, they would respect your decisions when it comes to your body and your readiness for sex.)
- **If you're married, you should have sex when your partner feels like it.**

(Facilitators' note: Regardless of your relationship status, you should only engage in sexual activity WHEN YOU WANT TO. Marriage does not mean you consent to have sex every time your partner feels like it.)

- **Guys should always initiate sexual contact.** (Facilitators' note: Anyone can initiate sexual contact. The belief that contact 'should' be initiated by a particular gender can put pressure on people, or feed into harmful attitudes that guys should be in control when it comes to sex.)
- **People shouldn't have sex before marriage.** (Facilitators' note: Remind the group that beliefs around sex before marriage may be informed by people's background, culture and religion. It's important that people shouldn't have sex before they are ready, whether they are married or not.)
- **People should be able to love who they want.** (Facilitators' note: In the UK this statement is supported by the law, but this doesn't mean that there isn't still stigma around relationships that don't fit into the traditional 'norms'. The exception to this is when 'love' involves a sexual or romantic relationship with children.)

Exercise 2: Exploring Healthy Relationships
Part 1
Have PowerPoint slide 1 up or draw a picture of a happy couple on the board.

Begin by exploring relationships in general, by asking the group: Why do humans need relationships?

▲ **PowerPoint slide 1**

Part 2
Get the students into small groups and ask them to discuss: What makes a healthy relationship? Ask them to record their ideas on Post-it notes (one idea per Post-it).

Ask the groups to feed back their ideas, and ask questions as you go along to unpick each concept further (e.g. if they have contributed 'trust' and 'respect', you could explore how you would know whether to trust someone or not, and ask what the signs are that someone respects you).

Part 3
After exploring the responses, ask the young people to work again in their group to try to put their Post-it notes in order of importance, with 'most important' at the top, and 'least important' at the bottom. (Facilitators' note: Explain that there is no right or wrong in this exercise. The young people should identify that what is important to one of them may not be important to another, which allows for a discussion around how 'one size does not fit all' when it comes to relationships.)

Part 4

After a discussion around their responses, show the group PowerPoint slide 2 or read out the additional ideas if there are any characteristics of a healthy relationship that they didn't identify:

HEALTHY RELATIONSHIPS

▷ Listening to each other's feelings, hopes and dreams
▷ Being equal (no one is controlling the other or has all the power and decisions are shared together)
▷ Supporting each other
▷ Acceptance (respecting who you are as individuals)
▷ Shared expectations
▷ Loyalty, commitment and honesty
▷ Respect (including consent, respecting sexual boundaries, respecting privacy and confidentiality – e.g. not sharing intimate parts of your relationship with others)
▷ Feeling safe
▷ Trust – you don't need to know where the other one is the whole time, or have access to each other's passwords, etc.
▷ Kindness (without expecting anything in return)
▷ Communication
▷ Accepting and respecting yourself and expecting the same from your partner

▲ **PowerPoint slide 2**

Part 5

Once the students have come up with and explored the characteristics of healthy relationships, ask the group:

1) How can you tell when a new relationship is healthy?
2) How can you tell that a new relationship is safe?
3) How do we resolve arguments in a healthy way?
4) When it comes to relationships, what does equal mean? (Facilitators' note: It can be interesting to explore the word 'equal' in this context. It's important that each person in a relationship is valued equally, but equality in a relationship may not be possible all the time.)
5) Is equality in relationships possible? (Facilitators' note: When equality in a relationship is not possible, it is still important to be aware of how someone might use their power or manipulate an imbalance of power to control, undermine or belittle others.)

Exercise 3: One Size Doesn't Fit All

Part 1

Show the group PowerPoint slide 3 or read the message about diversity in relationships:

RELATIONSHIPS ARE DIVERSE

We are all different and we all want and need different things.

This is why communication is so important.

Healthy relationships come in all different shapes and sizes.

▲ PowerPoint slide 3

Part 2

Ask the group:

1) Have you ever heard the word 'monogamous' or 'monogamy'?
2) (If yes) Does anyone know what it means?

After you have elicited feedback, show them PowerPoint slide 4 or read out the definition of monogamy:

MONOGAMY

The practice of only having one sexual or romantic partner.

We live in a society where monogamy – or only having one partner – is the norm and often the default.

Finding 'the one' is the theme of many films, songs, soaps and stories. This reinforces the idea that somewhere out there is your 'soulmate', and that once you've found this person, you will no longer have attraction or romantic feelings towards anyone else.

▲ PowerPoint slide 4

However, monogamy is not the only structure a relationship can take.

Part 3

Ask the group:

1) Have you ever heard the word 'polyamorous' or 'polyamory'?
2) (If yes) Does anyone know what it means?

After you have elicited feedback, show them PowerPoint slide 5 or read out the definition of polyamory:

POLYAMORY

The practice of, or desire for, intimate relationships with more than one partner, with the consent of all partners involved. Polyamory is described as a 'consensual, ethical and responsible alternative to monogamy'.[1]

The term 'polyamory' is from the Greek 'poly' meaning 'many or several', and the Latin 'amor' meaning 'love'.

Polyamory is not the same as cheating or being unfaithful because everything is done with the knowledge and permission of everyone else involved. There are many different forms including open relationships or exclusive relationships with more than two people.

▲ **PowerPoint slide 5**

Ask the group:

1)   What are the pros and cons of monogamy and polyamory?
2)   What are the challenges of a polyamorous relationship?

Part 4

Explain to the group that in addition to there being different ways that people can structure relationships, there are also different types of attraction. Ask the group if they can think of any different ways that people can be attracted to others.

After eliciting feedback, read out or show them PowerPoint slide 6 about types of attraction:

ATTRACTION ALSO COMES IN MANY SHAPES AND SIZES

Emotional attraction involves wanting to engage emotionally in intimate behaviour (e.g. sharing, confiding, trusting).

Romantic attraction involves wanting to engage in romantic relationships with others.

Sexual attraction involves sexual desire and erotic interests (e.g. wanting to be sexually aroused and touched and do the same for others). You can be sexually attracted to people that you don't have an emotional connection with or want to be in a romantic relationship with.

Some people identify as **asexual** and don't have sexual feelings towards others (and sometimes themselves) – they may still experience romantic or emotional attraction and connections and fall in love but don't express their attraction in sexual ways.

Some people identify as **aromantic** and don't have romantic feelings towards others or fall in love.

---

1   Klesse, C. (2016) 'Polyamory and its "others": Contesting the terms of non-monogamy.' *Sexualities 9*, 5, 565–583.

All of these types of attraction can be towards others of the same sex (**homosexual relationships**), others of a different sex (**heterosexual relationships**) or both (**bisexual relationships**).

▲ PowerPoint slide 6

Exercise 4: Managing Strong Emotions and Endings

Part 1

Start by asking the group what feelings they associate with being in a new relationship (e.g. happy, confident, excited, scared).

Show the group PowerPoint slide 7, or let them know:

IT'S NORMAL TO HAVE MIXED FEELINGS ABOUT THE PEOPLE YOU LOVE AND CARE FOR…

This is increased in teenagers because your brain has an over-sensitive **amygdala**, which is the part of your brain that controls emotions. This means you have even more intense experiences of your feelings.

It can be hard to recognize whether a relationship is meaningful or serious amidst all the other things that go hand in hand with it – e.g. attraction, infatuation, obsession, lust.

Relationships can sometimes change, and it can be hard to know when things are starting to go wrong.

▲ PowerPoint slide 7

Part 2

Write 'Break-Ups' and 'Endings' on the board. Ask the group to give you as many different words as possible that they associate with endings and break-ups and record their responses on the board (e.g. heartbreak, heartache, sadness, anger, loss, closure, grief, moving on, jealousy, hurt, pain).

Let the group know that we have a right to choose when to end a relationship.

Ask the group: If this is our right, what is our responsibility? (e.g. to let other people end a relationship and let them go if they choose to end it)

Ask the group to think of as many different reasons a relationship might end as they can.

After you've elicited feedback, show them PowerPoint slide 8, which shows common causes of break-ups:

WHY DO PEOPLE BREAK UP?
▷ Controlling or manipulative behaviour
▷ Unresolved arguments
▷ Withholding attention or affection
▷ Finding someone new/moving on

- ▷ Being incompatible
- ▷ Misdirected anger
- ▷ Trust issues, lying and cheating
- ▷ Selfishness
- ▷ Not communicating
- ▷ Resentment
- ▷ Feeling unsupported
- ▷ Peer pressure

▲ **PowerPoint slide 8**

Exercise 5: Ending a Relationship

Part 1

Ask the group: How do we know when it's time to end a relationship? (Facilitators' note: You can remind the group of the Early Warning Signs body map that we used in Workshop 3. Mention that feeling unsafe or uncomfortable about a relationship we are in, or around a person we are with, can be a sign that something isn't right.)

Part 2

Ask the group:

1) How do you know if ending something is the right thing?
2) What do you need in order to cope?
3) Does social media make break-ups more miserable?

Exercise 6: Speed Endings – Role Plays

Let the group know that you are going to role-play break-ups and endings, using different scenarios. The group can do this exercise sitting down in pairs or standing up if space allows. One option is to arrange the chairs in concentric circles, making it easy for the young people to face each other during the role plays and move on to the next person.

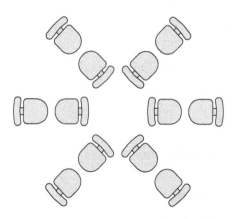

Remind them all that break-ups and endings are a sensitive subject that may bring up upsetting feelings in people, so it's important to remain respectful during this exercise. (Facilitators' note: It's also normal to laugh, giggle or be silly when we feel awkward or uncomfortable, so don't be surprised if this happens during the exercise.)

Part 1

Ask each pair to label themselves A and B. After revealing each scenario (which can either be read out or shown on PowerPoint), A and B have one minute to role-play what happens next. Let the group know that after each scenario A moves on to a different B to role-play the next scenario (like speed dating). (Facilitators' note: You can use a bell, alarm or timer to signal when the one minute is up; you may want to shorten or extend the time given when you see how the conversations are going.)

Scenario 1

Imagine A and B have been in a relationship and A is ready to end it. This is not a mutual break-up as B is willing to keep trying and wants to fight to stay together.

Have a one-minute conversation where A is breaking up with B.

- What sorts of things would they say?
- How could they say it?
- What sort of responses could B give?

▲ **PowerPoint slide 9**

At the end of the role play ask all the As in the pairs to move to a different B.

Scenario 2

Imagine A and B have been in an exclusive relationship and B notices that something doesn't feel right. B realizes they don't trust A any more and doesn't think they can stay in a relationship with no trust. A denies that there is any reason not to trust them and gets defensive.

Have a one-minute conversation where B is breaking up with A.

- What sorts of things would they say?
- How could they say it?
- What sort of responses could B give?

▲ **PowerPoint slide 10**

At the end of the role play ask all the As in the pairs to move to a different B.

Scenario 3

Imagine A and B have been in a relationship and A wants to end it. This time B also admits that they've noticed some difficulties in their relationship so the ending is more mutual.

Have a one-minute conversation where A starts talking about the difficulties in their relationship with B.

- What sorts of things would they say?
- How could they say it?
- What sort of responses could B give?

▲ **PowerPoint slide 11**

Part 2

At the end of the role plays, ask the group to give feedback about how they found it. What were the challenges and what made it easier?

At the end of the reflection, read out or show them PowerPoint slide 12:

WHEN IT COMES TO THE END...

Remember you have the right to end the relationship, and that your decision needs to be accepted and respected.

- Be clear on what you want.
- Practise how you might say it.
- Get support from others before, during and after ending a relationship.
- Talk about your feelings rather than blaming them (e.g. say 'I' more than 'you' to avoid the other person feeling attacked or becoming defensive).
- Choose a neutral and safe place, especially if you are worried about the reaction you might receive.
- Let someone know where you are and plan how you're going to get home.
- Share what's happening with someone you trust – it's OK to get support!
- Remember that lots of relationships don't work out – it's not your fault.
- Remember you have done nothing wrong by coming to this decision.

▲ **PowerPoint slide 12**

Exercise 7: Coping with Break-Ups

Part 1

Let the group know that break-ups can be hard even if the decision was mutual. It can leave people questioning if they did something wrong, whether there's something wrong with them, whether they're lovable or attractive to other people, whether they're good enough.

Ask the group to come up with as many ideas of ways to cope with a break-up as possible, either by writing them or down or just contributing ideas to a whole-group discussion.

Part 2

After you have elicited feedback from the group, read out or show them PowerPoint slide 13 about ways to cope with break-ups. These strategies can be helpful when the break-up was mutual, as well as when you were the initiator of the break-up or on the receiving end of it:

COPING WITH A BREAK-UP
- Do things that distract you.
- Do stuff that makes you feel good.
- Make a 'feel good' playlist.
- Find ways that make you less likely to get in touch with your ex (e.g. messaging a friend, writing a journal, being careful about how much you drink).
- Take care of yourself.
- Talk to people you trust.

▲ **PowerPoint slide 13**

Exercise 8: Agony Aunts and Uncles

Part 1

Briefly ask the group what they could do and how they could support a friend who they are worried about (e.g. try to have a conversation with them, ask them how they are, listen, let them know that they can come to you when they're ready, be non-judgemental, be trustworthy, don't gossip).

Part 2

Divide the young people into pairs. There are 12 letters exploring different relational challenges, which you can select or adapt depending on the age and context of the young people. Tell the group: 'Imagine you are an agony aunt or uncle and you have received one of the following letters. Your task is to write a response to the writer.'

Remind the group how brave it is for people to reach out for help, and ask them to make their responses sensitive and diplomatic.

Give each of the pairs one of the agony aunt/uncle letters (Resources and Handouts 7.1), and ask the pairs to consider the questions on PowerPoint slide 14 (or have the questions on the board or on sheets of paper to guide them while they are writing their responses).

QUESTIONS TO CONSIDER
- What does this person need to **hear** from you?
- What could you say to **reassure** them?
- What **non-judgemental** advice you could give them?
- Where or how could they get further **support**?

▲ **PowerPoint slide 14**

Trigger warning: These letters contain sexual language and describe behaviour that might be shocking or triggering to certain young people. Ensure that you read the letters before introducing them to the group to assess their suitability for the young people's age and the context of the session (see Disclaimer on page 12).

Letter 1

I'm 14 and I've been questioning my sexuality for about a year but I brushed it off as 'just a phase' and continued on with my life. Recently, I've kind of accepted that I like guys as well as girls but I can't really be certain because I've never hooked up with a boy. The problem is that I'm too scared to speak to anyone about it because I'm worried about people reacting to me differently. I'm also not sure what my family would think either. It's never been a topic discussed at home, so I honestly don't even know if they're homophobic! They never really teach you in school or anywhere how to come out, and if you don't come out, then how do you approach guys when you're out as everyone assumes you're into girls? If you're gay or bisexual, do you have to somehow find out if the other person is too before you try and get with them? I wouldn't even know how to tell a guy I was into him. I can't even tell my friends because I'm worried about it being spread in a way that everyone would judge me.

I don't really know what to do but I'm writing this letter just because I felt like I needed to tell someone.

Letter 2

I'm 16 and my partner broke up with me two months ago and I'm still struggling – I just want this pain to stop. I don't know if there's something wrong with me, but whenever I go through a break-up, it literally feels like the end of the world and that I'm totally unlovable and will never find anyone who wants to be with me. It just makes me not want to trust anyone again in case they just leave me.

I just want to not think about it but I see them at school every day, which just makes things worse because it's impossible to get them out my head. I can barely focus in my classes because my head is just going over and over what I did wrong or thinking about how much better things would be if we'd stayed together. I just

---

keep expecting it to get better but it just isn't. I honestly don't know if I'll ever be happy again.

Does anyone have any tips on how to come to terms with someone leaving you and move on? Thanks. Even just writing this has made me feel a bit better.

Letter 3

I'm 15 and I've been with my boyfriend for a year. He's my first love and we don't have any major issues, but I keep noticing little things he does that are bothering me. I'm not scared of him or worried that he'd physically harm me or anything – it's all just small things so I don't know how seriously I should take it. Like he's started asking me constant questions about what I'm doing and where I am and who I'm with – even if it's just me popping to the shop on the way home from school, he'll get pissed off that I didn't tell him first. If I don't message him back (like right away), he gets annoyed, even if he knows I'm out with family or whatever. He always asks who people are when they follow me on social media, like he's worried that I'm getting with other people or something. He even hates me hanging out with mates of mine that are male, even ones I've known forever. He asks me to check my messages and things, and it's got so annoying that I've just given up and given him my passwords because I've got nothing to hide anyway. The other day I was lying in bed just thinking, 'This is crazy, I shouldn't have to do stuff like this, I've done nothing wrong!' All these little things are building up and I don't want to resent him, but he's making it more likely that the thing he fears most (losing me) will actually happen. Apart from all this he's really sweet and thoughtful and loving, but all this is starting to get to me and I don't know what to do about it or whether it is all just little stuff that I should ignore.

Is this normal? Please help.

Letter 4

I'm 16 and my girlfriend has just accused me of being 'possessive and controlling'. She said that I'm trying to take her away from her friends and I need to trust her more. The truth is, I have actually started hating her hanging out with her mates and I get really jealous when she chooses to hang out with people other than me. One of her mates messages her all the time and it makes me feel paranoid, so I always ask her who she's messaging and ask her to show me. When she wants to post things on Insta, I ask her to show me first in case it's something that will give everyone the wrong impression or make her seem easy or flirty or something. Sometimes I tell her she shouldn't go out because I need her help or something, just to see if she'll choose me first. I sometimes buy her things or have a drama about something just so I can get her to stay with me, and if that doesn't work I start saying things like, 'Are you sure you want to go out like that? I think you look a bit cheap' and things to try and make her question herself and feel stupid so she doesn't go.

If I'm being honest with myself, I can't stand the thought of her having a life outside our relationship. Is she right to call me out on this?

Letter 5

I got really paranoid that my partner was messaging other people behind my back. They always talk on Snapchat and I just wondered, 'Why is that – why would they choose to socialize on a platform where everything is self-deleting?' I asked them if there was anything going on that I should know about and they always said no, but then I got their password and logged into their Snap and within a few seconds I received a message saying, 'Thx for the nude, ur well hot, when can we meet IRL?' When I told my partner what I saw, they denied that it was anything to do with them and we got into a massive row. They finally admitted it was them and they said they've sent nudes to a few different people, but nothing physical has ever happened and they're faithful to me otherwise. Obviously, this is a massive red flag, but when I said I didn't know if I could trust them, they begged and said they'd stop doing it.

I don't know what to do. Is it better to be alone than with someone you don't trust? Can you get trust back once it's been lost? How am I supposed to handle this?

Letter 6

I'm 15 and I recently found out that my parents are getting divorced. My whole world feels like it's crumbling down around me and I have no idea what's going to happen next. They haven't given me a reason, but I know they have been finding it hard to get along for a while, and arguing a lot. I'm finding it hard not to try to blame one of them, or work out what it was that made them decide to break up. And when I try not to blame them, I end up feeling like it was my fault somehow. I'm really scared of what this means for the future. I just feel devastated and don't know what my life will look like now.

I wish it could go back to the way it was. Does anyone have any advice on how to just accept it and move on?

Letter 7

I'm 14 and I'm not in a relationship, but I have a mate that I sometimes fool around with. We've talked about having sex for the first time together, just to get it over with. I feel like everyone else 'just does it' and it's just me left. We trust each other and have already seen each other mostly naked, so it kind of seems like a good idea. I told them that I would do it, but I think they want to have sex like SOON and I'm realizing that I'm not 100% sure. Sometimes when we fool around, I feel great afterwards, but last time I gave them oral it left me feeling a bit weird. Since I already said I was willing to before, how do I say that I've changed my mind without seeming like I was lying the whole time or leading them on? I'm worried that if we go for it, I'll feel icky after, or maybe even during, and it'll ruin it for both of us. But I'm worried that if I don't do it, then they'll just go and find someone that will and I'll have lost my chance!

Sorry if this is really naive, but I just want a safe place where I can get advice from other people. I can't really talk to my friends about this, and we all go to school together anyway, so I'd rather it didn't get out. I'm scared either way – I'll either get called frigid or everyone will find out that I've done it. What should I do?

Letter 8

Am I being paranoid? A peng guy added me on Snap and said he thought I was cute. He knew a few of my mates from school and we started talking and then met up in real life at McDonald's. We were with loads of other people but he just focussed on me, saying he was into me and wanted to get to know me better and stuff. He knows I'm younger (he's 21) but he said age doesn't really matter if you find someone you like and he told me I wasn't really like other 15-year-olds anyway. He started picking me up from school, buying me MaccyDs and stuff, and we spent all our time together. I told him I was a virgin and I wanted to take things slowly, and he said he wasn't in it for the sex and that he felt a connection to me. He was really sweet (and a good kisser!). When he took me to parties with his mates, he bought me alcohol and introduced me to his mates as his girl. It made me feel special and grown-up.

The only reason I feel paranoid is because I know others from school that have older boyfriends and they expect them to sleep with their mates for money and stuff. I feel like I do trust him, but how do I know that someone isn't being this nice just to get something out of me? Sometimes it feels too good to be true. My question is: How do you know if a relationship is safe and someone is trustworthy? I'm so confused!

Letter 9

I'm 17 and I've never had a partner and I don't really feel like I want one. I really enjoy having flings with people and getting with people at parties. I recently met up with someone to hook up, who I had sex with at a party a while ago, but when it came down to it, it didn't feel right. I thought there might be something wrong with me. We've already had sex and I was up for doing it again, but when they touched me, I tensed up. I wondered what had stopped me and then I realized it was probably the first time I would have fooled around with someone, or been naked, while I was sober. This might sound stupid, but this whole thing just made me realize that I'm always drunk, or at least tipsy when I get with people. I never feel coerced or out of control, but drinking definitely helps me feel turned on, confident and more sexy. I suggested we get something to drink and I was right – I felt more relaxed, and then more horny and then wanted to have sex (which we did!).

I'm just wondering if this is something that goes away over time, or when you're in a relationship or what? I don't want to have to drink every time I want to have sex, but it seems to be the only way I enjoy it! Do other people have similar experiences and what did you do about it? I'm hoping I'm not a total weirdo!

Letter 10

I've been hooking up with someone for a few years now. We're not exclusive and we both see other people, which we're honest about because both of us feel like you should use your teenage years to find out what you're into and experiment and stuff. Sometimes we watch porn together and try out some of the things we've seen, which is normally fun and silly, but I've noticed recently that the porn they put on is more hardcore and rough. We're normally really playful and both enjoy loads of foreplay, but this seems to have stopped, and last month they actually tried to choke me. I think I would have been cool if they asked me first if I'd like to try it, but it just surprised me and then I didn't really enjoy it because I tensed up. Our sex has got more aggressive and even watching porn together seems less playful. The other day they tried to have anal sex with me and it hurt so much I had to stop. They seemed a bit annoyed at me and said it had felt good for them, and I was just surprised that they didn't even seem to care about how I felt! I felt like I was disappointing them by not being able to do everything they do in porn. I don't know whether our sexual tastes are just different now or whether I'm being vanilla or what. Our sex life has always been more equal, but I feel like they're trying to dominate me, and I keep thinking maybe we should just have a 'safe word' or something. It would probably help me feel more in control but I don't know whether I should just stop having sex with them altogether. The last few times haven't been playful or fun and have left me feeling upset and confused. What do you think I should do?

Letter 11

I'm 16 and I'm in my first serious relationship. We've said 'I love you' to each other and met each other's parents. I'm allowed round to her house (as long as the bedroom door is open!) and everything feels really exciting and easy...except one thing. We're both religious, and when we met, we both decided that we didn't want to have sex before marriage. Both of us agreed that you shouldn't have sex just because everyone else is and that it's better to wait. We felt really strongly about this at the start, but recently she's started saying that she's curious to try things and worried about missing out and doesn't think it's as much of a big deal. I still don't want to have sex, but I also don't want to lose her. I feel like if she really loved me, she wouldn't be pushy about this and would respect where I'm at – especially as she understands my beliefs, used to feel the same and used to be supportive of them. It's not that I'm scared to try sex, and it's not like she's not the 'someone special' people say to wait for to lose your virginity with or anything – but I don't want to do it just because other people are and I still think it's really important to be married first. How come she's changed her mind and how can I get her to see that it's not fair to expect me to go through with this when it's against my values and my religion?

I feel really torn and I don't really know where to go from here... Please help!

Letter 12

I'm 16 and me and my girlfriend recently broke up. She started moaning at me that we weren't having enough sex and she wanted to be with someone who actually wanted to shag her. The truth is I do want to shag her but sometimes I can't get horny around her. When I'm not with her, I feel horny all the time and watch porn. Sometimes when she stays over and we try and have sex but it doesn't work for me...down there...I just go to the bathroom and watch porn and it seems like nothing is wrong. This sounds harsh, but she doesn't look or act like they do in porn and sometimes this turns me off. When we do have sex, I sometimes find it disappointing or have to fantasize about porn scenes to get turned on. I couldn't work out if it's just that I'm not sexually attracted to her any more or if it's that I'm not attracted to anyone normal. I met a girl at a party and we hooked up, but the same thing happened – I just couldn't get aroused. I ended up breaking down in front of her and told her all this and she suggested we watch porn to get me in the mood. This actually helped but I was focussing on the porn, not her, and she told me after that she had felt kinda empty and used. She left and said, 'Maybe you've got a problem', and since then I've felt like I have. I tried to cut down on how much porn I watched but it feels impossible.

Now I feel like I'll never be in a relationship again or be able to see girls the same way and I don't know what to do. It's hard to admit but I feel really pathetic and lonely. Is this just what my life is like now? Can't get it up without porn? Has anyone else been through this and what did you do?

When everyone has finished, you could invite each pair to briefly explain the issue that they have responded to and the advice that they provided. Consider ending with a game or grounding exercise. You can use the safe place or body scan exercises in Appendix 8, or find grounding techniques online.[2] For quick games you could consider 'Ultimate Rock, Paper, Scissors' or 'Count 21', which can be found in Appendix 9.

End the session with PowerPoint slide 15 and let the group know that there are many places they can go to get resources on this subject or seek support, and there are procedures in place for anonymous reporting. It is important for them to share any issues or concerns that they have about themselves or others related to this topic. Be mindful of the possible impacts and emotions that might be evoked for individuals from the discussion, and if a topic is emotive for someone, offer an opportunity to explore this outside the group, to ensure that they feel heard and safe.

SIGNPOSTING AND RESOURCES

If you are worried about your relationship or are concerned for someone else, help is available.

▷ **Childline** can be contacted online or by phone, any time, on 0800 1111.
▷ Childline also has some great advice about healthy and unhealthy relationships: www.childline.org.uk/info-advice
▷ **Stonewall** offers information and support for people who are LGBTQI+ and their allies. You can contact Stonewall's Information Service on Freephone 0800 0502020. Lines are open from 9.30am to 4.30pm, Monday to Friday.

▲ **PowerPoint slide 15**

---

2   For example, www.counselorkeri.com/2019/04/02/help-kids-manage-worry

Power, Control and Harassment

Helped me realize how important it is to consent w/o pressure

Session Overview

This workshop is about unhealthy relationships, including the warning signs for emotional abuse and coercive control. Sexual harassment is explored through scenarios, and the young people look at media messages about relationships through listening to popular songs. Finally, the group consider how they might support someone who is in an unhealthy, controlling and/or abusive relationship.

Info/Knowledge

In RSE young people should be taught how to identify behaviour in a relationship which is positive and supportive and behaviour which is exploitative and controlling. In April 2013 the domestic violence definition was strengthened to include coercive and controlling behaviour and extended to include victims aged 16 and 17.[1] However, the signs of peer-on-peer domestic abuse have been studied in children as young as 13[2] and can be identified in children even younger. Young people experience the highest rates of domestic abuse of any age group.[3] The NSPCC report: 'Partner exploitation and violence in teenage intimate relationships' found that 33% of girls and 16% of boys reported some form of sexual abuse within their

---

1   www.legislation.gov.uk/ukpga/2015/9/section/76/enacted

2   Barter, C., McCarry, M., Berridge, D. and Evans, K. (2009) 'Partner exploitation and violence in teenage intimate relationships.' NSPCC. Accessed on 24/2/2020 at www.nspcc.org.uk/globalassets/documents/research-reports/partner-exploitation-violence-teenage-intimate-relationships-report.pdf

3   Safe Lives (2017) 'Safe Young Lives: Young people and domestic abuse.' Accessed on 24/2/2020 at http://safelives.org.uk/sites/default/files/resources/Safe%20Young%20Lives%20web.pdf

relationship; 25% of girls (the same proportion as adult women) and 18% of boys reported some form of physical relationship abuse; and 75% of girls and 50% of boys reported some form of emotional relationship abuse.[4] Some young people will have witnessed violence and abuse at home, and may see this as a normal or acceptable way to behave. They may blame their partner, and sometimes family, friends and professionals collude by excusing or minimizing what is going on. It is difficult for the young person being abused to leave the relationship, and they may feel responsible for their partner's emotional state or violent behaviour. The young person's peers may exacerbate the problem with taunts: 'You allowed out tonight?' or 'Wow, where's your shadow?' Young people experiencing partner abuse may not realize that they are in an abusive relationship. They may also feel threatened. In the longer term, the young person may become unable or reluctant to form meaningful and supportive relationships.

While learning about the signs of abusive relationships is important, these resources cannot replace the professional duty of care placed upon adults to protect children and young people from abuse.

PSHE Association Curriculum Themes

▷ KS4 R5. To recognize when a relationship is unhealthy or abusive (including the unacceptability of both emotional and physical abuse or violence including 'honour' based violence, forced marriage and rape) and strategies to manage this or access support for self or others at risk (Note: This workshop doesn't cover 'honour' based violence or forced marriage)

▷ KS4 R7. To develop an awareness of exploitation, bullying, harassment and control in relationships (including the unique challenges posed by online abuse and the unacceptability of physical, emotional, sexual abuse in all types of teenage relationships, including in group settings such as gangs) and the skills and strategies to respond appropriately or access support

Exercises

▷ Exercise 1: Exploring Unhealthy Relationships
▷ Exercise 2: Relational Violence and Abuse
▷ Exercise 3: Media Messages about Relationships
▷ Exercise 4: Power, Control and Equality
▷ Exercise 5: Power, Control and Exploitation
▷ Exercise 6: Exploring Sexual Harassment
▷ Exercise 7: Equality and Upstanding

---

4   Barter, C., McCarry, M., Berridge, D. and Evans, K. (2009) 'Partner exploitation and violence in teenage intimate relationships.' NSPCC. Accessed on 24/2/2020 at www.nspcc.org.uk/globalassets/documents/research-reports/partner-exploitation-violence-teenage-intimate-relationships-report.pdf

Materials Needed

▷ Flipchart paper and pens
▷ Handout on Relational Violence and Abuse for Exercise 2 (Resources and Handouts 8.1)
▷ 'True' and 'False' cards for each table (optional) for Exercise 5 (Resources and Handouts 8.2)
▷ Access to YouTube
▷ Lyrics to songs if access to YouTube isn't available for Exercise 3[5]
▷ Handout on Sexual Harassment for Exercise 6 if no access to PowerPoint (Resources and Handouts 8.3)
▷ Scenarios for Exercise 6 (Resources and Handouts 8.4)
▷ Teen Equality Wheel handout for Exercise 7 if no access to PowerPoint (Resources and Handouts 8.5)

Learning Outcomes

By the end of this session:

• I can understand how different relationships affect how I'm feeling and know whether a romantic or sexual relationship is having a negative impact on my wellbeing
• I can recognize the red flags or early warning signs of an unhealthy or abusive relationship
• I can describe what harassment is
• I understand power and control and how this relates to child sexual exploitation
• I can support friends if they are in an unhealthy relationship, and know where to go for help if I am

At the beginning of the session, inform the group of the topic – *Power, Control and Harassment* – and point out that it requires the group to approach the discussions with a certain amount of maturity and sensitivity. Remind the group of the agreed expectations, particularly emphasizing confidentiality and the importance of treating one another with respect. Check that everyone is in agreement, looking for nods or verbal recognition that they're on the same page. Remind the group that if something comes up in the session that upsets them or makes them feel uncomfortable, they have permission to leave the room or find some space, and remind them of where they can go or who they can approach for support. Creating a safe environment is covered in more detail in the Introduction. Before starting, briefly set out what will be covered in the workshop.

---

5   'Love the Way You Lie' – www.azlyrics.com/lyrics/eminem/lovethewayyoulie.html; 'Hotline Bling' – https://www.azlyrics.com/lyrics/drake/hotlinebling.html; 'Sweet but Psycho' – www.azlyrics.com/lyrics/avamax/sweetbutpsycho.html

Exercise 1: Exploring Unhealthy Relationships

Part 1

Have PowerPoint slide 1 up, or draw a picture of two individuals looking miserable on the flipchart or board.

▲ **PowerPoint slide 1**

Part 2

Get the students into small groups and ask them to discuss: What are the signs that a relationship is unhealthy?

Part 3

Ask the groups to feed back their ideas, and ask questions as you go along to unpick each concept further (e.g. if they have contributed 'pressuring you' or 'isolating you from friends', explore how you would know whether this was happening or not).

Part 4

Ask the group: What are the early warning signs/red flags that a relationship is unhealthy? Refer back to the body map in Workshop 3 and the physical sensations we experience when we feel uncomfortable, threatened or unsafe.

Exercise 2: Relational Violence and Abuse

Part 1

Ask the group to do a thought shower of words they associate with 'violence' and 'abuse' and record their responses on the board.

   Ask the group:

1) Are 'violence' and 'abuse' always physical?
2) If not, what other forms might they take?

At the end of the discussion, read out or show the group PowerPoint slides 2 and 3, which outline different types of relational violence and abuse:

RELATIONAL VIOLENCE AND ABUSE

Relationship violence/abuse is a pattern of abusive and coercive* behaviours used to have power and control over an ex or current partner.

This behaviour tends to get worse over time.

There are four different types of violence and abuse:

Physical

Emotional

Verbal

Sexual

* Coercive means using force or threats to 'persuade' and manipulate others to do things.

▲ **PowerPoint slide 2**

Physical
The intentional use of physical force or power to hurt, intimidate, control or punish others, including punching, throwing/breaking things, hair pulling, etc.

Verbal
The intentional use of verbal abuse aiming to belittle, upset, threaten, frighten, intimidate or control others – for example, repeatedly putting someone down, saying they are worthless, gaslighting them (manipulating them to feel crazy/question their own sanity), blaming them for the abusive behaviour, threatening physical or sexual violence.*

Emotional
This includes coercive control – the intentional use of threats, humiliation and intimidation to harm, punish or frighten others, cause others to be dependent, isolate others from support, exploit, degrade or dehumanize others.*

Sexual
The intentional use of force, threats or intimidation to make someone do something sexual, or sharing intimate photos to shame, humiliate or control someone, etc.*

* Emotional, verbal and sexual violence can happen both online and offline.

▲ **PowerPoint slide 3**

Part 2

Keep PowerPoint slide 3 on the screen. It can also be given out as a handout (Resources and Handouts 8.1) so that the young people have it in front of them to refer to. Read out the following short scenarios (numbers 1–23) and ask the young people to identify which type of abuse they would use to describe what they have just heard. Let the group know that the scenarios might not always fit into just one category (e.g. all of them may fit into 'emotional abuse' as all violence has an emotional impact).

1) Controls your relationships/tells you who you can be friends with (online and offline). (Emotional)

2) Doesn't respect your sexual boundaries, won't take no for an answer and makes you feel guilty or immature for not trying things they want. (Emotional and sexual)

3) Spreads rumours or gossip about you. (Emotional and verbal)

4) Threatens to disclose your sexual orientation or gender identity to others. (Emotional and verbal)

5) Gaslights you and makes you feel crazy. (Emotional and verbal)

6) Dismisses violent behaviour – 'it was only a slap', 'you deserved it', 'I did it because I love you'. (Physical, emotional and verbal)

7) Refusing to use contraception. (Emotional and sexual)

8) Gives you gifts and then tells you that you owe them. (Emotional and verbal)

9) Tells you what to wear. (Emotional)

10) Blames their abusive behaviour on drink, drugs, stress, their past or you. (Emotional and verbal)

11) Choking you during sex without your permission or enthusiasm. (Physical, emotional and sexual)

12) Calls you names and puts you down, telling you you're stupid, ugly, useless. (Emotional and verbal)

13) Threatens to kill themselves if you leave them. (Emotional and verbal)

14) Shares intimate secrets about your relationship with others including showing naked pictures of you to their mates. (Emotional and sexual)

15) Tells you that no one else will ever love or put up with you. (Emotional and verbal)

16) Throws your phone against a wall. (Physical)

17) Denies that they are being abusive or controlling. (Emotional and verbal)

18) Physically intimidates you, throws things, glares at you, sulks. (Physical and emotional)

19) Threatens to tell your secrets if you leave them. (Emotional and verbal)

20) Promises they will change and begs you to stay. (Emotional and verbal)

21) Stonewalls you – the silent treatment, refusing to communicate. (Emotional)

22) Withholds affection to punish you. (Emotional)

23) Makes you share your passwords and accuses you of being untrustworthy. (Emotional)

Part 3

Finally, ask the group if they can think of any additional examples or scenarios based on things they have seen in the media that they want to share, and get the rest of the students to categorize these into sexual, emotional, physical or verbal violence.

Exercise 3: Media Messages about Relationships

Part 1

If you have the capacity to watch the music videos, then complete this exercise as a whole group. If not, then get the students into smaller groups. The lyrics for the songs can be found online.[6]

Play all three of the music videos before exploring the lyrics using questions from Part 2.

- 'Love the Way You Lie' – Eninem ft. Rihanna: www.youtube.com/watch?v=uel Hwf8o7_U (video length: 4 minutes 30 seconds).
- 'Hotline Bling' – Drake: www.youtube.com/watch?v=uxpDa-c-4Mc (video length: 5 minutes).
- 'Sweet but Psycho' – Ava Max: www.youtube.com/watch?v=WXBHCQYxwr0 (video length: 3 minutes 30 seconds).

▲ **PowerPoint slide 4**

Part 2

Elicit a discussion with the group, using the following prompts:

1) What messages do these songs send to the listeners about relationships? (Can they think of any lyrics to illustrate their answers?)
2) Do they dismiss or promote negative, unhealthy and abusive behaviour in relationships? (Can they think of any lyrics to illustrate their answers?)
3) If they haven't already come up, highlight the following lyrics and ask the group what they think about them:
   - 'You're tellin' me that I'm insane, Boy, don't pretend that you don't love the pain' (Ava Max)
   - 'I'm leaving you. No you ain't' (Eminem ft. Rihanna)
   - 'I like the way it hurts... I love the way you lie' (Eminem ft. Rihanna)
   - 'As long as the wrong feels right' (Eminem ft. Rihanna)
   - 'You started wearing less and goin' out more... Going places where you don't belong... Used to always stay at home, be a good girl' (Drake)
4) Are there any other lyrics the group want to explore from these songs?
5) Can the group think of any examples of songs that promote healthy, positive relationships?

---

6   'Love the Way You Lie' – www.azlyrics.com/lyrics/eminem/lovethewayyoulie.html; 'Hotline Bling' – https://www.azlyrics.com/lyrics/drake/hotlinebling.html; 'Sweet but Psycho' – www.azlyrics.com/lyrics/avamax/sweetbutpsycho.html

Exercise 4: Power, Control and Equality

Part 1

Read out or show the group PowerPoint slide 5:

Relational violence and abuse are all about **power** and **control**. It's normal for relationships to have ups and downs and conflict, and it's OK to have mixed feelings about people. When someone's behaviour in a relationship becomes about having power and control over someone else, it is a big warning sign that the relationship is not healthy.

DID YOU KNOW...?[7]

- **75%** of girls and **50%** of boys report some kind of emotional abuse while they are teenagers.
- **One in three girls** and **16% of boys** report that they have experienced sexual violence from a partner.
- **Almost half of gay or bisexual men** have experienced domestic violence from a partner or family member.
- **80% of trans people** have experienced some form of emotional, sexual or physical abuse from a partner or ex-partner.
- Relational violence includes so called 'honour'-based violence, female genital mutilation and forced marriage.

▲ **PowerPoint slide 5**

Part 2

Now that the group know that relational abuse is about power and control, ask them why people might be abusive towards others in relationships (e.g. they believe they have the right to control their partner(s), it is learned behaviour from the environment they grew up in or from the media and pornography).

Remind the group that abusive and violent behaviour is *always* a choice that somebody makes; there is no excuse or justification for it.

---

7   Sources: Barter, C., McCarry, M., Berridge, D. and Evans, K. (2009) 'Partner exploitation and violence in teenage intimate relationships.' NSPCC. Accessed on 24/2/2020 at www.nspcc.org.uk/globalassets/documents/research-reports/partner-exploitation-violence-teenage-intimate-relationships-report.pdf; Stonewall (2017) 'Domestic violence: What does the law say?' Accessed on 24/2/2020 at www.stonewall.org.uk/help-advice/criminal-law/domestic-violence; Scottish Transgender Alliance (2010) 'Out of sight, out of mind? Transgender People's Experiences of Domestic Abuse.' Accessed on 24/2/2020 at www.scottishtrans.org/wp-content/uploads/2013/03/trans_domestic_abuse.pdf

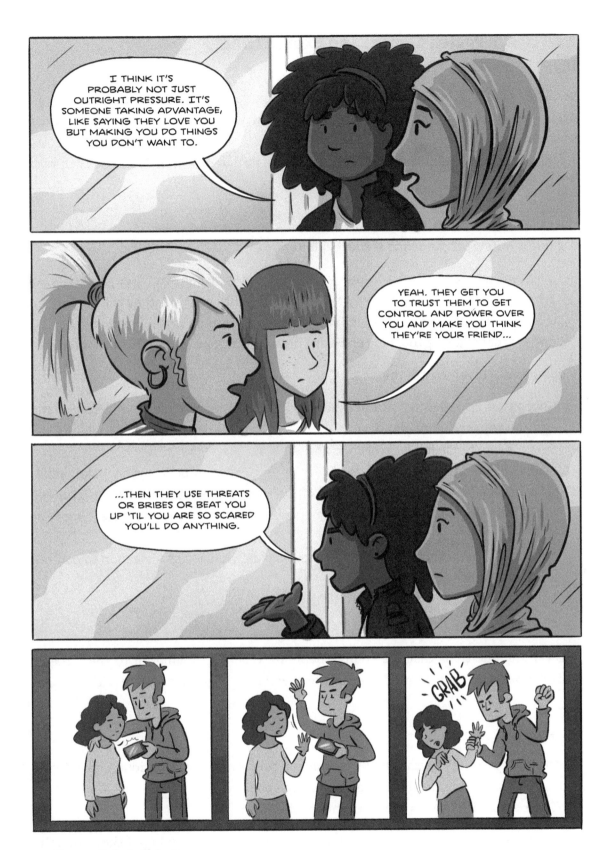

▲ **PowerPoint slide 6**

Exercise 5: Power, Control and Exploitation

Part 1

Show the young people PowerPoint slide 6 and ask the group whether they have heard of 'grooming' or 'sexual exploitation'. If so, ask them what they think it means and what they think it looks like.

Show them the definition of child sexual exploitation on PowerPoint slide 7 or read out the text:

WHAT IS CHILD SEXUAL EXPLOITATION?

A group of young people define sexual exploitation as:

> Someone taking advantage of you sexually, for their own benefit. Through threats, bribes, violence, humiliation, or by telling you that they love you, they will have the power to get you to do sexual things for their own, or other people's benefit or enjoyment (including touching or kissing private parts, sex, taking sexual photos).[8]

It is important to remember that:

- Anyone can be a victim of sexual exploitation – it can happen to boys and girls, of **any age** and any sexual orientation.
- Sexual exploitation is a form of child abuse.
- Sexual exploitation comes in many forms (e.g. peer-on-peer, by an older adult, someone being a boyfriend/girlfriend of the victim, at parties, as well as criminal exploitation including when gang or group members exploit young people to move or sell drugs for them).
- People who perpetrate sexual violence use sexual violence as a weapon to control, initiate and exert power over others.
- Sexual exploitation is **never the victim's fault**.

▲ **PowerPoint slide 7**

Answer any questions that the young people have before moving on to the 'True or False?' quiz (which may answer some of the questions the group come up with).

Part 2

Do the 'True or False?' myth-busting quiz about child sexual exploitation. A quiz can be a great way to capture the interest of the young people.

There are multiple ways you can conduct this quiz:

1) By reading out the statements and asking the group to stand up if they think the statement is true and remain seated if they think it's false.

2) Allowing small groups or pairs to discuss each question before presenting their answers to allow for further exploration of each statement. You can ask individual

---

8 Description of child sexual exploitation is from NSPCC: www.nspcc.org.uk/what-is-child-abuse/types-of-abuse/child-sexual-exploitation

students in the group why they have decided true/false before revealing the answer and the additional information.

3) You can give out 'True' and 'False' cards (Resources and Handouts 8.2).

4) You can have two or more groups competing against each other, with a prize to be won.

Statement	True or false?
People who perpetrate child sexual exploitation or groom young people are always older than the people they target.	**False:** There is no 'typical perpetrator' of CSE, and people exploiting young people can be any age, race or gender. They can sometimes be the same age as the victim (this is called peer-on-peer exploitation). Around one-third of child sexual exploitation is by other children and young people.[9]
Child sexual exploitation and grooming can be both online and offline.	**True:** Sometimes exploitation happens even if the people involved have never met. An example of this might be someone pretending to be a younger person online, creating a relationship with a child, asking for explicit images and then bribing the young person. The use of the internet makes it easier for potential sex offenders to meet, groom and abuse children. Around 16% of recorded sex offences involve an online element.[10]
Only girls get groomed.	**False:** Both boys and girls can be victims of grooming, although research suggests that boys and young men are less likely to report abuse and exploitation.[11]
Children and young people are normally exploited or abused by strangers.	**False:** 90% of children are abused by someone they know (i.e. family members and/or close friends). The people most likely to abuse children are those who have the most opportunity and access to them.[12]
Some people don't know they are being exploited.	**True:** Perpetrators of child sexual exploitation are clever and manipulative. They sometimes form a trusting or romantic relationship with their victims, and can make it seem as if the arrangement is 'mutually beneficial' (e.g. the victim gets something out of it such as access to alcohol, money, phones, gifts, status or initiation into a group or gang).
A quarter of all sexual offences recorded by the police are against children.	**False:** It's actually even more – one-third of police recorded sexual offences.[13]
Assaulting someone of the same gender is a homosexual act.	**False:** Sexual assault is ultimately about power, control or domination of the other person, rather than a sexual attraction to one specific gender.[14]

9   Hackett, S. (2014) *Children and Young People with Harmful Sexual Behaviours*. London: Research in Practice Reviews, 15.

10 Office for National Statistics (ONS) (2019) *Crime in England and Wales: Additional Tables on Fraud and Cybercrime*. Newport: ONS.

11 The Children's Society as part of the National CSAE Prevention Programme for England and Wales, in partnership with Victim Support and the National Police Chiefs' Council (NPCC) (2018) 'Boys and Young Men at Risk of Sexual Exploitation: A Toolkit for Professionals.' Accessed on 24/2/2020 at www.csepoliceandprevention.org.uk/sites/default/files/Boys%20and%20Young%20Men%20Toolkit.pdf

12 Radford, L., Corral, S., Bradley, C., Fisher, H. *et al.* (2011) 'Child Abuse and Neglect in the UK Today.' London: NSPCC. Accessed on 3/2/2020 at https://learning.nspcc.org.uk/media/1042/child-abuse-neglect-uk-today-research-report.pdf

13 Home Office (2019) *Police Recorded Crime and Outcomes: Open Data Tables*. London: Home Office.

14 www.know-means-no.co.uk/knowthetruth/index.html

Part 3

Elicit feedback from the young people about the quiz.

1) Did anything surprise them?
2) Did they learn anything new?
3) Do they have any questions?

Part 4

Show the group the definition of consent again on PowerPoint slide 8 or written on the board. Ask the group what they think of the comment that 'if there's power, it's not consent'.

A person consents if he or she agrees by choice with the freedom and capacity to do so.
– Sexual Offences Act 2003

▲ **PowerPoint slide 8**

Exercise 6: Exploring Sexual Harassment

Part 1

Ask the group:

1) How would you define sexual harassment?
2) Is sexual harassment different if it is online or offline?

After eliciting feedback, show the group the definition of sexual harassment in PowerPoint slide 9 or read out the text:

WHAT IS SEXUAL HARASSMENT?

Sexual harassment can be physical, verbal or emotional, and can take place online, in person and/or on physical surfaces such as graffiti on a toilet cubicle.

Anyone can be subjected to sexual harassment.

Sexual harassment often targets one or more of these characteristics: a person's appearance, body parts, sex, sexual orientation, gender identity, sexual experience and activities, disability/ability.

Sexual harassment is **unwanted** behaviour of a sexual nature which:

- violates someone's dignity
- intimidates, degrades or humiliates someone
- creates a hostile or offensive environment or makes someone feel exposed or unsafe.[15]

It is always the victim's **perception** of the behaviour that identifies it as harassment, not the **intentions** of the person doing the behaviour. Therefore, excuses like 'it was only fun', 'it was just banter' or 'they're really sensitive' aren't an effective defence when someone is accused of harassment.

▲ **PowerPoint slide 9**

Part 2

Ask the group whether they can think of any examples of sexual harassment from things they have seen in the media, on TV or in the news. Show them PowerPoint 10 to elicit further discussion.

---

15   Citizens Advice (2020) 'Sexual harassment.' Accessed on 3/2/2020 at www.citizensadvice.org.uk/law-and-courts/discrimination/what-are-the-different-types-of-discrimination/sexual-harassment

Part 3

SEXUAL HARASSMENT

Unwanted flirting	Crude jokes and gestures	Sexual favours	Unwanted touching	Unwanted sexually explicit	Cat calling
Pressuring someone after being asked to stop, saying 'you know you want it'	Humping gestures, unwanted crude comments or dirty jokes	Asking for sexual favours from someone – just because you've been nice doesn't mean you're into them	A slap on the bum, touching someone's hair, pulling someone's bra strap without their permission	pictures or comments sent on social media	Wolf whistles, or a sexually suggestive call in public, like saying someone has a nice bum

▲ **PowerPoint slide 10**

Part 4

Get the young people into small groups sitting at tables. Give each table a piece of flipchart paper and ask them to draw a line down the middle with 'Harassment' written at one end and 'Compliment' at the other.

Harassment ——————————————————————————————— Compliment

Part 5

Ask each group to cut out the scenarios (Resources and Handouts 8.4) and place them on the continuum where they think the scenario fits. The scenarios are purposefully vague to encourage communication and discussion between the students. Different students may have different ideas about where something goes, so explain that it's OK for them to put things in the middle or to disagree with each other over whether something is harassment or a compliment.

Trigger warning: These scenarios contain sexual language and describe behaviour which may be shocking or triggering to certain young people. Ensure that you read the scenarios before introducing them to the group to assess their suitability to the young people's age and the context of the session (see Disclaimer on page 12).

Pulling someone's bra strap.	A stranger offering you a lift home.	Someone leaving a sexual note in your locker.	Someone you know groping your bum.
Teasing someone for being a virgin.	Being called a ho, slag or a sket by a classmate.	Writing 'For good sex, call Jesse' and including a phone number on the bathroom wall.	Receiving a message from an unknown contact saying 'I'd like to get to you know you better'.
Leaving sexual notes in someone's locker after they have said to stop.	A stranger rubbing up against someone on the bus.	A partner touching your bum in public after you've told them to stop.	Smiling at someone while passing them in the hallway.
Following someone home after they've broken up with you.	Asking someone if they want to hang out.	Being whistled at and told to 'bring that over here'.	Giving someone a compliment.
Teasing someone about the clothes they are wearing.	Being approached by a group of guys/girls you do not know and them all asking for your number.	Being told to do something sexual to earn your place in a group or gang.	Someone continuously commenting on all your photos on Insta.
Someone taking your phone and saying you can only have it back if you sit on their lap/kiss them/ give oral sex.	Someone telling your friend they fancy you.	A friend touching your stomach, thighs and bum, and then laughing because 'it's just a joke'.	Getting messages on Instagram and Snapchat asking for naked pictures.
A friend of a friend taking photos up your skirt.	A picture or video being taken of you without your permission.	Someone continuing to message you and ask you out after you say 'No'.	Saying loudly in class the sexual things you want to do to one of your peers.
Someone remembering it's your birthday and sending you a GIF.	A stranger showing you porn while you're sitting next to them on the bus.	Someone sending you a porn video while you're at school.	Receiving a text that says 'You look hot in that outfit'.

Part 6

When each group has finished placing the scenarios on the continuum, ask the group:

1) How did you find the exercise?
2) Were any scenarios really hard to place?
3) If so, why was this? (e.g. they needed more information, more context)
4) Would they change any of the answers if you let them know that:
    - they were unable to leave the situation?
    - the other person involved was much older than them?
    - the other person was someone they were really into?
    - the other person had already been told that this behaviour made you uncomfortable and you had asked them to stop?

Part 7

Show the group the YouTube clip about sexual harassment from Disrespect NoBody:

www.youtube.com/watch?v=EyH2eGA1POo (video length: 30 seconds).

▲ **PowerPoint slide 11**

At the end of the video, remind the group that sexual harassment is 'unwanted' sexual attention and it can have lifelong consequences for both the person giving the attention and the person being targeted by the behaviour.

Ask the young people what the consequences of being sexually harassed might be (e.g. feeling exposed, feeling insecure, feeling unsafe, not trusting people, feeling suicidal, self-harm, feeling isolated, being confused, avoiding people/places, etc.).

Let the group know that a broader consequence of sexual harassment is the fact that it can normalize sexist behaviour and reinforce gender stereotypes (which we will explore further in Workshop 14).

At the end of the discussion, show the group PowerPoint slide 12 or let them know the 'Did you know...?' statistics:

DID YOU KNOW...?

- **85%** of women aged 18–24 have experienced unwanted sexual attention in public spaces.[16]
- **64%** of girls aged 13–21 in one study had experienced sexual violence or harassment at school or college in the past year, which included 39% having their bra strapped pulled and 27% having their skirts pulled up in the past week.[17]
- **6%** of male students have been subjected to sexual violence or sexual harassment while at school.[18]
- #MeToo shockingly revealed that **81%** of women and **43%** of men have experienced some form of sexual harassment or assault in their lifetimes. This was even higher for people with disabilities or gay or bisexual men.[19]

▲ **PowerPoint slide 12**

Exercise 7: Equality and Upstanding

Part 1

Show the young people the 'Teen Equality Wheel' to reinforce the discussion. This can either be on PowerPoint slide 13 or you can print this out and give one copy out per table for small groups to look at (Resources and Handouts 8.5). The Teen Equality Wheel outlines the sorts of behaviours we would expect to see in a healthy, safe relationship where individuals are not attempting to use power and control to manipulate others. The goal of all of the nonviolent behaviours explored around the outside is working towards relational equality.

The Teen Equality Wheel is a powerful model which can be used in a number of ways. It is worth looking at the website[20] for ideas if you wish to explore it further.

Ask the group:

1) Can you think of any examples of relationships in the media where people admit when they are wrong?
2) Can you think of any examples in the media where people make compromises that benefit everyone involved?
3) Can you think of any examples from the media where people manage conflict or disagreements without putting the other person down?

16 End Violence Against Women (2018) 'Parliamentary Committee to investigate sexual harassment in public places.' Accessed on 24/2/2020 at www.endviolenceagainstwomen.org.uk/parliamentary-committee-looks-at-sexual-harassment-of-women-and-girls-in-public-places

17 Girlguiding (2017) 'Girls' Attitudes Survey 2017.' Accessed on 24/2/2020 at www.girlguiding.org.uk/globalassets/docs-and-resources/research-and-campaigns/girls-attitudes-survey-2017.pdf

18 National Education Union (2019) '"It's Just Everywhere": A study on sexism in schools – and how we tackle it.' UK Feminista and NEU. Accessed on 24/2/2020 at https://neu.org.uk/advice/its-just-everywhere-sexism-schools

19 Stop Street Harassment (2018) 'The Facts Behind the #MeToo Movement: A National Study on Sexual Harassment and Assault: Executive Summary.' Accessed on 24/2/2020 at www.stopstreetharassment.org/wp-content/uploads/2018/01/Executive-Summary-2018-National-Study-on-Sexual-Harassment-and-Assault.pdf

20 www.theduluthmodel.org

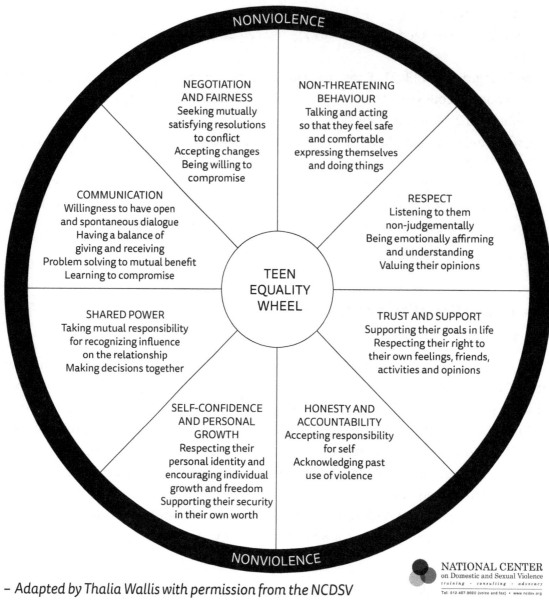

– Adapted by Thalia Wallis with permission from the NCDSV

▲ **PowerPoint slide 13**

Part 2

Ask the group what they could do if they were concerned about a friend experiencing any of the issues explored in this workshop (sexual, physical, emotional or verbal abuse or harassment, bullying behaviour or exploitation), or where there were red flags that their relationship was not based on the behaviours of the Teen Equality Wheel.

Part 3

After eliciting their feedback, show them PowerPoint slide 14 about being an Upstander or read out the text:

BEING AN UPSTANDER

Issues relating to abuse, harassment and exploitation are complicated. Many people experiencing these don't report what is happening to them for a range of reasons, including shame, humiliation, fear of being in trouble, fear of the person causing the harm, and sometimes not identifying what they are going through as abuse.

If you see something wrong or are worried about a friend, it is important that you act on this. Being a Bystander can send the message that what is happening is OK, which may make it even less likely this person will seek support.

TIPS FOR BEING AN UPSTANDER

- Tell your friend you are worried.
- Tell them why you are worried – with specific things you have noticed (e.g. changes in your friend's behaviour, appearance, mood, or things you have witnessed happening).
- Let them know you are bringing it up because you care.
- Remind them that it is not their fault.
- Seek help from a trusted adult if you think they are in danger, even if you have promised to keep it a secret.
- Put them in contact with Childline or CEOP to get help or make a report.
- Get support yourself – supporting a friend going through this is difficult and upsetting.

Remember: The golden rule of Upstanding is to intervene only if it's safe for you to do so.

▲ **PowerPoint slide 14**

End the session with PowerPoint slide 15 and let the group know that there are many places they can go to get resources on this subject or seek support, and there are procedures in place for anonymous reporting. It is important for them to share any issues or concerns that they have about themselves or others related to this topic. Be mindful of the possible impacts and emotions that might be evoked for individuals from the discussion, and if a topic is emotive for someone, offer an opportunity to explore this outside the group, to ensure that they feel heard and safe.

SIGNPOSTING AND RESOURCES

Sexual harassment is a criminal offence under the Equality Act 2010 (as it is a form of unlawful discrimination). Online harassment and stalking are also illegal.

If you experience any type of harassment, you have the right to file a police report. You don't need to have previously been subjected to someone's behaviour for it to be considered unwanted.

▷ **Childline:** In addition to the Childline Helpline, the website has ideas and advice about healthy and unhealthy relationships, including starting a relationship, telling someone you like them, where there is an age gap and breaking up: www.childline. org.uk/info-advice/friends-relationships-sex/sex-relationships/relationships

▷ **Stonewall** offers information and support for people who are LGBTQI+ and their allies. You can contact Stonewall's Information Service on Freephone 0800 0502020. Lines are open from 9.30am to 4.30pm, Monday to Friday.

▲ **PowerPoint slide 15**

Drugs, Alcohol and Consent

Made us think instead of us being told about things

Session Overview

This workshop looks at the myths and facts surrounding drug and alcohol use. It explores how drugs and alcohol impact on decision making and the ability to consent. It weighs up the pros and cons of using drugs and alcohol, and considers 'how much is too much'. It looks at media campaigns, and asks the young people what they would do if they were concerned about someone who was under the influence.

Info/Knowledge

Alcohol and drugs affect our ability to think and act rationally. They can lower our inhibitions, make us more sociable and make us less able to control our impulses, leading us to act without considering the consequences. They may make us less able to work out how we are feeling or enhance our feelings when we have little control over them. This can have serious consequences for our capacity to consent to sexual activity. Talking about sexual consent is complex and often difficult at the best of times, and when people are intoxicated, it makes negotiating sexual consent even more complicated. You may have to explore questions such as 'How drunk is too drunk to consent to sex?' or 'Is it rape if both people are intoxicated?' Before approaching this topic, be clear in your mind about the law and consent. It's important to emphasize the point with young people that even though someone is under the influence of drugs or alcohol, the responsibility for any sexual offences always lies with the person perpetrating the harm.

PSHE Association Curriculum Themes

▷ KS4 R18 To recognize the impact of drugs and alcohol on choices and sexual behaviour

Exercises

▷ Exercise 1: Quick Decision Making
▷ Exercise 2: Exploring Values and Beliefs – Group Debate
▷ Exercise 3: Alcohol, Drugs and Our Brains
▷ Exercise 4: Drugs, Alcohol, Sexual Behaviour and Consent
▷ Exercise 5: Under the Influence
▷ Exercise 6: Exploring Campaigns
▷ Exercise 7: Why? vs Why Not?
▷ Exercise 8: Role Play – 'Persuade Me'
▷ Exercise 9: How Much Is Too Much?
▷ Exercise 10: Skills Practice

Materials Needed

▷ 'Myth' or 'Fact' written on cards (optional) for Exercise 3 (Resources and Handouts 9.1)
▷ 'Myth or Fact?' handout for Exercise 3 (Resources and Handouts 9.2)
▷ Beer goggles or kaleidoscope glasses if you have the resources; these can be purchased from the FPA: www.fpa.org.uk/product/drunkbuster-twilight-vision-goggles
▷ Strong-flavoured sweets (e.g. aniseed, lemon sherbet, popping candy, sour sweets)
▷ Woollen gloves
▷ Access to headphones and loud music
▷ Access to YouTube
▷ 'Play', 'Pause' and 'Stop' cards (optional) for Exercise 9 (Resources and Handouts 9.3)

Learning Outcomes

By the end of this session:

• I can understand the effects of drugs and alcohol on decision making and the brain
• I can talk about how drugs and alcohol impact on sexual behaviour and consent
• I can use my knowledge to consider how much is too much in terms of capacity to consent
• I can be clear about where duty and responsibility lies in decision making

At the beginning of the session, inform the group of the topic – *Drugs, Alcohol and Consent* – and point out that it requires the group to approach the discussions with a certain amount of maturity and sensitivity. Remind the group of the agreed expectations, particularly emphasizing confidentiality and the importance of treating one another with respect. Check that everyone is in agreement, looking for nods or verbal recognition that they're on the same page. Remind the group that if something comes up in the session that upsets them or makes them feel uncomfortable, they have permission to leave the room or find some space, and remind them of where they can go or who they can approach for support. Creating a safe environment is covered in more detail in the Introduction. Before starting, briefly set out what will be covered in the workshop.

Exercise 1: Quick Decision Making

Part 1

Tell the group that you are going to give them some choices, and they have to make an instant decision. If they choose the first option, they stick their thumbs up in the air, and if they chose the second, they stick their thumbs down. Read out each 'Would you rather?' and then look around the room, commenting on the most popular response before moving on to the next conundrum.

Would You Rather?

- Free pizza or unlimited phone credit for life?
- Total respect or total power?
- Go out with someone you love or go out with someone who loves you?
- Fitting in or standing out?
- To travel in time or be able to fly?
- To be totally free or totally safe?
- To be the only person you know who has taken drugs or the only person who hasn't?
- To drop your phone down the toilet or drop your best friend's phone down the toilet?

Part 2

Ask the group:

1) What helped you make these decisions quickly? (e.g. instinct, past experiences, moral compass, what other people might think, our priorities and which option makes us feel the best)
2) What skills do we use to make decisions?

Exercise 2: Exploring Values and Beliefs – Group Debate

Ask the group to imagine that there is a line across the room. Explain to the group that one side of the room is 'Agree' and the other side is 'Disagree' (you can put up signs to make this clear). Let them know that when you read out a statement they are invited to stand where they feel they are on the line in relation to the statement. If it isn't possible for the young people to move about in the room, you can ask them to put up a hand or stand up if they agree, or give out the green, amber and red cards to each participant representing 'agree', 'neither agree nor disagree' and 'disagree' in Resources and Handouts 1.1. Reassure the group that there are no right or wrong answers, that they can stand in the middle if they are unsure and that they are able to move at any time if their opinion has been swayed. Remind the group to remain respectful when listening to and debating views and opinions that differ from their own. If the group find it hard not to talk over each other, you can use an object to represent a 'talking piece' which allows the person holding it permission to speak, while everyone else needs to listen until their turn with the talking piece (see Appendix 5).

When the young people have moved to where they want to stand, facilitate a debate between individuals or sides. Feel free to contribute to the debate (please note there are no facilitators' notes for this debate as all of the content will be explored throughout the workshop).

You don't need to go through all of the statements; pick those that seem most relevant to the group.

Once you have used a few statements, ask the group if they have any other ideas that they want to debate. It might help if the young people talk briefly in pairs to help them to come up with a statement.

- The drinking age should be reduced to 16.
- Drugs and alcohol can make you feel more confident.
- People do things they wouldn't normally do when they're drunk.
- It's easy to tell when someone's had 'too much'.
- If both people are drunk, then neither of them is responsible for what happens.
- Drinking makes you vulnerable.

Exercise 3: Alcohol, Drugs and Our Brains

Part 1

Read out or show the group PowerPoint slide 2, which is about the effects of alcohol on our brain and decision making:

DID YOU KNOW...?

Alcohol impairs people's decision making – it damages the 'dendrites' in your brain which send messages from your brain to your body.[1]

This can explain why, when people have drunk alcohol, they have slower reaction times – the brain takes longer to tell the body what it needs to do (e.g. walk in a straight line, type a text message, make a decision, notice our early warning signs).

▲ **PowerPoint slide 2**

Answer any questions the students might have so far on the effects of alcohol on the brain.

Part 2

Do the 'Myth or Fact?' quiz about drugs and alcohol with the group. A quiz can be a great way to capture the interest of the young people.

There are multiple ways you can conduct this quiz:

1) By reading out the statements and asking the group to stand up if they think the statement is a myth and remain seated if they think it's fact.

2) Using the handout (Resources and Handouts 9.2) and allowing small groups or pairs to discuss each question before presenting their answers to allow for further exploration of each statement. You can ask individual students in the group why they have decided myth/fact before revealing the answer and the additional information.

3) You can give out 'Myth' and 'Fact' cards (Resources and Handouts 9.1).

4) You can have two or more groups competing against each other, with a prize to be won.

---

1   Siegel, K. (2014) 'Beer before liquor: 13 biggest myths about alcohol, busted.' Accessed on 7/2/2020 at https://greatist.com/health/13-biggest-myths-alcohol

Facilitators' Answers

Statement	Myth or fact?
It's your fault if someone rapes you because you've drunk too much alcohol.	**Myth:** In law, a person consents to sexual activity 'if he or she agrees by choice, with the freedom and capacity to do so'. If a person is incapacitated or unconscious from having alcohol or drugs, they can't give consent to sex. Having sex with someone who is incapacitated through alcohol or drugs is rape. No one wants to be raped or sexually assaulted. 100% of the responsibility is with the person causing the harm.
Some people can't help raping others when they are drunk, stressed or had a difficult childhood.	**Myth:** Sexual assault is not caused by drugs and alcohol – it is the attacker committing the crime, not the substances they take. Most people under the influence of drugs and alcohol don't choose to rape someone. Being stressed or having a difficult past doesn't turn people into 'rapists' or justify sexual violence. There's no excuse.
Drinking three pints of beer or two glasses of wine can be considered 'binge' drinking.	**Fact:** Over 8 units of alcohol for men and over 6 units of alcohol for women is considered binge drinking. A pint of Stella is 2.8 units so 3 pints puts you over 8 units, and a large glass of wine can be just over 3 units.[2]
Using energy drinks as a mixer can make you more drunk than alcohol alone.	**Myth:** Energy drinks change our perception of how intoxicated we really are but have no physiological effect on how alcohol affects us.[3]
It is legal to give alcohol to a 6-year-old child.	**Fact:** The law in the UK states that it is against the law to give an alcoholic drink to anyone under the age of 5.[4] (Facilitators' note: This is a good point to use to illustrate that laws don't exist in isolation – just because it is not illegal to give alcohol to a 6-year-old does not mean that deliberately trying to get a 6-year-old drunk is not an offence, morally wrong and dangerous.)
People who have sex when they are drunk and regret it after often lie and say they were raped.	**Myth:** False allegations of rape are very unusual. Thinking that people make false allegations more than they do can be harmful if it means that victims of sexual violence don't report what happened for fear of not being believed, not being able to access the right help and not getting the justice they deserve. The media often focusses on false rape allegations, giving the impression that it's more common for people to lie about sexual violence than it actually is.[5]
You can sober up and avoid hangovers if you make yourself sick.	**Myth:** Alcohol gets absorbed into the bloodstream almost as soon as you drink it, so getting rid of a small amount by being sick probably won't make a lot of difference.

2   Alcohol Change UK (n.d.) 'Alcohol statistics.' Accessed on 3/2/2020 at https://alcoholchange.org.uk/alcohol-facts/fact-sheets/alcohol-statistics?gclid=EAIaIQobChMI65ejx76d4wIVq7ftChOvUgMbEAAYASAAEgLroPD_BwE

3   Siegel, K. (2014) 'Beer before liquor: 13 biggest myths about alcohol, busted.' Accessed on 7/2/2020 at https://greatist.com/health/13-biggest-myths-alcohol

4   Drinkaware (2019) 'The law on alcohol and under 18s.' Accessed on 3/2/2020 at www.drinkaware.co.uk/alcohol-facts/alcohol-and-the-law/the-law-on-alcohol-and-under-18s/?gclid=EAIaIQobChMIn8HJ3cCd4wIVDZPtCh2IHggWEAAYAyABEgLR4vD_BwE

5   Rape Crisis (n.d.) 'About sexual violence: Myths vs realities.' Accessed on 3/2/2020 at https://rapecrisis.org.uk/get-informed/about-sexual-violence/myths-vs-realities

It is illegal to buy alcohol for someone that is already drunk or appears drunk in a bar or club.	**Fact:** A person could be prosecuted for buying someone a drink in a bar and deliberately trying to get them more drunk.[6]
I can still be in control when I'm drunk.	**Myth:** Drinking impairs your judgement, which increases the chances that you will do something you'll later regret such as having unprotected sex or not checking for consent.
The drinking guidelines for men are higher because they have more muscles.	**Myth:** The current guidelines around alcohol consumption are now the same for men and women (they used to be different). All genders are advised by Drink Aware UK not to regularly drink more than 14 units a week. These guidelines are in place to reduce the risk of alcohol-related illnesses.[7] 14 units = 6 pints of beer of average strength (4%) or 6 glasses of 13% wine. If women are pregnant, they shouldn't drink at all.[8]
It's illegal for someone of legal drinking age (over 18) to buy alcohol for someone under 18.	**Fact:** The maximum fine for buying or supplying alcohol for people under 18 is £5000, and if you are a business such as a shop or off-licence, you can have your licence suspended even on a first offence. If you are found frequently selling alcohol to under-18s, the fine increases to £20,000 and you risk having your licence taken off you and a criminal record.[9]

Part 3

Elicit feedback from the young people about the quiz:

1) Did anything shock you?
2) Did you learn anything new?
3) Do you have any questions?

Exercise 4: Drugs, Alcohol, Sexual Behaviour and Consent

Ask the group:

1) What could be the consequences of being under the influence of drugs and alcohol on our sexual behaviour?
2) Can drugs and alcohol affect our ability to make decisions and to consent?

---

6   Drinkaware (2019) 'Buying alcohol.' Accessed on 3/2/2020 at www.drinkaware.co.uk/alcohol-facts/alcohol-and-the-law/buying-alcohol

7   Drinkaware (2019) 'How much alcohol is too much?' Accessed on 3/2/2020 at www.drinkaware.co.uk/alcohol-facts/alcoholic-drinks-units/how-much-is-too-much

8   NHS (2020) 'Drinking alcohol while pregnant: Your pregnancy and baby guide.' Accessed on 6/3/2020 at www.nhs.uk/conditions/pregnancy-and-baby/alcohol-medicines-drugs-pregnant

9   Home Office (2015) 'Policy paper: 2010 to 2015 government policy: Alcohol sales.' Accessed on 3/2/2020 at www.gov.uk/government/publications/2010-to-2015-government-policy-alcohol-sales/2010-to-2015-government-policy-alcohol-sales

(Facilitators' note: It can be helpful to link this discussion to the freedom and capacity aspect of the Sexual Offences Act 2003.)

After the end of the discussion, read out or show the group PowerPoint slide 3, which is about the effects of alcohol on sexual behaviour and consent:

DID YOU KNOW...?
According to the Crime Survey for England and Wales:

▷ **38%** of victims of sexual violence reported that the person who caused them harm was under the influence of alcohol.
▷ The same proportion (**38%**) said they were under the influence of alcohol themselves.
▷ **2%** said that they themselves were under the influence of drugs they had chosen to take.
▷ **6%** reported that they thought the person who harmed them had drugged them.[10]

▲ **PowerPoint slide 3**

Let the group know that although drugs and alcohol do influence people's ability to consent and to make decisions, there are many more factors that affect risky sexual behaviour such as social norms, the influence of pornography and the media, and peer influence on young people. These concepts will be explored further in other workshops.

Exercise 5: Under the Influence

You need access to some 'kaleidoscope glasses' or preferably 'beer goggles' (these are also called 'drunk goggles' or 'impairment goggles') to complete this exercise. This exercise can be completed in a classroom setting with one volunteer at a time.

Part 1

The volunteer needs to stand where everyone can see them with the glasses or goggles on, headphones playing a fast-beat music track and a strong-flavoured sweet in their mouth (e.g. aniseed, lemon sherbet, popping candy, sour sweets), and wearing woollen gloves or oven gloves.

Note: Ask the volunteers not to walk around while wearing 'beer goggles' as this can be unsafe.

Once the volunteer is ready, ask the other group members to suggest (appropriate) tasks for them to complete. Suggestions include:

10   Office for National Statistics (2017) 'Sexual offences in England and Wales: Year ending March 2017. Analyses on sexual offences from the year ending March 2017 Crime Survey for England and Wales and crimes recorded by police.' Accessed on 3/2/2020 at www.ons.gov.uk/peoplepopulationandcommunity/crimeandjustice/articles/sexualoffencesinenglandandwales/yearendingmarch2017

- Pat your head and rub your belly.
- Hop on one leg.
- Count in sevens up to 49.
- Point at four things beginning with G.
- Say the alphabet backwards.
- Whistle the *EastEnders* theme tune.
- Point at five blue things in the room.
- Tell a tongue twister or a joke.

If you complete this exercise, it is likely you'll have more than one student wanting a go. Wait for all volunteers to have a go before asking for feedback.

Part 2

After each student has given the task a go, ask how they found the exercise and whether they noticed a difference in their ability to focus and complete tasks.

At the end of the reflections, explain that this experience demonstrates how difficult the decision-making process is when your senses are overloaded, or just not functioning normally, such as when you are drunk or on drugs.

Exercise 6: Exploring Campaigns
Part 1

Show the group these two adverts:

- You Wouldn't Start a Night Out Like This – Know Your Limits:
  www.youtube.com/watch?v=8kScIRI7a4E (video length: 40 seconds).
- Alcohol – Know Your Limits (Superhero):
  www.youtube.com/watch?v=7F5o3NSHMoM (video length: 40 seconds).

▲ **PowerPoint slide 4**

Part 2

Lead a discussion around these campaigns:

1) What messages are these adverts trying to convey, and are they successful?
2) Which advert is more effective, and why?
3) Do you think adverts like these have an impact on the amount people drink?

Exercise 7: Why? vs Why Not?

Part 1

Create two columns on the board, one labelled 'Why?' and the other 'Why not?'

Part 2

Ask the group to come up with as many reasons as they can 'why' someone might use drugs and alcohol (the positives, the justifications) and 'why not' (the negatives, the consequences). Record their responses in the columns.

Some reasons they might come up with include:

Why?	Why Not?
• Makes people feel good • Social norms • Experimenting • Feeling more confident and less inhibited • Fun	• Affecting our level of control • Affecting our ability to communicate • Making us less likely to be aware of our surroundings • Increased aggressiveness • More vulnerable • More impulsive • It can be hard to know when you've had enough • They can damage our health • Alcohol and drugs are addictive

Exercise 8: Role Play – 'Persuade Me'

Part 1

Ask the group to get into pairs and label themselves A and B.

Explain that A is going to try to persuade B to drink alcohol, using as many reasons as possible why B should try it, and B is going to try to persuade A not to drink alcohol using as many reasons as possible why it's a bad idea. Give the pairs three minutes to complete the exercise.

Part 2

Elicit feedback on the exercise.

1) Whose argument was the stronger – A's or B's?
2) What's it like trying to say 'No' when someone is persuading you to do something?
3) What is the likely outcome of this conversation for each pair (B chooses to drink, or A chooses not to)?

If there is enthusiasm from the group, switch the roles around so that B is trying to persuade A to drink, and A is giving the reasons not to, and repeat questions 1 to 3.

Exercise 9: How Much Is Too Much?

Part 1

This exercise is a whole-group activity. Give each table or small group the coloured cards with 'Play', 'Pause' or 'Stop' on them (Resources and Handouts 9.3), and let them know you will be taking them through some scenarios and they need to have a conversation in their groups before presenting their cards:

- Amber = Pause
- Green= Play
- Red = Stop

Read out each scenario before inviting the students to vote, or go through the scenarios on the PowerPoint slides one by one.

Scenario 1

Bailey and Ash have been dating for two months and go to a friend's party together. Ash gets drunk and is stumbling around. Bailey asks if Ash wants to find a room to lie down in together and Ash mumbles in agreement. When they are alone together, Bailey starts kissing Ash. Bailey asks if it's OK and Ash mumbles 'Mmmmm'. Bailey gets turned on from the kissing and starts to undress Ash. Ash doesn't move while Bailey does this and doesn't seem particularly interested in sex.

    What should Bailey do?

▲ **PowerPoint slide 5**

After the students have voted, ask what their assumptions are about Bailey's and Ash's gender. Would it make a difference if Bailey was male and Ash female or vice versa? Would it make a difference if Bailey and Ash were the same gender?

Scenario 2

Casey and Dontae meet at a house party. They play spin the bottle and end up having to kiss each other multiple times. They are both tipsy but enjoying themselves. When the game is over, they sit outside together laughing and giggling about how many times the bottle landed on the two of them. They start kissing again more passionately, and Casey suggests they find somewhere more private. Dontae agrees and they go upstairs. Casey tells Dontae it's nice to be touched and they continue kissing and touching each other. They begin undressing each other.

    What should Dontae do?

▲ **PowerPoint slide 6**

After the students have voted, ask what their assumptions are about Casey's and Dontae's gender. Would it make a difference if Casey was male and Dontae was female or vice versa? Would it make a difference if Casey and Dontae were the same gender?

Scenario 3

Zia and Stevie have been hooking up for a few weeks but so far have only kissed. They have been in the park drinking and both having fun. Zia suggests they go for a walk away from the group and leads Stevie behind a tree. Zia starts kissing Stevie passionately, kissing Stevie's neck and trying to undo Stevie's trousers. Stevie says, 'I don't want to do anything else' and pushes Zia's hand away.

    What should Zia do?

▲ **PowerPoint slide 7**

After the students have voted, ask what their assumptions are about Zia's and Stevie's gender. Would it make a difference if Zia was male and Stevie was female or vice versa? Would it make a difference if Zia and Stevie were the same gender?

Scenario 4

Jules and Devin have been dating for a few months and have decided they are ready to have sex. They have a few drinks to help them feel more comfortable and relaxed. They start kissing, but Jules says, 'I'm finding it hard to focus' and is feeling drunker than expected. Devin is still keen for tonight to be the night, but Jules is feeling less sure and wants it to be special.

    What should Devin do?

▲ **PowerPoint slide 8**

After the students have voted, ask what their assumptions are about Jules's and Devin's gender. Would it make a difference if Jules was male and Devin female or vice versa? Would it make a difference if Jules and Devin were the same gender?

Scenario 5

Taja has been interested in Leo for months, but Leo keeps refusing Taja's requests on social media and telling Taja, 'I'm not interested.' Taja isn't taking Leo's no for an answer and keeps asking to meet up IRL. Leo decides to meet face to face to tell Taja, one final time, to leave them alone. Taja brings a bottle of tequila to the park. Leo tells Taja that this is going no further and that Taja is being pushy. Taja seems to accept this and suggests they just have fun together, offering Leo a shot. Leo accepts as it seems harmless enough and they are in a public space. After drinking and sitting

---

on the swings for a few hours, Leo feels drunk and realizes Taja has barely touched the tequila. Taja suggests they walk Leo home. Leo is stumbling and not able to walk straight. Leo throws up down their front, and when they get home Leo takes off their top before getting into bed. Taja gets in with Leo, snuggling up, placing a hand on Leo's chest and desperately wanting more to happen. Leo is lying with their back to Taja and saying they still feel sick.

What should Taja do?

▲ **PowerPoint slide 9**

After the students have voted, ask what their assumptions are about Taja's and Leo's gender. Would it make a difference if Taja was male and Leo female or vice versa? Would it make a difference if Taja and Leo were the same gender?

Part 2

Ask the group what they based their decision to vote Amber, Green or Red on. After eliciting feedback, show them PowerPoint slide 10.

HOW DRUNK IS TOO DRUNK?

If the answer to any of these questions is 'No', or even 'I don't know', then the other person is too drunk to consent:

1. Can this person communicate clearly?
2. Are they coherent?
3. Are they sober enough to know what is going on?
4. Are they enthusiastic?

Even if it is not **illegal**, it is still **unethical** to go ahead under these circumstances.

No one's sexual desires or expectations are more important than someone else's safety and wellbeing.

▲ **PowerPoint slide 10**

Stress the point that even if it's not illegal, it might still be an unethical or bad idea. And just to be clear: If there is ever *any* doubt, confusion or possible mixed messages, don't do it.

Exercise 10: Skills Practice

Part 1

Thinking about the scenarios we have just covered, ask the group to come up with ideas around what you could say if you were worried someone was too intoxicated to consent. Record these on the board or flipchart.

Part 2

After eliciting feedback, you can suggest:

- Do you still want to do this?
- Is this OK? Are you OK?
- Do you need a break?
- Are you having fun?
- What do you want to do next?

Part 3

Show the Causes of Rape graph (PowerPoint slide 10) and elicit any responses or questions from the group.

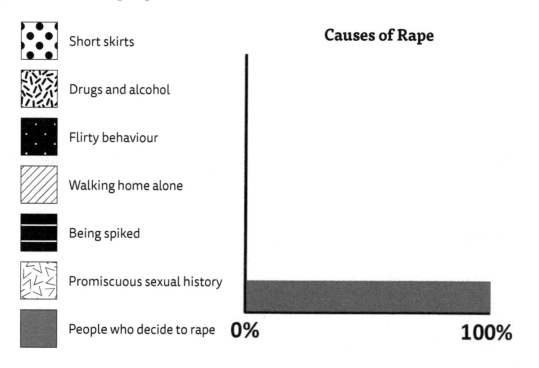

▲ **PowerPoint slide 11**

Part 4

Finally, read out or show the group 'What the law says' in PowerPoint slide 12:

WHAT THE LAW SAYS

- In situations when both people are drinking, charges are often brought against the person who is determined to have initiated sex, even if they're also intoxicated.
- Sex under the influence of alcohol is not automatically non-consensual, but alcohol makes it harder to determine if you have consent or to communicate whether you give consent. If in doubt – it's a 'No'.

- While alcohol can't be blamed for causing a crime, as we can see, we also can't pretend it has no effect on people's experiences.
- THERE IS NO SUCH THING AS 'SEX' WITH SOMEONE WHO IS PASSED OUT – this is always rape.

▲ **PowerPoint slide 12**

End the session with PowerPoint slide 13 and let the group know that there are many places they can go to get resources on this subject or seek support, and there are procedures in place for anonymous reporting. It is important for them to share any issues or concerns that they have about themselves or others related to this topic. Be mindful of the possible impacts and emotions that might be evoked for individuals from the discussion, and if a topic is emotive for someone, offer an opportunity to explore this outside the group, to ensure that they feel heard and safe.

SIGNPOSTING AND RESOURCES

If you have any questions or worries about drugs or alcohol and would like support, help is available.

▷ **Talk to Frank:** The website has lots of information about drugs and alcohol, and has a helpline, online support and a search facility for finding details of local and national services that provide counselling and treatment in England.
Helpline: 0300 1236600
www.talktofrank.com

▲ **PowerPoint slide 13**

Communication

This helped me understand myself and other people better

Session Overview

This workshop explores verbal and nonverbal communication through a series of games and activities. It considers communication and social styles, and looks at assertiveness, including ways to say 'No'. This session uses a variety of interactive games and techniques to explore different types of communication, understand communication styles and build confidence in assertiveness skills. As we discussed in Workshop 7, communication is a key component of healthy relationships.

Info/Knowledge

Consent seems so simple – surely 'Yes' means 'Yes' and 'No' means 'No'. Although saying 'Yes' or 'No' should be enough to communicate consent, the reality often isn't that straightforward. Words can have different meanings at different times, and our use of body language makes it possible for someone to be saying 'Yes' when their body is clearly communicating 'No' or vice versa. Unfortunately, many adults appear to find it hard to grasp, and when the nuances of culture, gender and context are added, the picture becomes even more ambiguous. When we enter a romantic and/or sexual relationship, our personalities and habitual behaviour translate over into our sexual relationships. A relationship where there is an imbalance of power will become a sexual relationship that is unequal. If two people can readily communicate their needs and wishes, their sexual relationship will have a similar vibe. A young person who struggles to assert their will in day-to-day situations may lack the ability to be assertive when it comes to sex. By teaching young people assertiveness and social communication skills, we hope to develop their confidence, independence and wellbeing in any situation.

PSHE Association Curriculum Themes

▷ KS3 R3. To further develop the communication skills of active listening, negotiation, offering and receiving constructive feedback and assertiveness

Exercises

▷ Exercise 1: Exploring Communication – Silent Birthday Line-Up
▷ Exercise 2: Verbal Communication and Active Listening
▷ Exercise 3: Nonverbal Communication and Teamwork
▷ Exercise 4: Types of Communication
▷ Exercise 5: Facts and Interpretations
▷ Exercise 6: Communication Styles
▷ Exercise 7: How to Be Assertive
▷ Exercise 8: Yes–No–Unsure

Materials Needed

▷ Flipchart paper and colouring pens
▷ Communication Styles handout if PowerPoint isn't available for Exercise 6 (Resources and Handouts 10.1)
▷ 'Passive', 'Passive-Aggressive', 'Aggressive' and 'Assertive' cards for Exercise 6 (Resources and Handouts 10.2)

Learning Outcomes

By the end of this session:

• I can describe different kinds of communication including verbal, nonverbal, body language, tone of voice and facial expressions
• I understand that both verbal and nonverbal communication are important when it comes to consent
• I can think about the differences between fact and interpretation, and how this affects how I communicate with others
• I can understand assertiveness, why it is important and explore when to use it
• I can explore 'Yes', 'No' and 'Maybe', and different ways these may be communicated
• I can understand that when it comes to sexual activity, 'Maybe' means 'No'

At the beginning of the session, inform the group of the topic – *Communication* – and point out that it requires the group to approach the discussions with a certain amount of maturity and sensitivity. Remind the group of the agreed expectations, particularly emphasizing confidentiality and the importance of treating one another with respect. Check that everyone is in agreement, looking for nods or verbal recognition that they're on the same page. Remind the group that if something comes up in the session that upsets them or makes them feel uncomfortable, they have permission to leave the room or find some space, and remind them of where they can go or who they can approach for support. Creating a safe environment is covered in more detail in the Introduction. Before starting, briefly set out what will be covered in the workshop.

Exercise 1: Exploring Communication – Silent Birthday Line-Up

Part 1

Explain that this exercise explores nonverbal and verbal communication.

Invite the group to stand up and indicate that one end of the room is 1 January and the other end is 31 December.

Explain that the task is for everyone to get into a line in order of when their birthdays are, *but* they can't speak to each other and have to do this in silence. They can use nonverbal communication to find out each other's birthdays and to get into the right order. You can time how long it takes them to get into order to make this activity more challenging.

Part 2

Once the group has formed a line, start at the January end of the line and invite people to call out their birthdays to check for accuracy.

Part 3

Explore how the exercise was for the group including:

1) What skills were required to get this right? (e.g. eye contact, patience, reading body language, gestures)
2) Were there any difficulties? If so, what would have made it easier?

Exercise 2: Verbal Communication and Active Listening

Part 1

Get the group into pairs, sitting back to back. Ask them to label each other A and B, and give each B a blank piece of paper. Explain that the aim of the exercise is to have the most accurate drawing of what person A describes to person B.

Part 2

Ask the As to use their imagination. For the duration of the exercise, the As are allowed to speak, and the Bs need to be silent but listening attentively. Bs are not allowed to ask questions.

A has three minutes to describe their house (or another building if they prefer), including their front door, any features, whether there are windows, curtains, whether there is more than one floor, while the Bs draw what is being described as accurately as possible.

Part 3

At the end of the three minutes, ask the As and Bs to compare what is on the sheet of paper with what A was describing.

Ask for feedback:

1) What went well and what was challenging?
2) What skills were required to accurately draw what the other person was describing?

Part 4

Ask the Bs:

1) What the As did well.
2) What they could have done differently to make their instructions clearer.
3) Whether there were questions that the Bs wanted to ask the As for clarification but couldn't.

Note: If you want to make this exercise competitive, you can give a prize or round of applause to the pair with the most accurate drawing.

Part 5 (Optional)

You can repeat the exercise with the Bs describing their own house (or other building) and the As listening to the instructions and drawing. You could simply repeat the same instructions, or introduce a new feature – for example, this time allowing the As to ask questions and clarify the descriptions.

After three minutes ask the As to compare their drawing with what B was describing. Ask the As:

1) what the Bs did well
2) what they could have done differently to make their instructions clearer
3) whether there was anything that B did as a result of going second and learning from the challenges of A's turn as the instructor?

Exercise 3: Nonverbal Communication and Teamwork

Part 1

Again, ask the group to get into pairs (or stay in the same pairs as for Exercise 2). Ideally, you need a bit of space for this exercise so the group can move around the room, but if this isn't possible, they can play it statically.

Part 2

Each group needs a pen. The aim of the exercise is for them not to drop the pen. The pair needs to hold the pen between them – putting pressure on either end of it (not holding on to the pen, just applying equal pressure so the pen stays between them) and move around, or move the pen up and down and backwards and forwards *without speaking*. Let the group know that you will say 'Go' and then time 60 seconds, and any pairs who have not dropped the pen within that time have won.

Part 3

Ask the group:

1)   What were the challenges of this exercise?
2)   What skills were needed to keep the pen up? (e.g. eye contact, team work)
3)   Did any pair manage to keep the pen from dropping for the duration of the exercise?
4)   What were the main reasons the pen fell down when it did drop? (e.g. loss of focus, making sudden movements that surprised your partner)

Exercise 4: Types of Communication

We've participated in some exercises exploring different types of communication. Ask the group if they can identify which types (e.g. nonverbal, verbal, body language) and then show them PowerPoint slide 2 or read out the categories of different types of communication:

COMMUNICATION
Verbal
▷ Language
   ○ Emphasis
   ○ Context
   ○ Interpretation
▷ Sounds
   ○ Volume
   ○ Tone of voice

Nonverbal
▷ Gestures
   ○ Facial expression
▷ Body language
   ○ Vibe/attitude
   ○ Eye contact
   ○ Posture

▷ Touch
  ◦ Physical closeness
▷ Sign language
▷ Written language
▷ Listening skills

▲ **PowerPoint slide 2**

Go through each type of communication with the group, answering any questions as you go along. At the end of the exploration, remind the group that when it comes to consent it requires verbal and nonverbal agreement from everyone involved.

Exercise 5: Facts and Interpretations

Part 1

Let the group know that there are many different things that complicate human interaction and communication, and show them PowerPoint slide 3 to emphasize the point.

COMMUNICATION IS CHALLENGING!

One challenge to successful communication is misinterpretation: everyone and anyone can misinterpret information, but it's even easier to misinterpret the world around you when you're a teenager. This is because your brain is wired to be the centre of your own universe, to be more self-conscious and truly feel like everyone is watching you!

The teenage brain is wired to make connections quicker than adults, and also wired not to have consequential thinking (e.g. if this happens, this will happen next...).

The part of the brain that controls reasoning is one of the last to develop!

This means teenagers are:

- more likely to be impulsive and irrational
- more likely to misread social cues
- more likely to misinterpret their own, or other people's, emotions
- more likely to think everything is to do with them
- less likely to think before they act!

▲ **PowerPoint slide 3**

Part 2

Let the group know that, as a teenager, it is important to be aware that you may jump to conclusions and interpret information as involving you – when it doesn't – or as threatening – when it isn't.

Part 3

As a whole group, go through each scenario, either reading them out and asking the follow-up questions or showing the PowerPoint slides and eliciting feedback as you go along (there are example answers/conversation starters for facilitators below).

Scenario 1: My best friend sees my WhatsApp message and doesn't respond

1. What might your interpretation be?
2. If you thought this was true, what might you do next?
3. What other reasons/alternative explanations could there be that are nothing to do with you?
4. How would you act if you considered another option?

▲ **PowerPoint slide 4**

Scenario 2: My partner is secretly messaging someone else

1. What might your interpretation be?
2. If you thought this was true, what might you do next?
3. What other reasons/alternative explanations could there be that are nothing to do with you?
4. How would you act if you considered another option?

▲ **PowerPoint slide 5**

Scenario 3: Someone is staring at me on the bus

1. What might your interpretation be?
2. If you thought this was true, what might you do next?
3. What other reasons/alternative explanations could there be that are nothing to do with you?
4. How would you act if you considered another option?

▲ **PowerPoint slide 6**

Scenario 4: Your friend posts a status saying 'I'm tired of these dickheads/skets'

1. What might your interpretation be?
2. If you thought this was true, what might you do next?
3. What other reasons/alternative explanations could there be that are nothing to do with you?
4. How would you act if you considered another option?

▲ **PowerPoint slide 7**

Scenario 5: Everyone on Insta has amazing lives, perfect bodies and is always on holiday

1. What might your interpretation be?
2. If you thought this was true, what might you do next?
3. What other reasons/alternative explanations could there be that are nothing to do with you?
4. How would you act if you considered another option?

▲ **PowerPoint slide 8**

Scenario 6: Someone is honking their horn at me

1. What might your interpretation be?
2. If you thought this was true, what might you do next?
3. What other reasons/alternative explanations could there be that are nothing to do with you?
4. How would you act if you considered another option?

▲ **PowerPoint slide 9**

Facilitators' Notes

Scenario 1: My best friend sees my WhatsApp message and doesn't respond

- Interpretations could include: They don't like me any more.
- What I might do next if I thought this was true: Cut them out or say something nasty about them.
- Alternative interpretation: Someone else had their phone and they didn't see the message; they're busy; there's something going on at home, etc.
- How would you act if you considered these options? Not fret about not getting a quick reply, check through friends that they are OK, message them again, have a conversation with them about your response.

Scenario 2: My partner is secretly messaging someone else

- Interpretations could include: They're seeing someone else; they don't like me any more; someone's disrespecting me and stealing my partner.
- What I might do next if I thought this was true: Demand that they tell me what's going on; watch them all the time; make them stop seeing or communicating with other people.
- Alternative interpretation: It's just a friend they messaged about a homework question; it's their cousin; they're arranging a surprise for me.
- How would you act if you considered these options? Be glad for them that they have other people in their life, and make sure I have my own friendships outside our relationship.

Scenario 3: Someone is staring at me on the bus

- Interpretations could include: They want to fight me; they're trying to intimidate me.
- What I might do next if I thought this was true: Tell them to stop staring; glare at them; punch them.
- Alternative interpretations: They think they recognize me; they're looking past me; they've had a terrible day; they're trying to draw me out.
- How would you act differently if you considered these options? Smile at them; ask them if everything is OK; look the other way; be the bigger person.

Scenario 4: Your friend posts a status saying, 'I'm tired of these dickheads/skets'

- Interpretation could include: I'm the dickhead/sket; I've done something to disappoint them.
- What I might do next if I thought this was true: Post a defensive response; write my own status targeting them.
- Alternative interpretations: It's not about you; someone has upset them; they're looking for a reaction; they're seeking attention in a negative way.
- How would you act differently if you considered these options? Check out what it is that has upset them; tell them it's not good to write cryptic messages as it can make people paranoid.

Scenario 5: Everyone on Insta has amazing lives, perfect bodies and is always on holiday

- Interpretations could include: My life is boring; I'm not good enough; I need to go on a diet.
- What I might do next if I thought this was true: Feel depressed, down and unsatisfied; post nasty things to make them feel bad.
- Alternative interpretations: Everyone posts their best selves, uses filters, etc.; some Insta characters are sponsored but don't say that they are.
- How would you act differently if you considered these options? Think about how my posts might affect people who read them; spend less time online; be a bit more authentic on social media; try to compare myself with other people less.

Scenario 6: Someone is honking their horn at me

- Interpretations could include: They're making a pass at me; they're disrespecting me.
- What I might do next if I thought this was true: Give them the finger; shout something at them; ignore them and feel self-conscious.
- Alternative interpretations: They might have been honking at someone else; they might have a child in the car pressing the horn.
- How would you act differently if you considered these options? Look around and check if the attention/horn is aimed at me before choosing how to respond.

Part 4

Ask the group if they have any other examples or scenarios of when they have misinterpreted information and acted on it without questioning the facts. How would they have responded differently if they had stopped and paused before responding?

At the end of the exercise, remind the group that interpreting information correctly over social media is even harder than in real life because we don't get to see all the nonverbal social cues of the other person!

Exercise 6: Communication Styles

Part 1

Let the group know that, on top of different types of communication, there are also different ways that we can choose to communicate: assertively, aggressively, passively and passive-aggressively. This is true of both verbal and nonverbal communication.

Show the group PowerPoint slide 10 or give them the handout (Resources and Handouts 10.1) which outlines characteristics of different communication styles. Go through each one, checking the young people's understanding and answering any questions as you go along.

Assertive	Passive	Aggressive	Passive-aggressive

Clear boundaries Aware of feelings Able to communicate feelings Able to say 'No' Honest and open Expressive Confident Able to see things from all perspectives and remain empathic towards self and others Uses a firm tone of voice and states things clearly Open and relaxed body language	Denies that they're angry Holds feelings in Doesn't hold their boundaries Can't say 'No' Avoids direct conflict at all costs Pleases other people over getting their own needs met Subtly manipulates others 'Pushover' Stays away from conflict Shy and withdrawing body language (slouches, withdraws, avoids eye contact)	Shows anger Doesn't listen to others Explodes Attacks Blames Interrupts others Judgemental towards others Manipulates to get what they want Controls others Intimidating body language (stares, glares, makes fists, takes over personal space, crossed arms, tight jaw) Gets what they want at the expense of others Hurts others to avoid being hurt	Denies that they're angry Is sarcastic Holds grudges – secretly plans to get others back/ make them pay Is resentful Indirect Avoids eye contact Gossips Gives people the silent treatment/ stonewalling Engages in hurtful banter Says something offensive followed by 'It's only a joke' Teases Indifference – 'whatever'

▲ PowerPoint slide 10[1]

Part 2

You will need eight volunteers who are happy to come up and role-play a reaction to different scenarios using the four communication styles. Have the 'Passive', 'Passive-Aggressive', 'Aggressive' and 'Assertive' cards ready (Resources and Handouts 10.2). Each volunteer will need to come up to the front and pick one of the communication styles without letting the rest of the group know which one. Before they begin, remind the young people that they can use body language, eye contact, tone of voice, gestures, facial expressions, etc. to convey their message.

Note: If students would prefer, you can have two volunteers per scenario so that each volunteer has someone else to react towards.

---

1   Images by Pete Linforth courtesy of Pixabay.

Then read out one of the scenarios to the whole group and ask the volunteer to role-play their reaction/response to the scenario using the communication style they picked. The rest of the group need to guess which communication style they are using.

Scenarios

1. A teacher has told you off for talking when it wasn't you.	5. One of your mates has asked out your ex.
2. A waiter has brought you the wrong order.	6. Someone has wrongly accused you of stealing from their shop.
3. Someone has accidentally broken your phone screen.	7. Someone has spread a rumour about you.
4. Someone has posted a picture of you on Insta that you want deleted.	8. Your partner has stood you up.

At the end of the exercise, ask the students what they noticed about the verbal and nonverbal communication of each of the communication styles, including body language, tone of voice, eye contact, facial expressions, etc.

Part 3

Show the group PowerPoint slide 11 or let them know that:

BEING ASSERTIVE

Being assertive means **clearly** and **confidently** letting someone know how you feel and what you need. It is based on **mutual respect** and is an empowering way to communicate.

Being assertive means taking your own needs into consideration, as well as the needs of others.

When it comes to our bodies, it is important to be assertive and to let people know what we are and are not comfortable with.

▲ PowerPoint slide 11

Let the group know that reacting to situations in an aggressive, passive or passive-aggressive way means that you are either ignoring your own needs or ignoring the needs of others. Show them PowerPoint slide 12[2] or draw the diagram on the board to illustrate the point, and answer any questions the group has on the diagram.

---

2   For more information about passive-aggressive behaviour, see: Dana G Coaching (n.d.) 'Are you passive aggressive or do you know someone who is?' Accessed on 6/2/2020 at https://danagatto.com/are-you-passive-aggressive-and-dont-even-know-it

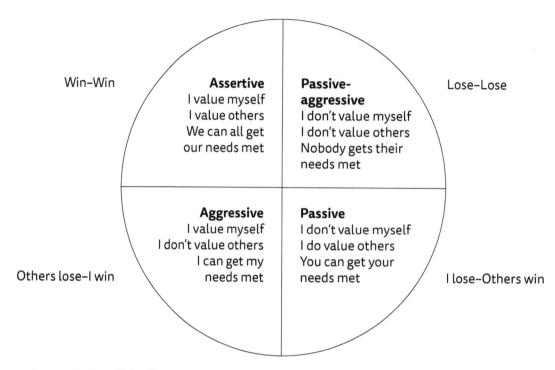

▲ **PowerPoint slide 12**

Exercise 7: How to Be Assertive

We are going to explore being assertive further, including barriers to being assertive and tips for assertive communication.

Part 1

Show the group PowerPoint slide 13, in which the character Tia is saying that sometimes it is hard to say things out loud. Ask the young people:

1) Why is this? (Facilitators' note: Explore ideas around guilt, disappointing or disagreeing with someone, not knowing what you want in the first place, being unsure, being pressured or someone trying to persuade us.)

2) When is it important to be assertive? (Facilitators' note: Explore ideas around peer influence, dealing with persuasion, ending a relationship, having difficult conversations, standing up to others, letting people know if you feel uncomfortable.)

3) What could Tia do to be more assertive in her relationship?

▲ PowerPoint slide 13

Part 2

After you have elicited feedback from the group, show them PowerPoint slide 14 or read out any ideas that they missed:

TIPS FOR ASSERTIVE COMMUNICATION
- **Practise** or **write down** what you want to say so you feel prepared.
- Talk **face to face** – it's easier to make a message clear if you are talking in person so the other person can hear your tone of voice and see your body language.
- Make **eye contact**.
- Be **clear** and **direct** about what you feel and need (people can't read your mind!).
- **Stay calm** – yelling or shouting may make the other person feel defensive rather than listening to what you are saying.
- **Don't apologize** for having needs in the first place.
- Use **'I' statements** to avoid blaming the other person – e.g. 'I don't like it when you...'; 'I feel uncomfortable when you...'; 'I like how it feels when you...'
- Use the **'broken record'** technique – repeat what you are saying so the message is clear and your boundaries are clear.

▲ PowerPoint slide 14

Part 3

After exploring the tips for assertive communication, ask the young people whether there might be times when being assertive could be a bad or dangerous idea. (Facilitators' note: Being assertive is about keeping safe and getting our needs met – if there is a concern that being assertive might make someone angry, aggressive, forceful or dangerous, then being assertive could cause more harm than good – in this instance they might need to ask an adult or friend for help.)

Exercise 8: Yes-No-Unsure

Part 1

In small groups (roughly four per group) ask the young people to come up with a list of ways that someone could show or say 'No', 'Yes' and 'Unsure' when it comes to consent. Ask them to include different forms of communication that we have explored during this workshop (e.g. verbal, nonverbal, aggressive, passive-aggressive, passive, assertive).

Note: This is a bit of a trick question as technically 'Unsure' means 'No' – if any of the students point this out, then adapt the exercise to just include 'Yes' and 'No' lists!

Get feedback from the groups about what sorts of things they had on their lists and then show them PowerPoint slide 15 or read out further ways someone could indicate 'No':

WAYS TO SAY NO! – VERBAL AND NONVERBAL

▷ No!
▷ Don't touch me
▷ Not saying anything at all
▷ I'm not ready
▷ I don't know how I feel about this
▷ Maybe another time, but not now
▷ I don't want to do this any more
▷ I've changed my mind
▷ Avoiding touching someone and being touched
▷ Moving away from their touch
▷ Looking sad or scared
▷ Saying or sounding as if they are in pain
▷ Get off me!
▷ I don't want to
▷ I would rather not...
▷ Don't pressure me
▷ I don't think I'm ready for that
▷ I would feel more comfortable if...
▷ This isn't working for me
▷ Looking away
▷ Pushing someone away
▷ Shaking their head no
▷ Silence or a trembling voice
▷ Not moving, freezing and lying still

▲ **PowerPoint slide 15**

Part 2

At the end of this discussion ask the group why it can be so hard to say 'No'. (e.g. sometimes it can feel awkward or uncomfortable to say 'No', especially if we are worried about disappointing or upsetting someone; sometimes we find it easier to hesitate or appear unsure and respond more passively because we're scared about hurting other people's feelings or being rejected.)

Part 3

Let the group know that everything in their 'Unsure' list can be put into their 'No' list. Remember: There are loads of ways that people can signal that they aren't consenting to sexual activity. If someone is unsure, it means 'No' (not 'persuade me' or 'keep trying'). If someone isn't saying anything at all, it also doesn't mean they are consenting – remember we may freeze or be unable to communicate in situations where we feel scared or uncomfortable. Show the group PowerPoint slide 16 to reinforce this point.

▲ **PowerPoint slide 16**

End the session with PowerPoint slide 17 and let the group know that there are many places they can go to get resources on this subject or seek support, and there are procedures in place for anonymous reporting. It is important for them to share any issues or concerns that they have about themselves or others related to this topic. Be mindful of the possible impacts and emotions that might be evoked for individuals from the discussion, and if a topic is emotive for someone, offer an opportunity to explore this outside the group, to ensure that they feel heard and safe.

SIGNPOSTING AND RESOURCES
If you are finding it hard to assert your needs, support is available.

▷ **Childline** can be contacted online or by phone, any time, on 0800 1111.
▷ In addition to the helpline, Childline offers information, advice and support on lots of issues relating to communication, including bullying and abuse; safety and the law; you and your body; your feelings; friends, relationships and sex; home and family; and school, college and work.
▷ Check out the website: www.childline.org.uk

▲ **PowerPoint slide 17**

Rape Culture

(Including Gender Double Standards, Sexual Objectification and Victim Blaming)

It was good to inform people (peers) that just because you may do things in your private life you don't need to be categorized as a 'slut'

Session Overview

This workshop looks at gender double standards, rape culture, sexual objectification and victim blaming, exploring the meaning of these terms and the harm these behaviours cause. A video and PowerPoint slide explore victim blaming in more detail, and the young people are asked to change the headlines for some front-page stories. Finally, the group consider rape culture, where they see it happening and how it might be challenged.

Info/Knowledge

The term 'rape culture' was first used by feminists in the United States in the 1970s to describe a group or society that blames victims of sexual assault and normalizes sexual violence.[1] It is a strong phrase to use, and it would be good if there was a common consensus that these opinions are unacceptable, although some people in positions of power and influence model attitudes and behaviours that we would not wish our children to emulate. RSE Guidance published by Brook, the PSHE Association and the Sex Education Forum states: 'Pupils should understand the impact of a pernicious culture that reinforces stereotyped and

---

1 Marshall University Women's Center (n.d.) 'Rape culture.' Accessed on 3/2/2020 at www.marshall.edu/wcenter/sexual-assault/rape-culture

gendered expectations for both boys and girls, including blaming victims for the abuse they experience and other cultural norms and negative stereotypes that they experience and observe.[2] In a study of 1000 young people aged 9–14 by School First News, 70% of girls and 60% of boys said that they had overheard sexist comments being made about their friends.[3] Many schools list 'respect' as a core value, and exploring what this means in practice through a 'whole-school' approach which challenges any elements of rape culture can help ensure that the school community is a safe environment for everyone.

School policies also need to reflect standards which challenge the normalizing of sexual violence. For example, excluding a student who has been the victim of sexism or sexual objectification to keep them safe sends students the message that you can't keep them safe in school, and ends up having a negative, rather than protective, impact on the victim.

This workshop and Workshop 12, which is about pornography, cover sensitive topics and are therefore deliberately placed towards the end of the series of workshops offered here, on the understanding that facilitators delivering these topics know the group and have a good rapport with the young people. It may be helpful to flag up early on with the group (and with parents/carers) that these topics will be covered. These sessions can also be introduced in response to attitudes or behaviours that young people present (e.g. 'slut-shaming' one another) or issues that they are asking about.

PSHE Association Curriculum Themes
▷ KS4 R17. To understand the pernicious influence of gender double standards and victim blaming

Exercises
▷ Exercise 1: Exploring Values and Beliefs – Group Debate
▷ Exercise 2: Definitions
▷ Exercise 3: Challenging Victim Blaming
▷ Exercise 4: Exploring Rape Culture
▷ Exercise 5: Dismantling the Pyramid

---

2   Brook/PSHE Association/Sex Education Forum (2014) *Sex and Relationships Education (SRE) for the 21st Century: Supplementary advice to the Sex and Relationship Education Guidance DfEE (0116/2000)*, p.9. Accessed on 27/1/2020 at www.pshe-association.org.uk/curriculum-and-resources/resources/sex-and-relationship-education-sre-21st-century. Please note that this document was published in 2014, in line with the previous Sex and Relationship Education Guidance (2000). Schools may still find it useful to consult this document but should also ensure they meet the criteria of the new updated statutory guidance (2019).
3   First News (2008) 'Are boys and girls treated the same?' Accessed on 3/2/2020 at https://schools.firstnews.co.uk/wp-content/uploads/sites/3/resources/FIRSTNEWS_605.pdf

Materials Needed

▷ Access to YouTube
▷ Cards with terms and definitions for Exercise 2 (Resources and Handouts 11.1)
▷ Worksheet with example statements to be cut out for Exercise 2 (Resources and Handouts 11.2)
▷ Handout with newspaper headlines for Exercise 3 (if no access to PowerPoint) (Resources and Handouts 11.3)

Learning Outcomes

By the end of this session:

- I can identify, understand and challenge distortions in popular culture and the media
- I can appreciate and accept difference
- I can understand the harmful impact of a culture that reinforces stereotyped and gendered expectations for both boys and girls
- I can understand how blaming victims reinforces harmful and negative stereotypes and places the responsibility for what happened on the wrong person
- I can be part of a healthy culture and sense of belonging with all members of the community

At the beginning of the session, inform the group of the topic – *Rape Culture* – and point out that it requires the group to approach the discussions with a certain amount of maturity and sensitivity. Remind the group of the agreed expectations, particularly emphasizing confidentiality and the importance of treating one another with respect. Check that everyone is in agreement, looking for nods or verbal recognition that they're on the same page. Remind the group that if something comes up in the session that upsets them or makes them feel uncomfortable, they have permission to leave the room or find some space, and remind them of where they can go or who they can approach for support. Creating a safe environment is covered in more detail in the Introduction. Before starting, briefly set out what will be covered in the workshop.

Have PowerPoint slide 1 with the image from *What Does Consent Really Mean?* on the screen as the students enter the room to set the scene for the workshop.

▲ **PowerPoint slide 1**

Exercise 1: Exploring Values and Beliefs – Group Debate

Ask the group to imagine that there is a line across the room. Explain to the group that one side of the room is 'Agree' and the other side is 'Disagree' (you can put up signs to make this clear). Let them know that when you read out a statement they are invited to stand where they feel they are on the line in relation to the statement. If it isn't possible for the young people to move about in the room, you can ask them to put up a hand or stand up if they agree, or give out the green, amber and red cards to each participant representing 'agree', 'neither agree nor disagree' and 'disagree' in Resources and Handouts 1.1. Reassure the group that there are no right or wrong answers, that they can stand in the middle if they are unsure and that they are able to move at any time if their opinion has been swayed. Remind the group to remain respectful when listening to and debating views and opinions that differ from their own. If the group find it hard not to talk over each other, you can use an object to represent a 'talking piece' which allows the person holding it permission to speak, while everyone else needs to listen until it is their turn with the talking piece (see Appendix 5).

When the young people have moved to where they want to stand, facilitate a debate between individuals or sides. Feel free to contribute to the debate (there are some facilitators' notes below that may be helpful discussion points).

You don't need to go through all of the statements; pick those that seem most relevant to the group.

Once you have used a few statements, ask the group if they have any other ideas that they want to debate. It might help if the young people talk briefly in pairs to help them to come up with a statement.

Note: All of the harmful and damaging assumptions that may have come up during this discussion will be challenged throughout this workshop and revisited at the end.

- Jokes about rape are harmless.
- It's more shameful to be raped than to have raped someone.
- Women have all the sexual power.
- Revealing clothes make you more likely to attract unwanted attention.
- Boys are more powerful than girls.
- Boys don't get raped.
- When girls are promiscuous, they are sluts; when guys are promiscuous, they are players.

Note: If any of the students ask what promiscuous means, you can define it as 'the act of having multiple casual sexual partners or experiences'.

At the end of the discussions, highlight how many of these statements are harmful myths which reinforce the negative gender stereotypes and dangerous cultural values that we will explore throughout this workshop.

Exercise 2: Definitions

Part 1

Create four cards with the terms 'Gender double standards', 'Sexual objectification', 'Victim blaming' and 'Rape culture', and separate cards with the definitions of those terms (Resources and Handouts 11.1). In small groups ask the students to try and match each term with the correct definition.

Once they have finished, check that the groups have correctly matched the terms to the appropriate description.

Term	Definition
Gender double standards	This is the belief that different genders are judged differently for the same behaviour – for example, guys being praised and rewarded for engaging in sexual activity, and girls being stigmatized, judged and 'slut-shamed' for similar behaviour.
Rape culture	This is an environment where sexual violence is not only prevalent but normalized, trivialized, excused and sometimes glamourized by the media and popular culture. This includes making sexist, homophobic or transphobic 'jokes' and 'banter'.
Victim blaming	This is the belief that when someone becomes a victim of sexual violence they did something (e.g. drank too much, dressed too provocatively, put themselves in a risky situation, trusted the wrong person) that invited or caused the behaviour. This keeps the responsibility with the victim instead of the person committing the offence.
Sexual objectification	This is the belief that a particular person is a mere object of sexual desire who exists purely for the sexual pleasure of another. It doesn't view that person as a whole human. It sees them instead as a combination of sexual parts (rather than as an individual with a complex personality, desires of their own and dignity) – for example, in heterosexual pornography women often exist purely for gratification and pleasure of men. This is not the same as being attracted to someone or finding someone good-looking or sexy.

Part 2

Let the group know that although all genders can be sexually objectified, society (including all genders) tends to objectify females the most. This feeds into a culture where females in particular often feel unsafe and many females report moderating their behaviour to try to avoid becoming a victim of sexual violence.

Show the group PowerPoint slide 2 and initiate a discussion about the double standards in the debate about breastfeeding. Ask them:

1) Is it acceptable for adverts to sexually objectify women (e.g. show them wearing skimpy bikinis)?

2) Is it acceptable that women are expected to be discreet while feeding their baby (which after all, is what breasts are for!)?

Part 3

Keep the students in small groups and give them the handout (Resources and Handouts 11.2), asking them to cut out each statement or situation and sort them into four categories: 'Sexual objectification', 'Victim blaming', 'Rape culture', 'Gender double standards'. The statements are examples of myths, beliefs and attitudes that reinforce harmful stereotypes that affect all genders. Explain that some of the cards may fit into more than one category. (There are example answers for facilitators below.)

▲ **PowerPoint slide 2**[4]

Note: You may like to create your own examples to reflect your context, or ask students to add their own examples from things that they see in the media.

Facilitators' Answers

- Sexual Objectification = SO
- Victim Blaming = VB
- Rape Culture = RC
- Gender Double Standards = GDS

Stay-at-home dads are seen as heroes, stay-at-home mums are not. (GDS)	Women shouldn't earn more than men. (GDS)	Men should have more sexual experience than women. (RC, GDS)
Using someone's lacy underwear as a 'reason' they got raped. (VB, RC)	Using someone's sexual history or mental state to discredit them in court during a rape case. (VB, RC)	Porn is mostly made for men because women don't masturbate. (GDS, SO)

---

4   Illustration courtesy of Tribune Content Agency.

Women are emotionally unstable. (GDS)	Only men watch porn. (GDS, SO)	Women exist for men's sexual pleasure. (SO, RC)
Only promiscuous women get raped. (GDS, VB)	Sex ends when a man ejaculates. (GDS, RC)	Women who enjoy sex are sluts. (GDS, RC, SO)
Boys with multiple sexual partners are players or legends, girls with multiple sexual partners are sluts or hoes. (GDS, SO)	When a girl says 'No', she really means 'Yes'. (RC, VB)	They should have left their abuser sooner. (VB)
Popstars wearing 'sexy' schoolgirl outfits. (SO)	A sports star who is charged with rape being given a short sentence to avoid it 'ruining their career'. (VB, RC)	Rape happens because 'men can't control themselves'. (RC)
Adverts using breasts to sell things like beer. (SO)	Women being shamed for breastfeeding in public when images of sexualized breasts are everywhere. (SO)	The media calling it 'non-consensual sex' instead of naming it as rape. (RC)
People being told they are 'overreacting' when they have been sexually harassed. (VB, RC)	People not believing victims/survivors of rape. (VB, RC)	Sexist, homophobic or transphobic 'banter'. (RC)
Teaching people how 'not to get raped' instead of 'how not to rape'. (VB, RC)	Magazines listing 'ways to please your man' and '100 things men don't like', etc. (SO, RC)	Normalizing and encouraging violence towards women, including prostitutes on video games such as Grand Theft Auto. (RC, SO)
Shaming women for getting angry while encouraging men. (GDS)	Assuming that people make false rape claims. (VB, RC)	Flirty people are more likely to get raped. (VB, RC)
Girls being told to wear their uniform a certain way so as 'not to distract the boys'. (VB, RC)	Female fancy dress outfits all being 'sexualized' (e.g. sexy nurse, sexy cat). (SO, RC)	Boys will be boys. (RC, GDS)
Lesbian porn is made for men's pleasure. (SO, RC)	Real men should be strong and muscly. (RC, SO)	

Part 4

Elicit some feedback from the group about how they found this exercise. Ask them:

1) Were there any statements that were really difficult to place or that clearly fit into more than one category?

2) Are the examples things that they recognize in the world around them? (Facilitators' note: Keep the focus on things the young people see in wider society rather than examples from their personal experience.)

3) Did any of the groups add their own examples? If so, what statements did they use and how did they categorize them?

Part 5

Ask the group what they think the impact of sexual objectification, rape culture, victim blaming and gender double standards are on society as a whole. After exploring the groups' feedback, you can show them PowerPoint slide 3 in case it adds any additional considerations:

**THE IMPACT OF SEXUAL OBJECTIFICATION, RAPE CULTURE,
VICTIM BLAMING AND GENDER DOUBLE STANDARDS**

- They put all the **responsibility** for sexual violence onto victims (e.g. telling women how to 'stay safe', 'avoid being raped' and 'wear clothes that don't attract unwanted attention'), rather than on the people who choose to harass, assault and rape them.
- Victim-blaming attitudes **isolate** the victim/survivor and can make it harder for them to speak out or seek support.
- Victim blaming also reinforces **shame** and may lead to the victim blaming themselves, adding to their trauma and suffering.
- Although both men and women can be victims of sexual violence, the majority of victims/survivors are women and the majority of perpetrators are men. Sexual objectification, rape culture, gender double standards and victim blaming all feed into this and allow, or sometimes even promote, this imbalance.

▲ **PowerPoint slide 3**

Answer any questions that that group have about the impact of gender double standards, rape culture, victim blaming and sexual objectification before showing the group the 'Did you know...?' statistics on PowerPoint slide 4:

DID YOU KNOW...?

▷ Approximately **4–5%** of adult sex offenders are women; **95–96%** are men.[5]
▷ **83%** of victims of sexual offences are women; **17%** are men.[6]

▲ **PowerPoint slide 4**

5   Knight, K. (2019) 'Predator women: How deviant babysitters abusing toddlers and twisted paedo "mistresses" are fuelling the rise of female sex offenders.' *The Sun.* Accessed on www.thesun.co.uk/news/5867301

6   Office for National Statistics (2017) 'Sexual offences in England and Wales: year ending March 2017.' Accessed on 3/2/2020 at www.ons.gov.uk/peoplepopulationandcommunity/crimeandjustice/articles/sexualoffencesinenglandandwales/yearending march2017#sexual-offences-recorded-by-the-police

Exercise 3: Challenging Victim Blaming

Part 1

Remind the group of the definition of victim blaming, or show them PowerPoint slide 5:

VICTIM BLAMING

This is the belief that when someone becomes a victim of sexual violence, they did something (e.g. drank too much, dressed too provocatively, put themselves in a risky situation, trusted the wrong person) which invited or caused the behaviour.

This keeps the responsibility with the victim instead of the person committing the offence.

▲ **PowerPoint slide 5**

Part 2

Watch the 'James is dead' video – a humorous cartoon created by Blue Seat Studios, which explores victim blaming with the example of someone who has been murdered at a party:

www.youtube.com/watch?v=Op14XhETfBw&t=29s (video length: 2 minutes 49 seconds).

▲ **PowerPoint slide 6**

Part 3

After you've watched the video, explore it with the group by asking:

1) What message is this video trying to convey?
2) What reasons were given for why James was to blame for his own murder? (See how many reasons the group can remember and then show PowerPoint slide 7 or read out the list):

REASONS WHY JAMES IS TO BLAME
▷ He was at the party on his own.
▷ He was drinking, which makes it harder to fight off a murderer.
▷ He made bad choices about who he was talking to.
▷ He was wearing a V-neck T-shirt.
▷ He was friendly and outgoing.
▷ He was talking to strangers at parties.
▷ He should have been more careful.
▷ He left his 'murder alarm' in his coat pocket.
▷ Nobody thinks it will happen to them.

- ▷ He let himself be murdered.
- ▷ It might have been assisted suicide.
- ▷ Maybe he wanted it to happen.
- ▷ Robert is definitely not a murderer.
- ▷ He's not a 'murderer murderer'.
- ▷ James was jailbait – he had that look.
- ▷ It's perfectly normal.
- ▷ Young people's lives are ruined just because they kill a few people.

▲ **PowerPoint slide 7**

Ask the group:

1) Are any of the reasons listed valid?
2) Who should take responsibility for what happened to James?

Part 4

To reinforce the point using a consent-related scenario, you could show the young people PowerPoint slide 8. Let them know that the characters are discussing a girl at their school who they heard has been raped and they are questioning who is responsible for what happened. Ask the group:

1) Are any of the reasons presented in the cartoon valid?
2) What might be the impact on the victim if they heard people discussing these 'reasons' why they were raped?

▲ **PowerPoint slide 8**

Part 5

Get the young people into small groups of three or four and show the group PowerPoint slide 9 or the handout (Resources and Handouts 11.3) showing different headlines from real newspaper stories. Each of the papers features a headline and/or strapline which blames the victim in some way.

Ask the groups to pick two or three headlines and to come up with a replacement headline which puts the responsibility with the person who caused the harm rather than the victim. Invite the groups to be creative and give them 5–10 minutes to do a thought shower of alternatives until they come up with their final responses.

If the young people are finding it hard to grasp this activity, you can use 'James is dead' as an example. If the headline read, 'Victim talked to strangers at parties and wound up dead', what could be the alternative headline? (Facilitators' note: Examples might be 'Party-goer took advantage of victim's friendliness to stick the knife in' or 'Murder on the dance floor: party-goer takes one man's life and ruins many people's night'.)

Note: The key to this exercise is always to keep the responsibility and focus on the person who committed the crime.

▲ PowerPoint slide 9

Part 6

Ask each group to present their favourite alternative headline to the rest of the students. To make this exercise more interactive, you could hold a vote for the best headline.

Elicit some feedback from the group about how they found this exercise:

1) How easy/hard was finding alternative headlines?
2) If you found it hard, why might that be?
3) Has this exercise made you more aware of how common and damaging victim blaming is?

Show the group PowerPoint slide 10 about the impact of victim blaming and why it is important to challenge it:

THE IMPACT OF VICTIM BLAMING

▷ Rape culture, gender double standards, sexual objectification and victim blaming can contribute towards hate crimes. A hate crime is an incident, which may or may not be deemed a criminal offence, which is perceived (by the victim or others) as being motivated by prejudice or hatred.

Did you know...?

▷ **85%** of hate crimes based on gender are towards women.[7]
▷ **75%** of women who have experienced hate crime report that the incident has had a long-term impact on them, and
▷ **63%** said they have changed their behaviour as a consequence.
▷ Despite this only **6.6%** of victims report these incidents to the police, which is partly due to factors including the 'normalization' of these incidents in wider society, fear of not being taken seriously or believed and/or fear of being blamed.[8]

▲ **PowerPoint slide 10**

Part 7

Show the group PowerPoint slide 11. This powerful image challenges the assumption that what you're wearing makes you more likely to become a victim of sexual violence.

7 Reynolds, E. (2019) 'Criminalising street harassment works. Britain must follow France's lead.' *The Guardian.* Accessed on 6/3/2020 at www.theguardian.com/commentisfree/2019/may/02/criminalising-street-harassment-britain-france-catcalling-groping

8 Mullany, L. and Trickett, L. (2018) 'Misogyny hate crime: New research reveals true scale of issue – and how the public are united against it.' *The Conversation.* Accessed on 3/2/2020 at https://theconversation.com/misogyny-hate-crime-new-research-reveals-true-scale-of-issue-and-how-the-public-are-united-against-it-100265

▲ **PowerPoint slide 11**

Part 8

Remind the group about being an Upstander instead of a Bystander. This means someone who speaks out or does something to support others, rather than just watching and doing nothing. Let the group know that anyone can be an Upstander regardless of their age, gender, sexual orientation, gender identity, background or experiences. Being an ally to others takes courage.

Look at the example on PowerPoint slide 12 of a young person being an Upstander to her friends who are victim blaming the girl in their school who they believe was raped.

▲ **PowerPoint slide 12**

Ask the group: Is there anything else the girls might have said to challenge the victim blaming she is hearing from her peers, and stand up for the girl who they are discussing?

Exercise 4: Exploring Rape Culture

Part 1

Remind the group of the definition of rape culture or show them PowerPoint slide 13:

RAPE CULTURE

This is an environment where sexual violence is not only prevalent, but normalized, trivialized, excused and sometimes glamourized by the media and popular culture.

This includes making sexist, homophobic or transphobic 'jokes' and 'banter'.

▲ **PowerPoint slide 13**

Start with a brief discussion around what the word 'culture' means. (Facilitators' note: Culture refers to the ideas, beliefs, social behaviour, communication, etc. that are shared by a society or a particular group of people.)

Part 2

Show the group PowerPoint slide 14 or read out the examples of rape culture:

EXAMPLES OF RAPE CULTURE

- People excusing, normalizing or minimizing sexual assault and violence
- People writing lyrics like 'Blurred Lines' and not understanding consent
- People believing that girls like to be pressured or persuaded to have sex
- Disrespecting boys and men by believing that they can't control their sexual urges/ expecting them to behave like animals
- Making sexist, homophobic or transphobic 'jokes' or 'banter'
- Stereotyping 'all men', 'all women', 'all gay people', etc. as the same

▲ **PowerPoint slide 14**

Part 3

Ask the group:

1) Where do you see this happening? (Facilitators' note: You could explore rape culture online, in music, in politics, in celebrity culture, in advertising, in video games (e.g. with prostitutes as 'props'), in gangs, etc.)
2) Are there elements of rape culture in our school?

Exercise 5: Dismantling the Pyramid

Part 1

Show PowerPoint slide 15 – the violence pyramid. This shows how small comments and actions contribute to a culture of violence, and how important it is to think critically and challenge rape culture.

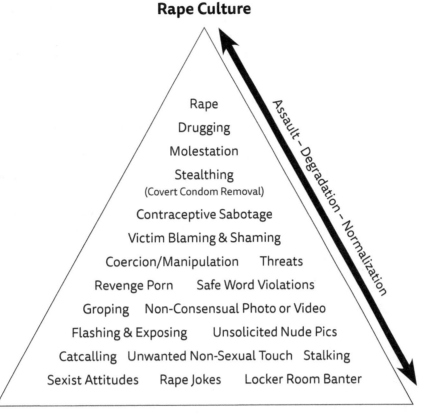

Rape Culture

Tolerance of the behaviours at the bottom supports or excuses those higher up. To change outcomes, we must change the culture.

**If you see something, say something!
Start the conversation today.**

– 11ᵗʰ Principle: Consent!
– www.11thprincipleconsent.org[9]

Even though things like sexist, homophobic or transphobic jokes may seem small or be passed off as 'just banter', they all contribute to a society that normalizes, trivializes and excuses sexual violence, which in turn contributes towards a culture of violence.

The foundations of a pyramid support everything else built on top. Shake, question and challenge the foundations and the whole structure collapses.

▲ **PowerPoint slide 15**

Part 2

The last part of this workshop explores how we can be an Upstander against some of the negative attitudes, beliefs and cultures discussed during this session.

Ask the young people what they, as a group, can do to challenge victim blaming, gender double standards, sexual objectification and rape culture. You could look at

---

9   'Rape Culture Pyramid' by 11th Principle: Consent!, used with permission, licensed under CC BY-NC-SA.

responses to all four categories at once, take them one at a time or just focus on one or two to explore (e.g. victim blaming and rape culture).

Here are some potential responses in case the group are finding it hard to come up with ideas.

Victim blaming	Gender double standards
Stop telling women to drink less, be less provocative, be less flirty, wear less sexy underwear, etc., as this leads to the belief that women are somehow at fault when they are assaulted. Keep the responsibility with the person who caused the harm, and don't let them make excuses that blame their victim (e.g. drugs or alcohol) for what they have done. Speak out if someone you are with is victim blaming. If someone tells you that they have been sexually assaulted, take them seriously, tell them it wasn't their fault and offer to support them.	Treat everyone as equal. Speak out if you notice gender double standards. Don't think of 'all men' or 'all women' (or all any other group) as the same.
Sexual objectification	**Rape culture**
Avoid objectifying people so they are not just seen as 'something to have sex with'. Don't buy into the media's messages about men, women, sex, relationships and violence. Speak out if someone you are with is objectifying women. 'Subjectify' women – see them as a whole person with a personality!	Avoid using language or jokes that degrade women. Speak out if someone you are with makes a sexist joke or uses language that degrades women. Don't buy into a culture that belittles rape and sexual abuse. Teach everyone about consent, and how to ask for and give consent.

Part 3

Give each young person a Post-it and ask them to write the words 'One thing I will do differently is...' across the top (see PowerPoint slide 16). Ask each of them to write something that they, as an individual, commit to doing that will contribute towards a society free from rape culture, sexual objectification, gender double standards and victim blaming.

There are different ways you can conduct the next part of the exercise depending on your group:

1) Ask each student to read out their 'one thing' to the rest of the group.
2) Ask each student to bring their Post-its to the front and then read out some or all of them (so they remain anonymous).

3) Ask the students to discuss their 'one thing' in small groups.

4) Ask each student to leave their Post-it behind and then make a collective 'group charter' with their ideas – for example, 'As a group, we are committed to challenging rape culture by...' (and then list the commitments they have made).

All of the above ways of conducting this exercise aim to allow the students to take ownership of their commitments, as well as witness the commitments of others, which allows for students to become better Upstanders and empowers them to challenge harmful attitudes, beliefs and behaviour.

▲ PowerPoint slide 16

Part 4

Finally, remind the group of the statements we explored at the start of the session or show them PowerPoint slide 17:

- Jokes about rape are harmless.
- It's more shameful to be raped than to have raped someone.
- Women have all the sexual power.
- Revealing clothes makes you more likely to attract unwanted attention.
- Boys are more powerful than girls.
- Boys don't get raped.
- When girls are promiscuous, they are sluts; when guys are promiscuous, they are players.

▲ PowerPoint slide 17

Ask the group:

1) Have any of their opinions or assumptions changed?
2) If so, which ones and how have they changed?

Note: This session could leave young people feeling anxious or vulnerable. If you sense that this might be the case, end with a game or something lighter.

End the session with PowerPoint slide 18 and let the group know that there are many places they can go to get resources on this subject or seek support, and there are procedures in place for anonymous reporting. It is important for them to share any issues or concerns that they have about themselves or others related to this topic. Be mindful of the possible impacts and emotions that might be evoked for individuals from the discussion, and if a topic is emotive for someone, offer an opportunity to explore this outside the group, to ensure that they feel heard and safe.

For further discussion on responses to victim blaming, you could show the group the following article on the BBC website: 'Victim blaming: Is it a woman's responsibility to stay safe?'[10] which includes comments by Jessica Taylor. Jessica Taylor is a speaker, researcher and writer in the field of sexual violence and mental health and the founder and owner of VictimFocus,[11] which provides research, consultancy, writing and speaking on forensic psychology, feminism and mental health.

SIGNPOSTING AND RESOURCES

If any of the issues in today's workshop affect you, support is available.

▷ **Childline** can be contacted online or by phone, any time, on 0800 1111.
▷ In addition to the helpline, Childline offers information, advice and support on bullying and abuse; safety and the law; you and your body; your feelings; friends, relationships and sex; home and family; and school, college and work.
▷ Check out the website: www.childline.org.uk
▷ **True Vision** is an online reporting facility where you can report hate crimes online, if you do not want to report directly to the police: www.report-it.org.uk/home
▷ **Police:** You can also report online hate material to the police: http://report-it.org.uk/your_police_force

▲ **PowerPoint slide 18**

---

10   www.bbc.co.uk/news/uk-england-45809169
11   www.victimfocus.org.uk

Pornography

All of the untalked about subjects were spoken about

Session Overview

This workshop starts with a definition of pornography and sets out what the law says. This is followed by a pornography quiz, an exploration of the various impacts of pornography and a section on mindful use of pornography.

Note: Many people refer to pornography simply as 'porn', and for the purposes of this workshop the terms are used interchangeably.

Info/Knowledge

Online pornography has become more accessible now than ever before. Its prevalence means that it is unlikely that young people will be able to filter it out of their lives entirely, and indeed young people are just as likely to stumble across it accidentally as to actively search for it. There is increasing evidence that pornography influences people's views and has a negative impact on their body image. Supplementary guidance developed by Brook, the PSHE Association and the Sex Education Forum state:

> Reports indicate that young people's interactions with pornography are distinctly gendered and that it can have negative effects on young people's attitudes to each other. Pornography can depict a lack of communication about choices, sexual consent and contraception, and often shows violent

and oppressive behaviours, which can be frightening and confusing, and make young people feel pressured to behave in particular ways.[1]

The quiz reveals that 88% of the most popular pornography depicts acts of aggression, leading to concern that it also makes violence sexy; worryingly, in a survey by the Children's Society, almost 22% of young people who had seen online pornography disagreed or strongly disagreed that sexual activities should be safe for everyone involved.[2]

A recent study by the NSPCC of over 1000 young people found that the majority of young people would like sex education in school to include discussion about the effects of seeing pornography, to help them deal with the feelings and behaviour that it can lead to, even if they admit it's a bit awkward. RSE can enable all young people to understand pornography's influence on gender expectations of sex. It builds on earlier learning about relationships, body image, consent and gender, which begins in primary school with discussions about the importance of loving and respectful relationships. DfE Guidance for RSE states: 'Pupils should know [that] specifically sexually explicit material e.g. pornography presents a distorted picture of sexual behaviours, can damage the way people see themselves in relation to others and negatively affect how they behave towards sexual partners.'[3] RSE provides opportunities to discuss body image and understand how pornographic pictures and videos are routinely edited and 'photoshopped'.

This session does not aim to shame or humiliate young people who access pornography, but to build their awareness and understanding around some of the issues that exposure to porn can create or exacerbate. It takes a public health approach, recognising that opening up this discussion is a balancing act between discussing adult themes with children and protecting them from harm. Teachers will know the young people in the group, and are encouraged to consult with parents/carers when preparing for this workshop.

Pornographic images must never be shown to pupils, and there is no need for facilitators to look at pornography to plan their teaching.

PSHE Association Curriculum and Themes
▷ KS4 R14. To understand the role of sex in the media and its impact on sexuality (including pornography and related sexual ethics such as consent,

1   Brook/PSHE Association/Sex Education Forum (2014) *Sex and Relationships Education (SRE) for the 21st Century: Supplementary advice to the Sex and Relationship Education Guidance DfEE (0116/2000)*, p.11. Accessed on 27/1/2020 at www.pshe-association.org.uk/curriculum-and-resources/resources/sex-and-relationship-education-sre-21st-century. Please note that this document was published in 2014, in line with the previous Sex and Relationship Education Guidance (2000). Schools may still find it useful to consult this document but should also ensure they meet the criteria of the new updated statutory guidance (2019).

2   The Children's Society (n.d.) 'NC15 and NC16: Introduction of mandatory Relationship and Sex Education for all children in all schools.' Accessed on 4/2/2020 at www.childrenssociety.org.uk/sites/default/files/sex-and-relationships-education-.pdf

3   Department for Education (2019) *Relationships Education, Relationships and Sex Education (RSE) and Health Education: Statutory guidance for governing bodies, proprietors, head teachers, principals, senior leadership teams, teachers*, p.28. Accessed on 27/1/2020 at https://assets.publishing.service.gov.uk/government/uploads/system/uploads/attachment_data/file/805781/Relationships_Education__Relationships_and_Sex_Education__RSE__and_Health_Education.pdf

negotiation, boundaries, respect, gender norms, sexual 'norms', trust, communication, pleasure, orgasms, rights, empowerment, sexism and feminism)

Exercises

▷ Exercise 1: Introduction to Pornography/Porn
▷ Exercise 2: Exploring Values and Beliefs – Group Debate
▷ Exercise 3: Pornography Quiz
▷ Exercise 4: World Café – Exploring the Impact of Porn
▷ Exercise 5: When it Comes to Porn...
▷ Exercise 6: Challenging Beliefs

Materials

▷ 'True' and 'False' cards for each table (optional) for Exercise 3 (Resources and Handouts 12.1)
▷ Pornography quiz printed out (optional) for Exercise 3 (Resources and Handouts 12.2)
▷ Flipchart paper and pens for Exercise 4

Learning Outcomes

By the end of this session:

- I can recognize the impact that pornography may have and challenge its portrayal of men, women, sex and relationships
- I can reflect on the messages we get from pornography about how different genders should behave sexually
- I can reflect on the impact that pornography has on our body image
- I can understand more about pornography and consent
- I can be more aware of how pornography might affect my expectations and behaviour
- I understand how pornography can be used mindfully and safely

At the beginning of the session, inform the group of the topic – *Pornography* – and point out that it requires the group to approach the discussions with a certain amount of maturity and sensitivity. Remind the group of the agreed expectations, particularly emphasizing confidentiality and the importance of treating one another with respect. Check that everyone is in agreement, looking for nods or verbal recognition that they're on the same page. Remind the group that if something comes up in the session that upsets them or makes them feel uncomfortable, they have permission to leave the room or find some space, and remind them of where they can go or who they can approach for support. Creating a safe environment is covered in more detail in the Introduction. Before starting, briefly set out what will be covered in the workshop.

Exercise 1: Introduction to Pornography/Porn

Part 1

Show PowerPoint slide 2 or let the group know the definition of pornography:

WHAT IS PORNOGRAPHY?

An image is pornographic if it can be reasonably assumed that it was produced solely or mainly for the purpose of sexual arousal. Porn is intended to be entertainment for adults, not sex education for young people.[4]

Porn is legal as long as:

- those who appear in it are aged **18** or over
- those watching it are **18** or over
- it does not contain anything defined as 'extreme' pornographic imagery (e.g. sex with animals, torture, or violent scenes which are life-threatening or could cause serious harm).[5]

▲ **PowerPoint slide 2**

Part 2

Ask the group:

1) What do you think about this definition of porn?
2) Would you change anything about it?
3) How can you tell what's porn and what's not, considering how many sexual images are out there? (Facilitators' note: Invite the young people to think about how often music videos have people behaving and dressing sexually – does this have the same intention of creating sexual excitement?)
4) Why is porn an important thing to discuss?

Exercise 2: Exploring Values and Beliefs – Group Debate

Ask the group to imagine that there is a line across the room. Explain to the group that one side of the room is 'Agree' and the other side is 'Disagree' (you can put up signs to make this clear). Let them know that when you read out a statement they are invited to stand where they feel they are on the line in relation to the statement. If it isn't possible for the young people to move about in the room, you can ask them to put up a hand or stand up if they agree, or give out the green, amber and red cards to each participant representing 'agree', 'neither agree nor disagree' and 'disagree' in Resources

---

4 BISH (2011) 'Porn laws – is it legal, is it right?' Accessed on 4/2/2020 at www.bishuk.com/porn/porn-what-is-legal-what-is-right
5 Crown Prosecution Service (2019) 'Obscene Publications.' Accessed on 4/2/2020 at www.cps.gov.uk/legal-guidance/obscene-publications

and Handouts 1.1. Reassure the group that there are no right or wrong answers, that they can stand in the middle if they are unsure and that they are able to move at any time if their opinion has been swayed. Remind the group to remain respectful when listening to and debating views and opinions that differ from their own. If the group find it hard not to talk over each other, you can use an object to represent a 'talking piece' which allows the person holding it permission to speak, while everyone else needs to listen until their turn with the talking piece (see Appendix 5).

When the young people have moved to where they want to stand, facilitate a debate between individuals or sides. Feel free to contribute to the debate (there are some facilitators' notes below that may be helpful discussion points).

You don't need to go through all of the statements; pick those that seem most relevant to the group.

Once you have used a few statements, ask the group if they have any other ideas that they want to debate. It might help if the young people talk briefly in pairs to help them to come up with a statement.

- Porn is a good place to learn about sex.
- Porn gives people unreasonable expectations about sex.
- Young people should be protected from porn.
- Porn makes sex more enjoyable.
- Porn is addictive.

Note: All of the harmful and damaging assumptions that may have come up during this discussion will be challenged throughout this workshop and revisited at the end.

Exercise 3: Pornography Quiz

Part 1

Explore the knowledge in the room with the interactive quiz. A quiz can be a great way to capture the interest of the young people.

There are many different ways you can choose to conduct this quiz:

1) Young people can complete the quiz individually (Resources and Handouts 12.2) and mark each other's answers.
2) You can get the young people in small groups and allow them to discuss what they think before deciding on an answer.
3) You can do this with the whole group and ask them to raise their hands for each statement (or hand out 'True' and 'False' cards; see Resources and Handouts 12.1) and then reveal the answers as you go along.
4) You can have two or more groups competing against each other, with a prize to be won.

Note: However you choose to conduct the quiz, it is important that you give the group the additional information in the answer column and allow space for reflection and/or questions as you work your way through.

Facilitators' Answers

	Statement	True or false?
1	More people access porn than Netflix, Amazon and Twitter.	**True:** Porn sites receive around 450 million unique visitors a month – this is larger than the number of visitors to Netflix (46 million), Amazon (110 million) and Twitter (160 million) combined![6] Porn is the most profitable industry in the world – it beats retail, technology and even entertainment (including Hollywood and all sports combined). Internet porn in the UK has more hits than social media, shopping, gaming, finance and travel.
2	Males and females access porn the same amount.	**False:** 70% of males and 30% of females report accessing porn.[7]
3	1 in 10 of all mobile searches are for pornography.	**False:** It's 1 in 5.[8]
4	In North Korea the punishment for viewing porn is seven years in prison.	**False:** False, involvement with pornography, even as a viewer, can result in 10–15 years in prison, and in some cases the death penalty.[9]
5	'Teen' is one of the most common words typed in alongside 'porn'.	**True:** A popular porn site reveals that 'teen porn' has been in the top 10 searches since it was number one in 2014, despite the average age of viewers being around 36 years old worldwide.[10] It is illegal to watch pornography if it involves someone under the age of 18 (this law is designed to protect young people). This is not the law in all countries, so some porn filmmakers manage to get around this by filming with under-18s in countries where the law allows it.
6	Most boys are exposed to porn for the first time aged 13.	**False:** The average age of exposure is 11[11] and 94% of young people had seen explicit material online by the age of 14.[12] As many as 1 in 10 visitors to porn sites is under the age of 10.[13]

6   Value Walk (2013) 'Porn sites get more visitors than Netflix, Amazon and Twitter.' Accessed on 4/2/2020 at www.valuewalk.com/2013/05/porn-sites-gets-more-visitors-than-netflix-amazon-and-twitter

7   Value Walk (2013) 'Porn sites get more visitors than Netflix, Amazon and Twitter.' Accessed on 4/2/2020 at www.valuewalk.com/2013/05/porn-sites-gets-more-visitors-than-netflix-amazon-and-twitter

8   Castleman, M. (2016) 'Dueling statistics: How much of the internet is porn?' *Psychology Today.* Accessed on 4/2/2020 at www.psychologytoday.com/gb/blog/all-about-sex/201611/dueling-statistics-how-much-the-internet-is-porn

9   Human Rights Council (2014) *Report of the Detailed Findings of the Commission of Enquiry on Human Rights in the Democratic People's Republic of Korea.* Accessed on 9/3/2020 at www.un.org/ga/search/view_doc.asp?symbol=A/HRC/25/CRP.1

10 Pornhub (2019) 'Pornhub Insights: The Year in Review.' Accessed on 9/3/2020 at www.pornhub.com/insights/2019-year-in-review#age

11 Randel, J. and Sánchez, A. (2016) 'Parenting in the digital age of pornography.' HuffPost. Accessed on 4/2/2020 at www.huffpost.com/entry/parenting-in-the-digital-age-of-pornography_b_9301802

12 Sellgren, K. (2016) 'Pornography "desensitising young people".' BBC News. Accessed on 4/2/2020 at www.bbc.co.uk/news/education-36527681

13 Fight the New Drug (2018) 'One in 10 visitors to hardcore porn sites is under 10 years old, study shows.' Accessed on 4/2/2020 at https://fightthenewdrug.org/data-says-one-in-10-visitors-to-porn-sites-are-under-10-years-old

7	Porn affects people's confidence.	**True:** Porn has a negative effect on people's confidence because of unrealistic expectations on body image leading both men and women to feel insecure about their bodies and sexual performance.[14]
8	Porn has no effect on men's ability to get an erection or to ejaculate with their real partners.	**False:** Lots of research shows a link between male erectile dysfunctions (e.g. not being able to get an erection or not being able to ejaculate) and the amount of time people spend watching porn. Unrealistic expectations and attitudes about sex can lead to future problems with sexual satisfaction.[15]
9	88% of top-rated porn scenes show aggressive acts towards women.	**True.**[16]
10	It is illegal to watch or buy porn if you are under 18.	**True:** It is only legal for those aged 18 and over to buy porn in the UK as long as it does not feature anyone under 18, sex with animals, scenes of rape or sexual assault and torture, or violent scenes which are life-threatening or likely to cause serious harm.
11	Boys are more likely to think that porn is realistic than girls.	**True:** 53% of boys compared with 39% of girls think porn is realistic.[17]
12	Porn is addictive.	**True:** Although porn addiction isn't in the manual for mental health problems in the same way that drug addiction and gambling addiction are, there are multiple studies which show it has an addictive effect on our brains – e.g. not being able to stop watching porn, porn having a negative effect on our relationships and needing to watch more extreme and hardcore porn to experience the same level of sexual arousal.[18]

cont.

14 Fight the New Drug (2019) 'How watching porn can give you warped self-image and low self-esteem.' Accessed on 4/2/2020 at https://fightthenewdrug.org/watching-porn-worse-sex-bad-self-esteem

15 Park, B.Y., Wilson, G., Berger, J., Christman, M. *et al.* (2016) 'Is internet pornography causing sexual dysfunctions? A review with clinical reports.' *Behavioral Sciences 6*, 3, 17. Accessed on 4/2/2020 at www.ncbi.nlm.nih.gov/pmc/articles/PMC5039517

16 Castleman, M. (2016) 'Dueling statistics: How much of the internet is porn?' *Psychology Today.* Accessed on 4/2/2020 at www.psychologytoday.com/gb/blog/all-about-sex/201611/dueling-statistics-how-much-the-internet-is-porn

17 Martellozo, E., Monaghan, A., Adler, J.R., Davidson, J., Leyva, R. and Horvath, M.A.H. (2016) '…I wasn't sure it was normal to watch it…' Accessed on 4/2/2020 at www.mdx.ac.uk/__data/assets/pdf_file/0021/223266/MDX-NSPCC-OCC-pornography-report.pdf

18 Pietrangelo, A. (2019) 'Everything you need to know about pornography "addiction".' Accessed on 4/2/2020 at www.healthline.com/health/pornography-addiction. See also 'The Great Porn Experiment', a Ted X talk by Gary Wilson. Accessed on 4/2/2020 at www.youtube.com/watch?v=NbP_ehYHfsk

	Statement	**True or false?**
13	People who watch porn are more likely to be violent towards women.	**True:** Porn can give people harmful messages about how to treat women and contribute to people being violent and aggressive. Porn can reinforce the idea that women are sex objects, which holds us back from more equal and progressive gender roles.[19] However, some studies say that porn actually decreases violence towards women and girls as porn can give people an outlet for feelings of sexual aggression or violent fantasies.[20]
14	Porn changes people's sexual preferences (preferences for what turns them on, not sexual orientation).	**True:** 64% of males and 42% of females said their preferences have been influenced by porn.[21]
15	Porn makes you less likely to cheat on your partner.	**False:** Lots of studies show that porn makes people more likely to cheat on their partners[22] and less committed and intimate in relationships.[23]

Part 2

After you've completed the quiz and revealed the answers, elicit feedback from the group:

1) Did you learn anything new?
2) Did anything shock you about the answers?
3) Is porn itself harmful or is it the way people use it that is?

---

19   Weinberg, M.S., Williams, C.J., Kleiner, S. and Irizarry, Y. (2010) 'Pornography, normalization and empowerment.' *Archives of Sexual Behavior 39*, 6, 1389–1401; Doring, N.M. (2009) 'The internet's impact on sexuality: A critical review of 15 years of research.' *Computers in Human Behavior 25*, 5, 1089–1101.

20   Weir, C. (2014) 'Is pornography addictive?' *Monitor on Psychology 4*. Accessed on 4/2/2020 at www.apa.org/monitor/2014/04/pornography

21   Jameson, S. (2018) 'Come here often? A study of 740 men and women's ejaculation habits.' Bad Girls Bible. Accessed on 4/2/2020 at https://badgirlsbible.com/come-here-often

22   Braithwaite, S.R., Coulson, G., Keddington, K. and Fincham, F.D. (2015) 'The influence of pornography on sexual scripts and hooking up among emerging adults in college.' *Archives of Sexual Behavior 44*, 1, 111–123; Maddox, A.M., Rhoades, G.K. and Markman, H.J. (2011) 'Viewing sexually-explicit materials alone or together: Associations with relationship quality.' *Archives of Sexual Behavior 40*, 2, 441–448.

23   Minarcik, J., Wetterneck, C.T. and Short, M.B. (2016) 'The effects of sexually explicit material use on romantic relationship dynamics.' *Journal of Behavioral Addictions 5*, 4, 700–707; Maddox, A.M., Rhoades, G.K. and Markman, H.J. (2011) 'Viewing sexually-explicit materials alone or together: Associations with relationship quality.' *Archives of Sexual Behavior 40*, 2, 441–448.

Exercise 4: World Café – Exploring the Impact of Porn

Part 1

Write the following headings at the top of four sheets of flipchart paper, with one heading per sheet:

1) The impact of pornography on...sexual expectations (how we 'should' behave sexually)
2) The impact of pornography on...body image (males and females)
3) The impact of pornography on...our beliefs about consent
4) The impact of pornography on...relationships

Split the group into four smaller groups and allocate each of them a themed flipchart sheet. Each group will visit and contribute to all of the themes on the flipchart paper.

For each piece of paper, the groups have three minutes to record all the ways that pornography might impact the theme of their flipchart paper – for example, the impact of pornography on sexual expectations, the impact of pornography on body image. After three minutes each group moves on to the next piece of paper and adds to what the previous group has contributed. All groups will have a chance to comment on every piece of flipchart paper.

You can do this like speed dating, ringing a bell or having an alarm every three minutes when the students need to move on to the next theme.

Part 2

After the groups have had three minutes on each table ask them for feedback about what they came up with.

Note: Be sure to let the group know that the impact of porn on these areas of our lives isn't always negative, and they can record any positives that come to mind as well.

Part 3

Read out the following ideas or show the group PowerPoint slides 3–6 in case there are ideas they hadn't considered:

THE IMPACT OF PORN ON SEXUAL EXPECTATIONS
(HOW WE 'SHOULD' BEHAVE SEXUALLY)

- Porn can shape what we think is realistic. **Five out of ten boys and four out of ten girls think porn is realistic.**[24]
- Porn often fails to include consent, communication, contraception and respect.
- Porn often depicts violent or oppressive behaviour, especially towards women.
- Porn can change people's sexual tastes and behaviours and often involves 'taboo' sexual acts.
- Porn may cause people to associate pleasure with risk taking and harming others (e.g. sites most visited by children under 10 include 'brutal gang bang', 'sleep assault' and 'crying in pain').
- Porn may cause people (especially males) to associate their sexual worth with being powerful, dominant and in control (and reinforce toxic masculinity).
- Porn creates the illusion that people can orgasm on demand, and that all women can orgasm from penetrative sex, which is not the case.
- Porn can make sex seem less shameful and encourage people to explore and experiment in a playful way.
- Porn can increase our imagination for what's possible.
- Porn can normalize fantasies that people may have so they don't feel like they're the only one.

▲ PowerPoint slide 3

THE IMPACT OF PORN ON BODY IMAGE

- ▷ Exposure to porn is linked to dissatisfaction with your body.
- ▷ Porn does not show people with average bodies and rarely shows difference in body shape and size, which can cause people to think that 'sexy' comes in only one shape and size.
- ▷ Porn markets people as objects and contributes to the sexual objectification of individuals.
- ▷ Porn often shows women performing for men rather than seeking their own sexual gratification.
- ▷ Porn normalizes having no pubic hair and having plastic surgery, which can cause people to feel unsatisfied with their appearance.

---

24 Martellozo, E., Monaghan, A., Adler, J.R., Davidson, J., Leyva, R. and Horvath, M.A.H. (2016) '...I wasn't sure it was normal to watch it...' Accessed on 4/2/2020 at www.mdx.ac.uk/__data/assets/pdf_file/0021/223266/MDX-NSPCC-OCC-pornography-report.pdf; Fight the New Drug (2018) 'One in 10 visitors to hardcore porn sites is under 10 years old, study shows.' Accessed on 16/3/2020 at https://fightthenewdrug.org/data-says-one-in-10-visitors-to-porn-sites-are-under-10-years-old; Bish UK (2020) 'A guide to sex, love and you. For everyone over 14.' Accessed on 16/3/2020 at www.bishuk.com

▷ Porn can make males think they need to perform and worry about their penis size, how much they ejaculate, how long they can last for, etc.

▷ There is a difference between looking sexy, and feeling it – many people in porn learn to pose in ways that make them look most appealing to the camera, rather than in a position that feels natural or comfortable.

▲ PowerPoint slide 4

THE IMPACT OF PORN ON OUR BELIEFS ABOUT CONSENT

- In one study, **87%** of boys and **77%** of girls who responded felt that pornography failed to help them understand consent.[25]
- Porn often shows a lack of communication about choices, consent, safe sex and contraception in sexual relationships.
- Porn sends the message that people are horny, sexually available and 'up for it' the whole time.
- Research indicates that porn can increase levels of sexual aggression and increase acts of sexual violence.
- Lots of things happen in porn without the participants seeking permission beforehand.
- People don't say 'No' in porn or change their minds.

▲ PowerPoint slide 5

THE IMPACT OF PORN ON RELATIONSHIPS

- Porn can make it seem easy to find a partner (or multiple partners).
- Porn can cause people to compare their sexual partners with performers in porn, and can find their partner less attractive or less of a turn-on as a result.
- Porn can cause people to feel unsatisfied with their sex life.
- Watching too much porn can increase the likelihood of developing sexual problems such as not being able to ejaculate.
- Porn can make sex seem like a performance, rather than an intimate and playful act.
- Porn can be an outlet for feelings of sexual aggression or violent fantasies that helps people not act these ideas out in their relationships/in real life.
- Some people expect their partner to do things that they've seen in porn that they may be uncomfortable with.
- Porn can unite people and encourage them to explore things together.

▲ PowerPoint slide 6

Part 4

Show the group PowerPoint slide 7 showing some dialogue between two young people, one of whom assumes everyone is 'up for it' as they are in porn. Ask the group:

---

25 Sellgren, K. (2016) 'Pornography "desensitising young people".' BBC News. Accessed on 4/2/2020 at www.bbc.co.uk/news/education-36527681

1) What other messages could the other boy say to challenge his harmful beliefs about porn?

2) What needs to be done to reduce the harmful effects of pornography? (Facilitators' note: This could include communicating with sexual partners, education around porn, knowing what we like and how to ask for it, knowing that porn doesn't convey real sex, etc.)

▲ **PowerPoint slide 7**

Part 5

Show the group PowerPoint slide 8, which outlines some challenges in a relationship. Ask the group:

1) If you were the girl's friend and you heard her say this, what advice would you give her?

2) What advice would you give her partner?

▲ PowerPoint slide 8

Exercise 5: When it Comes to Porn...

Although there are many negative and harmful effects of pornography, we need to be careful not to shame students who have accessed or do access pornography, and give them the skills they need to view porn with a critical eye. This can be a protective factor for exposure to porn.

Part 1

Let the group know that even though it is illegal to watch porn if you are under 18, many young people still access and watch porn. It's OK and normal to feel curious about sex and to experiment, and it's important to be aware of how to do this safely so that you don't harm yourself or others. Using porn safely increases the chance your experience will be positive rather than damaging.

Part 2

Show the group PowerPoint slide 9 or read out the 'When it comes to porn...' dos and don'ts before asking the group whether they have any questions.

It is normal for teenagers to be curious, but porn is made for adults. The law tries to protect under 18's from accessing porn because the effect on their undeveloped brains and health is different from adults. Here are some healthy and unhealthy ways that people can use porn.	
Healthy	**Unhealthy**
Use porn wisely – stay **aware** and in **control** of how much they watch.	Assume that everyone watches porn.
Get to know their own body, and show sexual partners how they like to be touched (they don't need porn for this!).	Share things that they have seen online with other people – not everyone is interested in what they are watching and some things online may disgust or distress people.
Continue **exploring** their body and sexual fantasies without the use of porn.	Expose younger people to porn.
Seek out **ethical porn** (where the performers are fully consenting, not exploited and paid well) or **feminist porn** (where the focus is on female pleasure).	Use porn too regularly. Assume that porn is real. Let porn replace real people or relationships.
Slow down – sex and masturbation are not a race.	Keep any worries or concerns to themselves – if they are worried about something, there are places they can go to get non-judgemental help and advice.
Report anything they see online that is shocking or makes them feel uncomfortable.	
Notice if their porn habits change – e.g. if they need increasingly hardcore images to feel aroused then their porn use may be becoming problematic.	

▲ **PowerPoint slide 9**

Part 3

For young people aged 16 and over

For young people who are using porn it could be helpful to reinforce the message that what you see in porn is a performance and does not reflect sexual interactions in real life. The authors would not recommend this approach for children under 16 and suggest that parents/carers are consulted. Let the group know that there are far more silly, playful and serious elements of sex than mainstream porn gives credit to.

Show them the illustration by Hazel Mead on PowerPoint slide 10. Respond to any questions or reflections that might arise whilst discouraging any personal disclosures (see Disclaimer on page 12).

▲ **PowerPoint slide 10**

Exercise 6: Challenging Beliefs

Remind the group of the statements you covered at the beginning of the workshop in the agree/disagree exercise (on PowerPoint slide 11) and elicit any feedback on whether any of their thoughts have developed or changed:

- Porn is a good place to learn about sex.
- Porn gives people unreasonable expectations about sex.
- Young people should be protected from porn.
- Porn makes sex more enjoyable.
- Porn is addictive.

▲ **PowerPoint slide 11**

End the session with PowerPoint slide 12 and let the group know that there are many places they can go to get resources on this subject or seek support, and there are procedures in place for anonymous reporting. It is important for them to share any issues or concerns that they have about themselves or others related to this topic. Be mindful of the possible impacts and emotions that might be evoked for individuals from the discussion, and if a topic is emotive for someone, offer an opportunity to explore this outside the group, to ensure that they feel heard and safe.

SIGNPOSTING AND RESOURCES
If anything in today's workshop has affected you, support is available.

▷ **Childline** has information and advice about porn, including facts about porn and staying safe if you are using it. You can write in with your questions at Ask Sam and read what other young people are asking about: www.childline.org.uk/get-support/ask-sam

▷ **Fight the New Drug** is a campaign to raise awareness of the harmful effects of pornography: https://fightthenewdrug.org

▲ **PowerPoint slide 12**

Positive Sexuality

Really helpful towards self-confidence :)

Session Overview

This workshop starts with an exploration of values and beliefs, followed by a quiz looking at myths and facts about sexuality. After considering readiness for sex, the 'Wheel of Consent' model is introduced to practise language to do with asking for and giving consent.

Info/Knowledge

Sexuality is an important part of who we are, including our sexual thoughts and feelings, our attractions and our behaviours. We want young people to develop an understanding of positive sexual behaviour, both with themselves and with others, so that when they develop intimate relationships, these are not only respectful and safe, but also playful, loving and fulfilling. We can support young people by talking openly with them about sex and sexuality, which empowers and equips them with the skills to talk openly with each other. Thinkuknow identifies the qualities of positive sexuality as shared enthusiasm, equality, empathy, communication and knowledge.[1] Betty Martin developed the Wheel of Consent model as a tool for adults to explore the complexity of consent, and it has been adapted here for teenagers for the first time.

Some adults are concerned that teaching about positive sexuality exposes young people to concepts that they are too immature or inexperienced to understand and makes them more likely to experiment sexually. The PSHE

---

1   Thinkuknow (n.d.) 'Supporting positive sexual behaviour.' Accessed on 7/2/2020 at www.thinkuknow.co.uk/parents/articles/ Supporting-positive-sexual-behaviour

Association points out that the age at which people first have sex in Britain has changed very little over the past decade and that RSE 'contributes to reducing early sexual activity, teenage conceptions, sexually transmitted infections, sexual exploitation and abuse, domestic violence and bullying'.[2] Talking about positive sexuality with young people is a protective factor for risky or harmful sexual behaviour, and ensures that their information doesn't come solely from pornography or each other.

PSHE Association Curriculum Themes

▷ KS3 R5. That relationships can cause strong feelings and emotions (including sexual attraction)
▷ KS3 R15. To consider different levels of intimacy and their consequences
▷ KS3 R16. To acknowledge and respect the right not to have intimate relationships until ready
▷ KS3 R17. About readiness for sex and the benefits of delaying sexual activity
▷ KS4 R20. To understand and respect others' faith and cultural expectations concerning relationships and sexual activity
▷ KS4 R21. To assess readiness for sex

Exercises

▷ Exercise 1: Exploring Values and Beliefs – Group Debate
▷ Exercise 2: My Personal Values and Beliefs
▷ Exercise 3: Myth or Fact?
▷ Exercise 4: Readiness for Sex
▷ Exercise 5: Masturbation and Self-Pleasure
▷ Exercise 6: Practising Consent Agreements – The Wheel of Consent
▷ Exercise 7: Frequently and Non-Frequently Asked Questions

Materials Needed

▷ Worksheet on attitudes and beliefs for Exercise 2 (Resources and Handouts 13.1)
▷ Myth or Fact? worksheet for Exercise 3 (Resources and Handouts 13.2)
▷ 'Myth' and 'Fact' cards for each table (optional) for Exercise 2 (Resources and Handouts 13.3)
▷ Access to YouTube
▷ Wheel of Consent handouts for Exercise 6 (Resources and Handouts 13.4)

---

2 Brook/PSHE Association/Sex Education Forum (2014) *Sex and Relationships Education (SRE) for the 21st Century: Supplementary advice to the Sex and Relationship Education Guidance DfEE (0116/2000)*. Accessed on 27/1/2020 at www.pshe-association.org.uk/curriculum-and-resources/resources/sex-and-relationship-education-sre-21st-century

Learning Outcomes

By the end of this session:

- I can reflect on my attitudes and beliefs, and how they impact my behaviour around sex and relationships
- I understand that sexual acts should be pleasurable for everyone
- I have explored readiness for sex
- I have thought about touch, who it is for and how to communicate my needs in relationships

At the beginning of the session, inform the group of the topic – *Positive Sexuality* – and point out that it requires the group to approach the discussions with a certain amount of maturity and sensitivity. Remind the group of the agreed expectations, particularly emphasizing confidentiality and the importance of treating one another with respect. Check that everyone is in agreement, looking for nods or verbal recognition that they're on the same page. Remind the group that if something comes up in the session that upsets them or makes them feel uncomfortable, they have permission to leave the room or find some space, and remind them of where they can go or who they can approach for support. Creating a safe environment is covered in more detail in the Introduction. Before starting, briefly set out what will be covered in the workshop.

Exercise 1: Exploring Values and Beliefs – Group Debate

Ask the group to imagine that there is a line across the room. Explain to the group that one side of the room is 'Agree' and the other side is 'Disagree' (you can put up signs to make this clear). Let them know that when you read out a statement they are invited to stand where they feel they are on the line in relation to the statement. If it isn't possible for the young people to move about in the room, you can ask them to put up a hand or stand up if they agree, or give out the green, amber and red cards to each participant representing 'agree', 'neither agree nor disagree' and 'disagree' in Resources and Handouts 1.1. Reassure the group that there are no right or wrong answers, that they can stand in the middle if they are unsure and that they are able to move at any time if their opinion has been swayed. Remind the group to remain respectful when listening to and debating views and opinions that differ from their own. If the group find it hard not to talk over each other, you can use an object to represent a 'talking piece' which allows the person holding it permission to speak, while everyone else needs to listen until their turn with the talking piece (see Appendix 5).

When the young people have moved to where they want to stand, facilitate a debate between individuals or sides. Feel free to contribute to the debate (there are some facilitators' notes below that may be helpful discussion points).

You don't need to go through all of the statements; pick those that seem most relevant to the group.

Once you have used a few statements, ask the group if they have any other ideas that they want to debate. It might help if the young people talk briefly in pairs to help them to come up with a statement.

- **Sex should be enjoyable for everyone.** (Facilitators' note: There are lots of benefits to sex, including deepening your relationship(s), releasing tension, pleasure and feeling good – and babies! Foreplay is important in making sure that everyone involved has an enjoyable and pleasurable time.)
- **Orgasming is the goal of any sexual activity.** (Facilitators' note: Lots of sexual acts give people pleasure and it doesn't always lead to, or have to lead to, orgasms. There are many factors that impact on whether people can orgasm or not.)
- **Only guys masturbate.** (Facilitators' note: Both girls and boys masturbate, and it is totally normal to be curious about your body and have a sexual relationship with yourself. Religious beliefs often affect people's views on masturbation.)

Exercise 2: My Personal Values and Beliefs
Part 1

Give each of the young people the handout (Resources and Handouts 13.1) and ask them to finish the sentences as quickly as they can, without overthinking their responses. Let the young people know in advance that they will not be required to reveal any of their answers to the group unless they choose to, so they are encouraged to be as honest as possible.

Note: Alternatively, you can read out the beginning of the sentences and the group can write their responses on their own paper as you go along.

People are...

Men and women are...

Sex is...

Porn is...

Relationships are...

Masturbation is...

In a relationship, partners should...

Trust is...

Religion is...

Break-ups are...

Betrayal is...

Men should...

Women should...

Consent is...

Marriage is...

Life is...

One rule I live by is...

Part 2

Lead a discussion about the worksheet with the group, reminding them that they don't need to share their answers if they choose not to. Explain that often the first things that come to mind in an exercise like this are our unconscious values and beliefs – we might not even be aware that we have them! Our values and beliefs about sex, relationships and life have an effect on how we think and behave towards ourselves and others. As long as our attitudes and beliefs are not harmful to ourselves or others, then we have the right to live by them.

Part 3

Ask the group:

1) Did any of your responses surprise you?
2) Did you learn anything about yourself?
3) Where do our beliefs and values come from? (Facilitators' note: This could include parents/carers school, the media, society, religion, culture and personal experiences.)
4) Do our values and beliefs stay the same throughout our lifetime? (Facilitators' note: Remind the group that, even though values and beliefs sometime seem 'fixed', it's OK to change our minds and live by different values than those we are taught.)
5) Which values would you want to pass on to your own children?

Exercise 3: Myth or Fact?

Part 1

Now move on to the 'Myth or Fact?' quiz. A quiz can be a great way to capture the interest of the young people. Adapt the questions and topics to be age-appropriate to your group if necessary.

There are multiple ways you can conduct this quiz:

- By reading out the statements and asking the group to stand up if they think the statement is a fact and remain seated if they think it's a myth.

- Allowing small groups or pairs to discuss each question before presenting their answers to allow for further exploration of each statement. You can ask individual students in the group how they came to each conclusion before revealing the answer and the additional information.
- You can give out 'Myth' and 'Fact' cards (Resources and Handouts 13.3).
- You can have two or more groups competing against each other, with a prize to be won.
- You can print out Handout 13.2 and ask the students to complete the quiz as individuals and then mark each other's answers.

Facilitators' Answers

Statement	Myth or fact?
Most young people lie about having sex.	**Fact:** Many young people claim to be more experienced than they actually are. The average age in the UK for people having sex for the first time is 18.3 according to a study by Durex.[3]
The clitoris is more sensitive than a penis.	**Fact:** The clitoris contains 8000 amazingly sensitive nerve endings, double the number of nerve endings in the glans of a penis.[4]
Dolphins have homosexual/bisexual sex.	**Fact:** Dolphins[5] and other species of animal engage in homosexual or bisexual sex, which suggests they sometimes have sex for pleasure and intimacy rather than just reproduction. This is also true of many other animals including elephants,[6] lions[7] and gorillas.[8]
Men don't fake orgasms.	**Myth:** In a study of over 2000 people from Europe and the USA it was found that 27% of men have faked an orgasm; according to the same survey, 68% of women had as well.[9]
Most women don't orgasm through penetration alone.	**Fact:** Only 25% of women reliably orgasm just through penetration.[10]

3   Joe (2016) 'Here's the average age people lose their virginity around the world.' Accessed on 31/1/2020 at www.joe.ie/fitness-health/heres-the-average-age-people-lose-their-virginity-around-the-world-564505
4   Wolf, A.S. (2017) 'The clitoris has 8,000 nerve endings (and nine other things we learned from a new artwork).' *The Irish Times.* Accessed on 4/2/2020 at www.irishtimes.com/life-and-style/health-family/the-clitoris-has-8-000-nerve-endings-and-nine-other-things-we-learned-from-a-new-artwork-1.2947694
5   Bagemihl, B. (1999) *Biological Exuberance: Animal Homosexuality and Natural Diversity.* New York, NY: St. Martin's Press, p.339.
6   Bagemihl, B. (1999) *Biological Exuberance: Animal Homosexuality and Natural Diversity.* New York, NY: St. Martin's Press, pp. 427–430.
7   Srivastav, S. (2001) 'Lion, without lioness.' *TerraGreen: News to Save the Earth,* 15–31 December 2001.
8   Yamagiwa, J, (1987) 'Intra- and inter-group interactions of an all-male group of virunga mountain gorillas (*Gorilla gorilla beringei*).' *Primates 28,* 1, 1–30.
9   Alexander, B. (2010) 'Sorry, guys: Up to 80 percent of women admit faking it.' Sexploration on NBC News. Accessed on 4/2/2020 at www.nbcnews.com/id/38006774/ns/health-sexual_health/t/sorry-guys-percent-women-admit-#.XFAgaM_7RTZ
10   Lloyd, E.A. (2006) *The Case of the Female Orgasm: Bias in the Science of Evolution.* Cambridge, MA: Harvard University Press.

Fish have penises.	**Fact:** Some resemble a human penis, others don't, and some fish have them on their heads![11]
Women love men ejaculating on their face.	**Myth:** While 42% of men prefer ejaculating on women's faces, only 13% of women said they like it. This is likely a myth that has come from 'money shots' in pornography. There are many other myths from porn.[12]
There's no such thing as 'losing your virginity'.	**Fact:** Sex means different things to different people, and the idea of 'losing your virginity' is very heteronormative (based on a penis penetrating a vagina). In reality, having sex for the first time can involve different things for everyone. There are some people (including some lesbian, gay, pansexual and bisexual people) who will never have penetrative sex by a penis but do not identify as 'virgins'. The myth of 'losing your virginity' is also associated with 'breaking your hymen', but not all females have a hymen in the first place, and they are different for everyone. Many activities that aren't sex can break a hymen, so this is not a good indication of whether someone has had sex before or not.

Part 2

After you've completed the quiz and revealed the answers, elicit feedback from the group:

1) How did you find the quiz?
2) Did you learn anything new?
3) Did anything shock you about the answers?

---

11 Brackett, C. (n.d.) '10 bizarre facts about fish penises and sex rituals.' Weird Nature. Accessed on 4/2/2020 at www.ranker.com/list/strange-facts-about-fish-penises/crystal-brackett

12 Jameson, S. (2018) 'Come here often? A study of 740 men and women's ejaculation habits.' Bad Girls Bible. Accessed on 4/2/2020 at https://badgirlsbible.com/come-here-often

Part 3

Let the group know that Durex (the world number-one brand for condoms) compiled a list of ages people have sex for the first time across the globe, and broke this down into the average age in each country.

Show the group the world map on PowerPoint slide 2 and ask the group to identify:

1) the country with the youngest average age that people have sex for the first time (answer: Iceland)
2) the country with the oldest average age that people have sex for the first time (answer: Malaysia).

THE AVERAGE AGE THAT PEOPLE HAVE SEX FOR THE FIRST TIME[13]

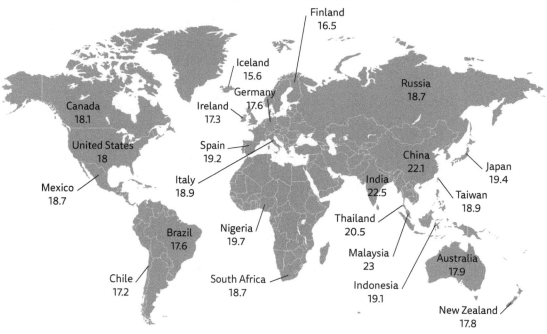

▲ PowerPoint slide 2

Exercise 4: Readiness for Sex

Part 1

Show young people PowerPoint slide 3 or read out the statements and statistics:

13   Durex (2012) *The Face of Global Sex 2012*. Slough: Reckitt Benckiser.

READINESS FOR SEX

Having sex too soon is the biggest regret of young people who have had sex for the first time.

The National Survey of Sexual Attitudes found that:

Nearly **40%** of young women and **26%** of young men did not feel that their first sexual experience had happened 'at the right time'.

50% of young women and **40%** of young men felt they had sex for the first time when they weren't sober enough to have consented, or because they were acting on peer pressure.

20% of young women and **10%** of young men felt that they and their partner had not been equally willing to have sex for the first time.[14]

▲ **PowerPoint slide 3**

Part 2

Elicit a discussion about how the group feels about these statistics. Did anything shock or surprise them?

---

14   Palmer, M.J., Clarke, L., Ploubidis, G.B. and Wellings, K. (2019) 'Prevalence and correlates of "sexual competence" at first heterosexual intercourse among young people in Britain.' *BMJ Sexual & Reproductive Health 45*, 2, 127–137. Note that these figures apply only to heterosexual couples and we are unaware of equivalent existing research studies relating to LGBTQI+ communities.

Part 3

Next, ask them to discuss in small groups: How do you know if you're ready to have sex? Ask the students to write a list of questions they would suggest to a friend (or younger sibling) to assess readiness for sex.

After about three minutes, ask for some feedback from the groups so they can hear as many different questions and perspectives as possible, before showing them PowerPoint slide 4 or reading out the suggested questions:

HOW DO PEOPLE KNOW IF THEY'RE READY?

▷ Does it feel **right**? [tick]
▷ Do they **trust** the person they want to have sex with? [tick]
▷ Are they **equally willing** to have sex? [tick]
▷ Do they feel **comfortable** with this person? [tick]
▷ Would they feel able to **change their mind**? [tick]
▷ Can they **talk** to this person openly about their fears, worries or concerns? [tick]
▷ Can they talk about **contraception and protection**, and is this a shared decision? [tick]
▷ Are they both open, honest and mature enough to discuss **STIs**? [tick]
▷ Do they feel under any **pressure** to have sex? [cross]
▷ Are they having sex because they think everyone else is and they don't want to be left behind? [cross]
▷ Are they having sex because they're worried about what will happen if they don't (e.g. their partner might leave them)? [cross]

▲ **PowerPoint slide 4**

Part 4

Show the young people the YouTube video 'Screwball!', which depicts the story of two young people who are considering having sex for the first time:

www.youtube.com/watch?v=OC7xv3wOauk&has_verified=1 (video length: 12 minutes 20 seconds).

▲ **PowerPoint slide 5**

At the end of the video ask the group:

1) What did they think of the video?
2) What led to the couple making the decision not to have sex?
3) What expectations did each of the characters have about their first time?

Note: After watching this video young people may ask, 'What's a vulva?' It's important that they know the correct terms for sexual anatomy. Vulva: the part of female genitals that is outside of the body, including the labia, clitoris, vaginal opening and the opening of the urethra (your pee-hole). Many people say 'vagina' when they are actually referring to the vulva.

Exercise 5: Masturbation and Self-Pleasure

Although many people masturbate, this topic can cause embarrassment, shame and dread in both facilitators and young people. The fact that it can be so hard to talk about then reinforces the sense of shame, stigma and guilt around the topic, which is why it is so important to normalize masturbation. The questions below aim to explore masturbation in a light-hearted, non-shaming way. Before starting this conversation, be aware of your audience, and consider the different cultural and religious attitudes to sexuality and masturbation. The young people within your group may be getting a range of different messages at home.

Ask the group:

1) What other words do people use to describe masturbation? (Facilitators' note: There are many creative terms for masturbation that the group may enjoy sharing – e.g. menage-a-moi, me-some, spanking the monkey, playing the clitar, riding the unicycle, charming the snake, procrasturbating and many, many more.)

2) Is masturbation only for single people? (Facilitators' note: People in relationships can also masturbate – it's still important to have a healthy relationship with your own body. Not everyone masturbates but anyone can – regardless of their age, gender, gender identity, religion, sexual orientation, etc.)

3) Is masturbating too much dangerous? (Facilitators' note: There is no such thing as masturbating too much unless it gets in the way of other parts of your life such as school or relationships, and as long as you're doing it in an appropriate place (in private) and at an appropriate time. There are many myths about how masturbating is dangerous – e.g. it makes you go blind – which are damaging and reinforce the shame and stigma around masturbation.)

4) Is masturbating good for you? (Facilitators' note: Masturbation has many positive effects such as relaxation, the release of stress and tension, improved confidence, acceptance of your body and body image, boosting your mood and helping you sleep, and can even reduce period cramps in females. There is nothing dirty or shameful about masturbation.)

Exercise 6: Practising Consent Agreements – The Wheel of Consent

Part 1

This exercise uses a simplified version of the Wheel of Consent developed by Betty Martin. It would be helpful to familiarize yourself with the model before teaching this exercise.[15]

You could show PowerPoint slide 6 while introducing the Wheel of Consent:

▲ **PowerPoint slide 6**

Part 2

Ask the group:

1) Raise your hand if you have ever been annoyed because someone has taken a chip without asking.
2) Raise your hand if you have ever felt pleased when someone offered you a chip.
3) Raise your hand if you have ever felt obliged to give someone a chip when you didn't really want to.
4) Raise your hand if you have ever felt good because you shared your chips.

Elicit some of the feelings involved with sharing chips (anger, anxiety, annoyance, happiness, envy, greed...). At this point you could touch on the different rules and expectations around the making, offering, sharing and eating of food in different cultures.

Explain that, even with chips, relationships can be complicated!

---

15   A basic introduction can be found at: https://schoolofconsent.org/wheel-explained

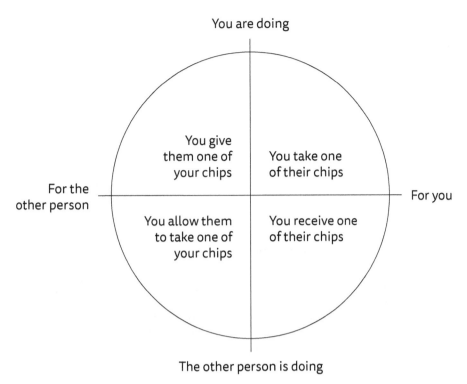

You are doing

You give them one of your chips

You take one of their chips

For the other person

For you

You allow them to take one of your chips

You receive one of their chips

The other person is doing

▲ **PowerPoint slide 7**[16]

Part 3

Show PowerPoint slide 7 or create the diagram on the whiteboard or flipchart. Talk the group through the diagram. The right half of the diagram is about chips that are for you to eat; it is about you taking or receiving the other person's chips. The left half of the diagram is about chips for the other person to eat, with you either giving them a chip or allowing them to take one of yours. Now show them that in the top half of the diagram, you are the person 'doing' – either taking their chip or giving them one of yours. In the bottom half the other person is 'doing', either taking one of your chips or giving you one of theirs.

Divide the class into groups. Give each group a copy of the diagram (Resources and Handouts 13.4). Give the group four cards, each with one of the sentences below (Resources and Handouts 13.5):

| 'Do you want one of my chips?' |
| 'Can I have a chip?' |
| 'Go ahead, have one!' |
| 'That's nice of you, cheers!' |

---

16   The Wheel of Consent is reproduced with kind permission from Betty Martin.

Part 4

Get the group to put each sentence in the correct section of the diagram. It should look like this:

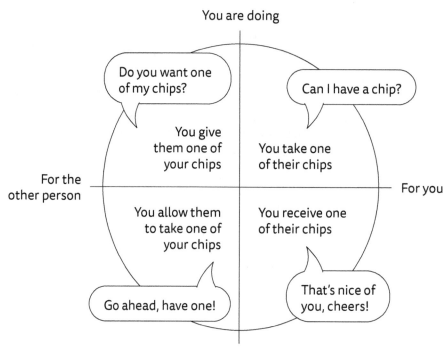

▲ **PowerPoint slide 8**[17]

You could explain that you can usually get away with nicking someone's chip without asking permission, but even with chips this can cause a fight if you are not in agreement.

Part 5

Explain that we will now think about when you are in a relationship with someone. Look at the diagram again. All of the feelings that we identified with sharing chips you could have with sex and consent, which are also about giving and taking. Think back to all the things we learned about unhealthy relationships in Workshop 8, where there are issues around equality, power and coercion.

Explain that we will look at each of the four segments of the diagram in turn.

Say to the group: 'What might happen when you have two people in an unhealthy relationship who have both ordered chips, in relation to the top right corner of the diagram?' They may say that you would keep taking their chips without asking. Now explore the other three corners.

You may get something like the diagram on PowerPoint slide 9:

---

17   The Wheel of Consent is reproduced with kind permission from Betty Martin.

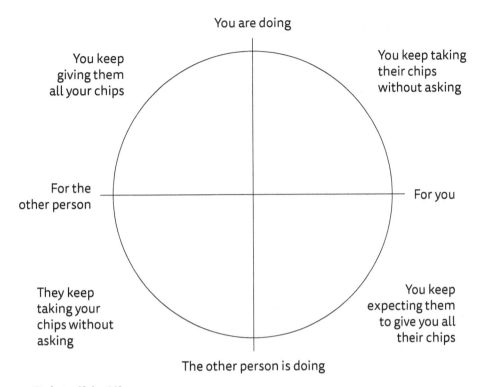

▲ PowerPoint slide 9[18]

If appropriate, you could mention that unlike the healthy examples of sharing that we started with, these are the 'shadow' sides where there isn't consent. You could say that if you were the person in the top left, you would be acting like a rescuer or do-gooder; if you were the person in the bottom left, your behaviour would be passive and a bit like a doormat; if you were the person in the top right, you would be disrespectful and stealing; and if you were the person in the bottom right, you would be acting in an entitled or spoilt manner.

Part 6

Explain that what we know about consent is that if someone is in an unhealthy relationship generally, it is likely to be unhealthy when it comes to consent and sex. If someone is in a healthy relationship generally, it is likely to be healthy when it comes to consent and sex. Even how people share chips could be a sign of whether they are in a healthy or unhealthy relationship.

Part 7

Explain to the group that touch is really important – we want it in our lives! In a healthy and equal relationship, both people will feel pleasure and want to give pleasure to their partner. You always need the consent of both people to keep both of you safe and happy,

---

18   The Wheel of Consent is reproduced with kind permission from Betty Martin.

so that someone isn't touching you when you don't want it, or you are touching them and they don't want it. Stress that this applies to same-sex relationships as much as to heterosexual relationships.

Both need to agree! But there are different types of consent agreement. Write up on the board these questions:

- Who is it for?
- Who is doing it?

Part 8

Give each group a copy of the Wheel of Consent diagram below and/or show PowerPoint slide 10. Talk the group through the four sections of the diagram:

- You touch them the way they want – this is giving.
- You touch them the way you want – this is taking.
- They touch you in the way you want – this is receiving.
- They touch you in the way they want – this is allowing.

'Who is doing, and who is it for?'

You are doing

Giving   Taking

You touch them the way they want | You touch them the way you want

For the other person — For you

They touch you the way they want | They touch you the way you want

Allowing   Receiving

The other person is doing

▲ **PowerPoint slide 10**[19]

---

19   The Wheel of Consent is reproduced with kind permission from Betty Martin.

Part 9

Start by going through a couple of examples. Write on the board or flipchart: 'How do you like that?' Ask the group: 'Who is doing?' (you are doing) and 'Who is it for?' (for the other person). The correct section is therefore 'Giving'. Now write on the board or flipchart: 'Is it OK if I touch you here?' Ask the group: 'Who is doing?' (you are doing) and 'Who is it for?' (for you). The correct section is therefore 'Taking'.

Give each group the sentences on strips of paper (Resources and Handouts 13.6; you may want to print some more). Their task is to sort out the sentences into the four quarters in the diagram. Explain that in this exercise you are the one asking the question (not the other person).

Some of the strips cover more than one quadrant and can be put over the lines or in the middle. You could either give the groups all of the sentences at once, or break them into sets of four (one for each quadrant) which is an easier task.

Set 1

'How would you like to be touched?'	Giving
'Do you mind if I...?'	Taking
'Will you...?'	Receiving
'You can keep going if you want to'	Allowing

Set 2

'Would you like me to?'	Giving
'Is it OK if I keep going?'	Taking
'Do you mind rubbing my back?'	Receiving
'You can go ahead, it's OK'	Allowing

Set 3

'Do you want me to keep going?'	Giving
'Is it OK if I touch you down there?'	Taking
'Please keep going, that's great'	Receiving
'Do you like doing that to me?'	Allowing

Others

'Do you want me to stop?'	Giving or taking
'Let's stop now'	All/any of them
'Do you want to just cuddle?'	Giving
'Yes, that sounds great'	All/any of them
'Yes, I will'	Giving
'Go ahead, that's good'	Receiving or allowing
'Is this fun for you?'	All/any of them
'Are you all right?'	All/any of them
'How does that feel?'	All/ any of them
'OK, but please be a bit gentle'	Allowing
'Do you like what I'm doing to you?'	Giving
'Is it OK if I touch you here?'	Taking
'Are you OK?'	All/any of them
'Can we try something new?'	All/any of them
'Would you like to touch me there?'	Allowing

Note: If the group is able to sit in a circle without tables, the Wheel of Consent exercise can be done with the whole group using floor art. Create the diagram from PowerPoint slide 10 on the floor using masking tape to create the lines, and A4 paper for the text. Hand out the sentences on strips of paper so that everyone has at least one. In turn, ask the young people to read out what is on their strip of paper, and then place the paper in the appropriate section on the floor. Alternatively, they could stand in that part of the wheel to read out their sentence.

Part 10

You could summarise the exercise by asking the group whether they agree with the following:

1) It is OK to ask for what you want
2) It is important to ask other people what they want
3) It is OK to say 'Yes'
4) It is OK to say 'No'.

Mention that the Wheel of Consent was developed by Betty Martin. You could say that, in Betty's model, if you are inside the circle, there is consent, and if you are outside the circle, there is no consent. You could explain that being able to talk openly about consent can avoid real problems. Here is an example.

If you're doing something but you haven't agreed who it's for, you can easily end up with a situation where you are touching someone else on their body, because you think it's what *they* most want right now, but meanwhile the other person thinks you are touching them there because it's what *you* most want to do right now, so they are letting you do that. And in reality, it's not what *either* of you most wants to be doing! You'd both rather be doing something else, but you haven't communicated your needs so neither of you realizes that! Then it's good for one person to speak: 'I'd like it even more if you touched me there' or 'I'd like to touch you somewhere else now, are you OK with that?' etc...

Part 11

Finally, elicit any feedback from the group about how they found this exercise. It could be helpful to have a handout of the Wheel of Consent for the young people to take away. You could remind them how we started the exercise looking at sharing chips, and that giving, receiving, taking and allowing apply to many situations in life, as well as those involving touch and sex.

Exercise 7: Frequently and Non-Frequently Asked Questions

At the end of the session ask the young people to put any anonymous questions they want to ask on a Post-it. You can:

1) Read these questions out there and then, if you feel you have the knowledge to respond to what might come up.
2) Collect the Post-its and let the group know that you will explore the questions and responses in a future session.
3) Invite a school nurse, sexual health nurse or professional from a sexual health clinic to come and speak to the group with responses to their questions.

End the session with PowerPoint slide 11 and let the group know that there are many places they can go to get resources on this subject or seek support, and there are procedures in place for anonymous reporting. It is important for them to share any issues or concerns that they have about themselves or others related to this topic. Be mindful of the possible impacts and emotions that might be evoked for individuals from the discussion, and if a topic is emotive for someone, offer an opportunity to explore this outside the group, to ensure that they feel heard and safe.

SIGNPOSTING AND RESOURCES

There are answers out there for any question you might have about sex, your sexual health or relationships. Here are a couple of places to look:

▷ **Brook** has loads of information and support on sexual health, relationships and wellbeing. Check out their website: http://brook.org.uk
▷ **The Survivors Trust:** Information about specialist support for women, men and children who have survived rape or sexual violence. For advice and support, phone 08088 010818. https://thesurvivorstrust.eu.rit.org.uk/contact

▲ **PowerPoint slide 11**

Gender Expectations

I learnt: Don't judge people by stereotypes

Session Overview

This workshop starts off by defining 'sex' and 'gender', and looks at the pressures that boys and girls experience from the cultural expectations and stereotypes relating to their gender. This theme is further explored through media adverts and the everyday language that people use that reinforce gender stereotypes.

Info/Knowledge

Children from a young age learn that their behaviour, preferences and aspirations are bound by unwritten rules and expectations around male and female roles. These rules are simply assumptions, reinforced by marketing and distorted media messages, which can be limiting to a young person's development and life opportunities. By building awareness and challenging gender-based stereotypes and expectations, young people can take an active part in combating a culture that implies that our gender defines who we are and limits us. If you have the space and resources, it can be quite powerful to run this session with individuals who identify as male and female separately, and then bring them together at the end to reflect on the session and discuss. Although this session explores issues affecting 'boys' and 'girls', we also acknowledge non-binary gender identities and explore these in Workshop 16.

PSHE Association Curriculum Themes

▷ KS3 R14. To understand the role of sex in the media and its impact on sexuality (including pornography and related sexual ethics such as consent, negotiation, boundaries, respect, gender norms, sexual 'norms', trust, communication, pleasure, orgasms, rights, empowerment, sexism and feminism)

▷ KS4 R17. To understand the pernicious influence of gender double standards and victim blaming

Exercises

▷ Exercise 1: Exploring Values and Beliefs – Group Debate
▷ Exercise 2: Sex, Gender and Gender Identity
▷ Exercise 3: Gender Identity
▷ Exercise 4: Exploring Gender Expectations and Pressure
▷ Exercise 5: Exploring Gender Stereotypes in the Media
▷ Exercise 6: Societal 'Norms'
▷ Exercise 7: If I Could Ask Anything, It Would Be…

Materials Needed

▷ Access to YouTube
▷ 'Agree' and 'Disagree' cards for Exercise 1 (Resources and Handouts 14.1)

Learning Outcomes

By the end of this session:

- I can understand the difference between sex and gender
- I can recognize the pressure of gender expectations on young people, where this comes from and its impact
- I can make up my own mind about whether these gender expectations are realistic and fair
- I feel able to think about what my peers and I might do individually and collectively to resist gender-based pressure
- I can challenge gender-based stereotyping and discrimination

At the beginning of the session, inform the group of the topic – *Gender Expectations* – and point out that it requires the group to approach the discussions with a certain amount of maturity and sensitivity. Remind the group of the agreed expectations, particularly emphasizing confidentiality and the importance of treating one another with respect. Check that everyone is in agreement, looking for nods or verbal recognition that they're on the same page. Remind the group that if something comes up in the session that upsets them or makes them feel uncomfortable, they have permission to leave the room or find some space, and remind them of where they can go or who they can approach for support. Creating a safe environment is covered in more detail in the Introduction. Before starting, briefly set out what will be covered in the workshop.

Exercise 1: Exploring Values and Beliefs – Group Debate

Ask the group to imagine that there is a line across the room. Explain to the group that one side of the room is 'Agree' and the other side is 'Disagree' (you can put up signs to make this clear). Let them know that when you read out a statement they are invited to stand where they feel they are on the line in relation to the statement. If it isn't possible for the young people to move about in the room, you can ask them to put up a hand or stand up if they agree, or give out the green, amber and red cards to each participant representing 'agree', 'neither agree nor disagree' and 'disagree' in Resources and Handouts 1.1. Reassure the group that there are no right or wrong answers, that they can stand in the middle if they are unsure and that they are able to move at any time if their opinion has been swayed. Remind the group to remain respectful when listening to and debating views and opinions that differ from their own. If the group find it hard not to talk over each other, you can use an object to represent a 'talking piece' which allows the person holding it permission to speak, while everyone else needs to listen until their turn with the talking piece (see Appendix 5).

When the young people have moved to where they want to stand, facilitate a debate between individuals or sides. Feel free to contribute to the debate (there are some facilitators' notes below that may be helpful discussion points).

You don't need to go through all of the statements; pick those that seem most relevant to the group.

Once you have used a few statements, ask the group if they have any other ideas that they want to debate. It might help if the young people talk briefly in pairs to help them to come up with a statement.

- **Real men shouldn't cry.** (Facilitators' note: There is technically no such thing as a 'real man'. It can be helpful to mention that this is a stereotype that can be damaging – e.g. it can lead to boys feeling unable to share their emotions, which can contribute towards poor mental health and relationship problems.)
- **Girls should wear make-up.** (Facilitators' note: Girls should wear whatever they want! It can be helpful to explore people's motivation to wear make-up – is it individual expression and preference, or pressure from the media and advertising to conform to the unrealistic expectations they set?)
- **Women should always take the man's surname if they get married.** (Facilitators' note: Traditionally this has been the case. However, there has been a shift in attitudes in Western societies and many people now challenge the assumption that the female should always take the man's name, viewing it as outdated. Some people argue that this tradition is an example of everyday sexism.)
- **Pink is for girls.** (Facilitators' note: It can be helpful to mention that this is a stereotype which can be harmful as it assumes that all girls are into the same things.)

Exercise 2: Sex, Gender and Gender Identity

Part 1

In pairs or small groups, ask the young people to discuss what they think the difference between our 'sex' and our 'gender' is, and then ask for feedback.

Part 2

Read out or show them the definitions in PowerPoint slide 2:

SEX, GENDER AND GENDER IDENTITY

Sex refers to the **biological** differences between males and females (e.g. genitalia and genetic differences).

Gender is more difficult to define. It often refers to the perceived 'roles' of a male or female in society (**gender role**) or to an individual's concept of themselves (**gender identity**).

Sex has a basis in science whereas gender is a socially constructed way for people to identify with their sex. People don't always identify with the sex they were born with (**gender incongruence**, or **gender dysphoria** if accompanied by discomfort or distress).

▲ **PowerPoint slide 2**

Part 3

Ask the group the following questions and elicit feedback. You can either have this discussion with the whole group, or ask them to discuss in smaller groups to begin with.

1) Do sex and gender affect how we think and feel? If so, how? If not, how come?
2) Do sex and gender affect our experiences and the way we are treated? If so, how? If not, how come?

Part 4

Show the group PowerPoint slide 3 or read out the statistics:

THE EQUALITY SURVEY

Over 1000 9–14-year-olds were surveyed by a children's newspaper[1] which discovered that...

- Over **50%** of all the young people they surveyed felt that girls are more likely to be judged on their physical appearance than boys.

---

1   First News (2018) 'Are boys and girls treated the same?' Accessed on 17/3/2020 at https://schools.firstnews.co.uk/wp-content/uploads/sites/3/resources/FIRSTNEWS_605.pdf

- **63%** of girls feel they are treated differently because of their gender.
- **52%** of boys feel they are treated differently because of their gender.

▲ PowerPoint slide 3

Part 5 (Optional)

You can follow up this slide by showing the young people the Equality Survey from *First News* which adds more young people's voices on their experiences of being stereotyped:

https://schools.firstnews.co.uk/wp-content/uploads/sites/3/resources/FIRST
NEWS_605.pdf

It is on page 11.

Exercise 3: Gender Identity

Show the following clip 'Girl toys vs boy toys: The experiment' by Doctor Javid:

www.youtube.com/watch?v=nWu44AqF0il (video length: 3 minutes 25 seconds).

▲ PowerPoint slide 4

Lead a discussion with the group about what they noticed in the video. Let the group know that the process of learning gendered behaviours considered 'appropriate' for one's sex is called 'gender role socialization'.

Exercise 4: Exploring Gender Expectations and Pressure
Part 1

Ask the group what the word 'stereotype' means to them and elicit feedback. Then show them PowerPoint slide 5 or read out the definition of a stereotype:

WHAT ARE STEREOTYPES?
A widely held, but fixed and oversimplified image or idea of a particular type of person or thing.
– Oxford Dictionary

Stereotyping is a form of prejudice.

▲ PowerPoint slide 5

Part 2

▲ **PowerPoint slide 6**

Put up PowerPoint slide 6 to set the scene for this activity. Draw the outline of a male and a female on the board (alternatively, you can split the group into smaller groups and get them to work on flipchart paper to create their own stereotypical male and female).

Ask the group to contribute all the different traits, characteristics and stereotypes they associate with each gender. Record their responses around the image on the board or ask them to record responses on their flipchart paper. Unlike the PowerPoint slide, the speech bubbles have been filled in here to give facilitators an idea of responses they can expect from the group.

Part 3

Lead a discussion with the group about where these ideas come from. (Facilitators' note: This could include peers, the media, family, culture, societal 'norms', religion, etc.)

Ask the group:

1)   Do these expectations and stereotypes put pressure on us to act in a certain way and try to fit in?
2)   What messages do we get about the roles we 'should' take on in relationships because of our gender?

Part 4

Show the group PowerPoint slide 7 or say the statement 'Fitting in is important'. Ask the group to stand up (or put up a hand) if they agree with the statement and to stay seated if they don't. Seek some opinions from both sides of the debate about why they believe what they do.

Fitting in is important

▲ **PowerPoint slide 7**

Comment on your observation of the group's response to this statement and then lead a discussion about what the consequences of not fitting in, or living up to these expectations might be.

Note: You could show PowerPoint slide 8 and ask the group if they agree with the young people on the slide. Are there any additional consequences they want to add? (Facilitators' note: This could include stigma, being left out/excluded, humiliated, bullied, disappointment, being judged, etc.)

Part 5

Ask the group how it feels to have so many external and internal expectations and pressures on them.

▲ **PowerPoint slide 8**

Part 6

Ask the group to stand up (or put up a hand) if they agree with the following statements (asking them to sit back down after each one):

1)   Stand up if you think living up to these pressures is realistic.
2)   Stand up if you think the pressure is unfair.
3)   Stand up if you want to live in a society where individual differences are celebrated and encouraged.

If the majority of the group has stood up for each of these statements, you can lead a discussion about what they can do individually and as a group to work towards resisting pressure from others (or ourselves) to be a certain way so we can live these values.

Part 7 (Optional)

Give each young person a Post-it and ask them to write the words 'One way I can resist pressure is...' across the top (see PowerPoint slide 9). Ask each of them to write something that they, as an individual, commit to doing that will contribute towards a society where difference is celebrated and encouraged, and people feel free to be themselves.

There are different ways you can conduct the next part of the exercise depending on your group:

1) Ask each student to read out their 'one thing' to the rest of the group.
2) Ask each student to bring their Post-its to the front and then read out some or all of them (so they remain anonymous).
3) Ask the students to discuss their 'one thing' in small groups.
4) Ask each student to leave their Post-it behind and then make a collective 'group charter' with their ideas – for example, 'As a group, we are committed to resisting pressure/celebrating difference...' (then list the ideas they have come up with).

All of the above ways of conducting this exercise allow the students to take ownership of their ideas, as well as witness the ideas of others, which allows for students to become better Upstanders and empowers them to challenge harmful stereotypes, attitudes and beliefs.

▲ PowerPoint slide 9

Exercise 5: Exploring Gender Stereotypes in the Media
Part 1

Explain that advertising sends strong and powerful messages about how we 'should' act, live, look, think and feel.

Part 2

Explore each of the adverts below (PowerPoint slide 10) with the group and then lead a discussion about what messages the adverts send to the audience (using the questions provided as prompts). Let the group know that the most recent adverts are played first and the oldest ones last (you can let them know the year of each advert as you go along).

GILLETTE – THE BEST MEN CAN BE (2019)

www.youtube.com/watch?v=koPmuEyP3a0 (video length: 1 minute 45 seconds).

- What message is this advert sending about how men should behave in society?
- What stereotypes is this advert trying to challenge?
- Is it effective?

SNICKERS – YOU'RE NOT YOU WHEN YOU'RE HUNGRY (2014)

www.youtube.com/watch?v=MqgjTZQiySw (video length: 1 minute 19 seconds).

- Why do you think this advert was banned from being shown on television?
- What is this advert saying about how men should behave in society? Is this a harmful message?
- Do you think this advert is a fair representation of men?
- What does misogyny mean? (Facilitators' note: Misogyny means showing mistrust, dislike, contempt or ingrained prejudice against women and can contribute to sexual violence towards women.)

ALWAYS – #LIKE A GIRL (2014)

www.youtube.com/watch?v=XjJQBjWYDTs (video length: 3 minutes 18 seconds).

- What message is this advert trying to challenge about how girls are perceived?
- Is it effective?

WEETABIX CHOCOLATE – SIBLING RIVALRY (2013)

www.youtube.com/watch?v=3Z7h6RGvtYA (video length: 40 seconds).

- What stereotypes about boys and girls does this advert reinforce? Are they harmful?
- Is this an effective way of advertising Weetabix?

ASDA – CHRISTMAS ADVERT (2012)

www.youtube.com/watch?v=RHUFZSa7JNc (video length: 1 minute 16 seconds).

- What stereotypes about how men and women 'should' behave are reinforced in this advert?

NUTS MAGAZINE – DON'T EXPECT ANY HELP ON A THURSDAY (2004)

www.youtube.com/watch?v=3vVQv8A7W1A (video length: 1 minute 58 seconds).

- What stereotypes does this advert reinforce about men and women?

YORKIE – IT'S NOT FOR GIRLS (2002)

www.youtube.com/watch?v=HGvjGJ9II9Q (video length: 1 minute).

- What stereotypes about boys and girls does this advert reinforce?
- Do you think this advert is more offensive to males or females?

▲ **PowerPoint slide 10**

Part 3

Read out or show the young people PowerPoint slide 11 about advertising regulations, and ask the questions on the slide, eliciting their responses as you go along:

DID YOU KNOW...?

In 2019 the ASA (Advertising Standards Authority) banned UK adverts from:

- including stereotypes which are likely to cause harm or offence (e.g. passive dads, men who can't cook/clean, women taking care of the home or struggling to park a car)
- suggesting people will be more romantically successful if they transform their bodies using new products.

This was a conscious step to challenge gender stereotyping affecting how people view themselves and others, and to reflect the changing and more progressive standards of society.

1. Do you think these new laws are effective from what you've seen so far?
2. Did the more recent adverts have different messages from the older ones?
3. Do you think there should be tougher regulations on gender stereotypes in advertising?

▲ **PowerPoint slide 11**

Exercise 6: Societal 'Norms'

Part 1

In small groups, ask the students to come up with as many different messages or phrases that reinforce gender stereotypes as they can, and ask them for feedback. (Facilitators' note: If the groups are getting stuck, you can give them some examples – ladies first, girls don't know the offside rule, be more ladylike, throw like a girl, man up, boys don't cry, boys will be boys, grow a pair, etc.)

Part 2

Ask the group: What is the impact of some of the messages and phrases you came up with? (Facilitators' note: For example, for males, they imply that men should be strong, and shouldn't show emotions or ask for help, etc. – this can make men feel that they can't talk about or express emotions and bottle things up more, which can lead to men only feeling comfortable to express anger, which may then make them more likely to be controlling or abusive, or be unable to speak out if they become a victim of domestic or sexual violence. For females, these messages suggest that women are naturally weak, fragile, emotional and sensitive and are there to be seen as pretty objects (ladylike).)

Read out or show the group PowerPoint slide 12:

All these messages reinforce **harmful stereotypes** about gender.

Many of these phrases suggest that **strength** and **weakness** are naturally part of our gender and suggest that some characteristics are valuable and desirable and others are not.

For example, having gender double standards such as men being seen as 'assertive' (positive trait) and women being seen as 'bossy' (negative trait) for the same behaviour.

Some of these messages also suggest that **'strength'** is all about physical strength – whereas there are many different types of strength, including **emotional strength** and **resilience**.

▲ **PowerPoint slide 12**

Part 3

Ask the group:

1) How do these stereotypes impact people who don't fulfil gender 'norms' such as the trans community? (Facilitators' note: For example, isolating and excluding people from having a sense of belonging, fetishizing the trans community, judging and stigmatizing difference.)

2) How do people within their peer group/community reinforce gender stereotypes? (Facilitators' note: For example, using derogatory language, bullying behaviour directed at individuals or groups who don't conform to the gender 'norms'.)

Before moving on to Exercise 7, read out or show the group PowerPoint slide 13:

Gender shouldn't be a barrier to:

- us reaching our goals, ambitions or potential
- us feeling good about ourselves
- us being treated fairly and respectfully.

▲ **PowerPoint slide 13**

Exercise 7: If I Could Ask Anything, It Would Be…

At the end of the session ask the young people to put any anonymous questions about today's topic on a Post-it. Let them know that any questions that ask about specific group members won't be included.

If you have time in this session, read out the anonymous questions and put them to the group, adding any information you feel is relevant to the discussion. Otherwise, 'park' these questions until the next session and open up a discussion around what the young people asked.

End the session with PowerPoint slide 14 and let the group know that there are many places they can go to get resources on this subject or seek support, and there are procedures in place for anonymous reporting. It is important for them to share any issues or concerns that they have about themselves or others related to this topic. Be mindful of the possible impacts and emotions that might be evoked for individuals from the discussion, and if a topic is emotive for someone, offer an opportunity to explore this outside the group, to ensure that they feel heard and safe.

SIGNPOSTING AND RESOURCES

Your sexuality and gender identity are part of who you are. However you're feeling, support is available for you.

▷ **Childline:** In addition to phone and online support, Childline has webpages on sexuality, gender identity, coming out, homophobic and transphobic bullying: www.childline.org.uk/info-advice/your-feelings/sexual-identity
▷ **Stonewall** offers information and support for people who are LGBTQI+ and their allies. You can contact Stonewall's Information Service on Freephone 0800 0502020. Lines are open from 9.30am to 4.30pm, Monday to Friday.

▲ **PowerPoint slide 14**

Resilience, Self-Esteem and Body Image

> I thought this session was important to help people realize it is OK not to be 'perfect'

Session Overview

This session is about exploring and normalizing emotions, why we have them and why they are important, as well as providing an introduction to the range of different emotions we have. It also looks at positive body image and self-esteem, which are some of the foundations for resilience.

Info/Knowledge

Emotional resilience is the ability to adapt to stressful situations and cope with life's challenges. Emotional resilience requires us to be aware of our feelings and how we react in times of stress. People who lack resilience may become overwhelmed and resort to unhealthy coping mechanisms to deal with crises. Why is this important in the context of consent? We know that resilient, emotionally switched-on young people are less vulnerable to becoming victims of crime, including criminal and sexual exploitation and sexual and domestic violence. We can help young people build resilience by strengthening their self-belief, enabling them to practise interactive and presenting skills, and supporting them in knowing their worth and getting their voices heard.

PSHE Association Curriculum Themes

▷ KS4 R1. Strategies to manage strong emotions and feelings
▷ KS4 R29. The role peers can play in supporting one another (including

helping vulnerable friends to access reliable, accurate and appropriate support)

Exercises

▷ Exercise 1: Emotional Alphabet Icebreaker
▷ Exercise 2: Exploring Emotions
▷ Exercise 3: Emotional Health
▷ Exercise 4: Body Image
▷ Exercise 5: Exploring Resilience
▷ Exercise 6: A Resilient Mindset

Materials Needed

▷ Internet access to watch video
▷ Resilience Mindset worksheet for Exercise 6 (Resources and Handouts 15.1)

Learning Outcomes

By the end of this session:

- I can understand why emotions are important
- I can explain what resilience is and think about factors that affect my own, and others' resilience
- I can understand why feeling and expressing a range of different emotions can make me more resilient
- I can understand self-esteem and how it is connected to body image and resilience
- I can understand what might affect my self-esteem and how this can impact my emotional wellbeing
- I have a range of tools to help me build self-esteem and self-worth
- I can understand self-care, why it is important and assess how good I am at taking care of myself emotionally and physically

At the beginning of the session, inform the group of the topic – *Resilience, Self-Esteem and Body Image* – and point out that it requires the group to approach the discussions with a certain amount of maturity and sensitivity. Remind the group of the agreed expectations, particularly emphasizing confidentiality and the importance of treating one another with respect. Check that everyone is in agreement, looking for nods or verbal recognition that they're on the same page. Remind the group that if something comes up in the session that upsets them or makes them feel uncomfortable, they have permission to leave the room or find some space, and remind them of where they can go or who they can approach for support. Creating a safe environment is covered in more detail in the Introduction. Before starting, briefly set out what will be covered in the workshop.

Exercise 1: Emotional Alphabet Icebreaker

Use the emotional alphabet icebreaker to start exploring the topic of emotions. This can be done with a ball, with the group standing in a circle; if you have limited space, you can have the group in their normal seats and go round the room pointing at each individual as you go along. The idea of the game is to get from A to Z with a different emotion for each letter of the alphabet – so, for example, the first person may say 'A for Anxious', the second person 'B for Brave', the third person 'C for ...', etc. until you get all the way to Z. If young people get stuck when it is their turn to respond, they can ask for help from other students. Ask the others to remain quiet unless help is requested. Not all of the letters have an obvious emotion, so give the group permission to be creative (e.g. 'Zany', 'Zealous', 'Quizzical', 'Quirky', 'X-cited', etc.).

Exercise 2: Exploring Emotions

Part 1

Begin the session by asking the group: Why are emotions important and why do we have them?

Record their answers on the board or flipchart. After you have elicited feedback from the group, show them PowerPoint slide 2 or mention any ideas that they didn't come up with:

WHY DO WE HAVE EMOTIONS?
▷ They help us connect to each other and form relationships.
▷ They help us communicate with each other.
▷ They give us information on how we are and how to respond to different situations.
▷ They help us survive (e.g. respond to danger or threat).
▷ They affect how we think and behave.
▷ They can motivate us and help us make decisions.
▷ Life would be boring without them.
▷ They make us unique.

| Haha | Angry | Love | Sad | Wow | Like |

▲ **PowerPoint slide 2**

Part 2

Explain to the group that they are going to do an Emotional Literacy Quiz.

Get the students into about six groups and give them some paper to record their answers. A quiz can be a great way to capture the interest of the young people and to explore the knowledge in the room. This quiz is interactive and each question has different actions that the participants are expected to complete or perform. Some of the questions might require them to finish first or to select a volunteer to do some acting. You can ask the groups to make a 'team name' to make this quiz more competitive.

Before starting the quiz, let the group know that you will:

- add points for supportive comments/encouragement between team members
- add points for appropriate celebration when a team gets a point
- subtract points for any negative comments, booing or putting people down.

Quiz

1) Write down five other words you could use to describe 'sad' (the first team to say 'stop' and share their answers gets two points, the second team gets one point).

2) Ask each team to select a volunteer to come up to the front. Show the volunteers the word 'anxious' – they need to act this out and the first team to guess gets a point.

3) Write down five different songs that have the word 'love' in the title.

4) Write down six different ways you could tell if someone was 'angry' (the first team to say 'stop' and show their answers gets two points, the second team gets one point).

5) Ask each team to select a volunteer to come up to the front. The volunteers need to take it in turns to do the best fake laugh. Once they have all had a go, ask the group to vote for the best fake laugh and give that team two points.

6) Give the groups two minutes per image to come up with the best caption for the pictures on PowerPoint slides 3–6. After you have elicited feedback from each group, allocate two points to the winning team for each caption, and one point to the runner-up.

7) Ask each team to select a volunteer to come up to the front. Show them each a different emotion, written on a card (e.g. jealousy, disgust, fear, embarrassment, joy, surprise, hatred, insecurity). Each volunteer has one minute to try to describe the feeling to their team without saying the word itself. If they say the word itself, they don't get a point; if their team guesses the emotion within the minute, they get one point.

▲ **PowerPoint slide 3**[1]

▲ **PowerPoint slide 4**

1   Images courtesy of Shutterstock.

▲ PowerPoint slide 5

▲ PowerPoint slide 6

Exercise 3: Emotional Health

Part 1

Let the group know that it is often easy to know how to look after ourselves physically, but it's harder to know how to keep our minds healthy. Ask the group:

1) What does 'emotional health' mean?
2) What do we need to feel emotionally healthy?

Part 2

Show the group PowerPoint slide 7 or read out the definitions of confidence and self-esteem:

SELF-ESTEEM AND CONFIDENCE
A big aspect of emotional health is self-esteem and confidence.

Self-esteem is how you think and feel about yourself – for example, how much you like, respect and accept yourself.

Confidence is being comfortable and secure with how you look, think, feel and behave.

Body image is how you feel about your appearance and body, and can affect your confidence and self-esteem. It is not what we see in the mirror, but how we **feel** about what we see.

▲ **PowerPoint slide 7**

Part 3

Show the group the Cycle of Self-Esteem on PowerPoint slide 8 or draw the cycle on the board. Explain that how we feel about ourselves affects how we behave, which in turn affects how other people perceive us, treat us and respond to us.

The cycle of self-esteem

▲ **PowerPoint slide 8**

Part 4

Explore the Cycle of Self-Esteem by asking the young people the following questions. Can the young people come up with any specific examples?

1) If someone feels self-conscious, how might they behave? How might other people perceive and treat them?

2) If someone feels confident, how might they behave? How might other people perceive and treat them?

3) If someone feels depressed, how might they behave? How might other people perceive and treat them?

At the end of the discussion, read out or show the group PowerPoint slide 9:

People with low self-esteem or self-worth often assume that other people are more important than them, and put themselves last as a result.

When it comes to consent and relationships, it's important not to give up your own needs to please other people.

It's important to remember that your own needs are important.

▲ **PowerPoint slide 9**

Exercise 4: Body Image

Part 1

Explain that, although confidence is about more than just our appearance, how we feel about how we look can affect our confidence and self-esteem in a range of ways and situations.

Show the group PowerPoint slide 10 or read out the 'Did you know...?' statistics:

DID YOU KNOW...?

- **20%** of primary school girls have been on a diet.[2]
- Nearly **5 out of 10** teenage boys want to change their body.[3]
- **8 out of 10** teenage girls are unhappy with their body image.[4]
- **56%** of teenage boys report feeling pressure from social media to look a certain way.[5]
- **87%** of girls aged 11–21 think females are judged more on their appearance than their ability.[6]
- The number of boys being hospitalized for eating disorders is increasing, including a condition called **'Bigorexia'** which is characterized by an obsession with body shape and muscle definition.[7]

---

2   Girlguiding (2013) 'Girls' Attitudes Survey 2013.' Accessed on 14/3/2020 at www.girlguiding.org.uk/globalassets/docs-and-resources/research-and-campaigns/girls-attitudes-survey-2013.pdf

3   Rawlins, S. (2018) 'Body dissatisfaction: It's not just teenage girls.' Shout Out UK. Accessed on 14/2/2020 at www.shoutoutuk.org/2018/03/29/body-dissatisfaction-its-not-just-teenage-girls

4   Rawlins, S. (2018) 'Body dissatisfaction: It's not just teenage girls.' Shout Out UK. Accessed on 14/2/2020 at www.shoutoutuk.org/2018/03/29/body-dissatisfaction-its-not-just-teenage-girls

5   Hassall, H. (2018) 'Mental health: How body image pressure for boys has led to rise in hospital cases.' CBBC Newsround. Accessed on 6/2/2020 at www.bbc.co.uk/newsround/46301970

6   Girlguiding (2013) 'Girls' Attitudes Survey 2013.' Accessed on 14/3/2020 at www.girlguiding.org.uk/globalassets/docs-and-resources/research-and-campaigns/girls-attitudes-survey-2013.pdf

7   Hassall, H. (2018) 'Mental health: How body image pressure for boys has led to rise in hospital cases.' CBBC Newsround. Accessed on 6/2/2020 at www.bbc.co.uk/newsround/46301970

- Trans young people are at high risk for dissatisfaction with their bodies, making them particularly vulnerable to eating disorders.

▲ **PowerPoint slide 10**

Part 2

Ask the group: What affects our body image? (Facilitators' note: For example, we are surrounded by idealized images of how people 'should' look. Often women are depicted as 'sexy, skinny and glamourous' and men are depicted as 'manly, muscly and strong'. Sometimes it's not just the media but the adults around us and our peers that put pressure on us to meet these unrealistically high standards.)

Part 3

Show the group PowerPoint slide 11 depicting 'before' and 'after' shots of models whose images have been photoshopped, and/or show the videos (PowerPoint slide 12) and ask the group: What impact does photoshopping, endless filters and constant pressure on young people to look a certain way have on people's body confidence? (Facilitators' note: Answers could include eating disorders, depression, self-harm, suicide, judgement, bullying behaviours, anxiety, self-consciousness.)

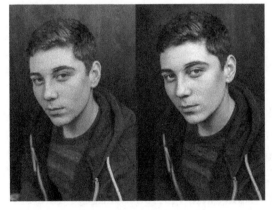 

▲ **PowerPoint slide 11**[8]

MAKING A MODEL'S FACE MORE MASCULINE
www.youtube.com/watch?v=Rg6YrdTFKmI (video length: 3 minutes 54 seconds; as this is quite long, you could start watching at 3.27).

BODY EVOLUTION
www.youtube.com/watch?v=xKQdwjGiF-s (video length: 59 seconds).

▲ **PowerPoint slide 12**

---

8   Images courtesy of Shutterstock.

Part 4

Show the group PowerPoint slide 13, or read out the quote.

Ask the group: What do you think about the quote from Dr Gail Dines? (Facilitators' note: Industries rely on people feeling dissatisfied with their appearance so they can sell more products! This is why it's so important to view everything in the media with a critical eye.)

If tomorrow, women woke up and decided they really liked their bodies, just think how many industries would go out of business.
– Dr Gail Dines

Would you say this is true of males as well?

▲ **PowerPoint slide 13**

Ask the group: Can you think of any celebrity role models who promote positive body image? After eliciting feedback, read out or show the group PowerPoint slide 14 about body image:

Our bodies come in all different shapes and sizes, but in the media they tend to come in one shape and one size!

Don't judge or shame people for how they look. **Difference is beautiful!**

▲ **PowerPoint slide 14**

Exercise 5: Exploring Resilience

Part 1

Let the group know that having negative body image can be one thing that makes us feel less emotionally healthy as it likely causes us to feel critical of ourselves, makes us compare ourselves with other people and often makes us feel not good enough.

Ask the group: What other things in our environment make us feel less emotionally healthy? (Facilitators' note: Prompt the group to think of things from a range of different environments – e.g. the media, family, school, exams, our friends and relationships.)

Note: You can conduct this as an interactive 'World Café' exercise. Have a sheet of flipchart paper on tables, with one the following headings on each: 'Media', 'Family', 'School and exams', 'Peers and relationships' (add any more categories that feel relevant). Ask the young people to visit each table in small groups and provide feedback on how these aspects of life affect our emotional health. Remind the group to talk in general terms about the impact of family, friends, relationships, etc. on a person's emotional health, rather than share information about their own personal experience.

Part 2

Let the group know that our ability to stay emotionally healthy and confident in challenging and stressful situations is called 'resilience'. Ask the group to come up with as many different words as they can that they associate with resilience and record these on the board (e.g. bouncing back, believing in yourself, managing stress, coping, staying strong, etc.).

Part 3

Explain to the group that staying resilient and believing in ourselves often depends on self-awareness. If we know our strengths and qualities, can challenge negative thought patterns, and can communicate our needs and how we feel, we are more likely to be able to manage stress and feel confident.

Part 4

Give each of the students a plain piece of paper and ask them to draw around their hand. Then give them five minutes to think of 5 different strengths, qualities or things they like about themselves, and write one on each finger and thumb on the hand. Challenge them to come up with things that *are not appearance-related*.

After they have completed this individually, ask the students to get into pairs and to give each other three compliments that *are not appearance-related*. If they choose to, they can add the compliments they have received to their hand.

Elicit feedback from the group about how they found this exercise and let them know that people often find this hard to do because it is common to hear and remember more negative news, feedback and comments about ourselves than positive ones. Encourage the students to take their picture home with them.

Part 5

Refer back to the Rights and Responsibilities activity in Workshop 2 (for every right we also have a responsibility to respect the rights of others), and ask them to finish the sentences:

- I have a right not to be judged... I have the responsibility to... (e.g. accept others)
- I have the right to thrive/reach my potential... I have the responsibility to... (e.g. see the potential in others, not limit others, not hold others back)
- I have the right to receive encouragement and praise... I have the responsibility to... (e.g. praise, compliment and encourage others/be kind)

Exercise 6: A Resilient Mindset

Part 1

Explain to the group that because we often hear more negatives than positives, we sometimes start criticizing ourselves and putting ourselves down.

Give each of the young people the Resilient Mindset worksheet (Resources and Handouts 15.1). Reassure the group that they will not need to show their answers to anyone else, but before you get them to complete the worksheet, ask them whether they recognize any of the 'self-doubt' mindset statements on the left-hand side of the page.

Let the group know that challenging self-doubt and self-criticism actually changes the way that our brain thinks and helps us see the world, others and ourselves more positively!

Ask the students to complete the resilient mindset side of the handout individually to practise challenging negative ways of thinking.

Examples for Facilitators

Self-doubt mindset	Resilient mindset
This is too hard.	Just because things are challenging doesn't mean I should give up.
I might as well not try.	It's better to try and fail than not try at all.
I can't do this.	I can do this/I can at least try.
I'm not good enough.	I am good enough/important/valued.
Everyone else can do it.	Everyone makes mistakes and learns from them. Maybe I'm misinterpreting things – I don't know whether others are struggling.
I'm so stupid.	I'm smart, and I have strengths, qualities and potential.
What's the point?	Even when they seem meaningless, it's good to give things a go.
I'll probably fail.	I'll definitely fail if I don't even try; if I give it a go, I might get something out of it.

Part 2

Ask the group for feedback on how they found this exercise. Ask if any of the students wants to share any of their resilience mindset responses and let the young people know that if they continue noticing when they have negative self-beliefs, they can begin to challenge self-doubt and negative self-talk.

Bring the session to a close by showing the group PowerPoint slide 16 or reading out the tips for confidence and self-esteem.

At the end of the tips, ask the young people whether they have anything they would add to the list.

BUILDING CONFIDENCE AND SELF-ESTEEM

▷ Remind yourself that you are **important**.

▷ **Believe** in yourself and your right to be loved and respected.

▷ Have personal **goals** and **aspirations**.

▷ Take **pride** and acknowledge when you have done something good.

▷ Keep a journal of **positive** things about yourself, or things you are **grateful** for.

▷ **Challenge yourself** to be honest about what you do and don't want (this will help you feel in control of the choices in your life).

▷ Take care of yourself and make time to do the things you **enjoy**.

▷ Understand that you will make mistakes (everybody does) – the trick is to **learn** from them.

▷ Don't compare yourself with other people – we are all **different** and **unique**.

▷ **Try** new things.

▷ Hold your head up **high**.

▷ Find things that make you **laugh**.

▲ PowerPoint slide 15

End the session with PowerPoint slide 16 and let the group know that there are many places they can go to get resources on this subject or seek support, and there are procedures in place for anonymous reporting. It is important for them to share any issues or concerns that they have about themselves or others related to this topic. Be mindful of the possible impacts and emotions that might be evoked for individuals from the discussion, and if a topic is emotive for someone, offer an opportunity to explore this outside the group, to ensure that they feel heard and safe.

SIGNPOSTING AND RESOURCES

If you are affected by any of the issues raised in today's workshop, help and support are available.

▷ **Childline:** In addition to the helpline and online support, Childline offers tips for building confidence and self-esteem on the website: www.childline.org.uk/info-advice/your-feelings/feelings-emotions/building-confidence-self-esteem

▷ **The Children's Society** runs therapeutic support, befriending, and counselling and advice services for young people who are in need of mental health support, and also has information and ideas about self-esteem on the website: www.childrenssociety.org.uk/mental-health-advice-for-children-and-young-people/self-esteem

▲ PowerPoint slide 16

Equality, Diversity, Inclusion and Individuality

I think that we should be who we are

Session Overview

This workshop explores some of the terms relating to gender identity and sexual orientation, and through the 'equality journey' charts the history of celebrating diversity. In considering celebrities with different gender identities, the young people are asked how they and society might become more inclusive and accepting of diversity and individuality.

Info/Knowledge

Our understanding of gender is constantly evolving, and this has never been more apparent; research shows that young people today have a significantly different perspective on gender to previous generations. Many consider gender to be on a spectrum rather than male/female binary. The same is true for sexual orientation; a 2015 YouGov poll revealed that nearly half of young people describe themselves as 'not 100 per cent heterosexual'.[1] This can feel challenging or even disturbing for those of us who grew up in what may have felt like a more black-and-white world, although diversity in gender identification and sexual orientation has occurred throughout history and across the globe. Our identity is of huge importance, and young people need to be allowed space to explore their own understanding about their gender and sexuality, and be given agency in

---

1   Dahlgreen, W. and Shakespeare, A.-E. (2015) '1 in 2 young people say they are not 100% heterosexual.' YouGov. Accessed on 5/2/2020 at https://yougov.co.uk/topics/lifestyle/articles-reports/2015/08/16/half-young-not-heterosexual

their choices and expressions. It can be challenging for young people who exist outside of traditional norms, and RSE is a place to emphasize the importance of respect, empathy and tolerance when it comes to expressions of individuality. Questions around this topic can be confusing, and a workshop about consent is a great opportunity to explore these complex issues and ensure that your own practice and the school community is fully inclusive and accepting of diversity. After all, consent applies to everyone equally.

PSHE Association Curriculum Themes
▷ KS4 R14. To understand the role of sex in the media and its impact on sexuality (including pornography and related sexual ethics such as consent, negotiation, boundaries, respect, gender norms, sexual 'norms', trust, communication, pleasure, orgasms, rights, empowerment, sexism and feminism)
▷ KS3 R24. About the difference between assigned/biological sex, gender identity and sexual orientation
▷ KS3 R25. To recognize that there is diversity in sexual attraction and developing sexuality
▷ KS3 R26. The terms associated with sex, gender identity and sexual orientation and to understand accepted terminology
▷ KS3 R27. About the unacceptability of sexist, homophobic, biphobic, transphobic, racist and disablist language and behaviour, the need to challenge it and how to do so

Exercises
▷ Exercise 1: Stand Up If...
▷ Exercise 2: Exploring Values and Beliefs – Group Debate
▷ Exercise 3: Difference and Diversity
▷ Exercise 4: Exploring Gender and Sexuality as a Spectrum
▷ Exercise 5: The Equality Journey and Celebrating Difference
▷ Exercise 6: Respecting, Accepting and Celebrating Difference
▷ Exercise 7: Inclusion

Materials Needed
▷ Genderbread Person handout if not using PowerPoint for Exercise 4 (Resources and Handouts 16.1)
▷ Handout of Terms and Definitions for Exercise 4 (Resources and Handouts 16.2)
▷ Access to YouTube

Learning Outcomes

By the end of this session:

- I can define and understand terminology around gender identity and sexuality
- I can explore different gender identities and challenge stereotypes/assumptions
- I can explore different sexual orientations and challenge stereotypes/assumptions
- I can respectfully describe LGBTQI+ issues affecting young people
- I can discuss hate crimes and the importance of challenging 'isms' and 'phobias' (e.g. homophobia, biphobia, transphobia, etc.)
- I know where to go for support

At the beginning of the session, inform the group of the topic – *Equality, Diversity, Inclusion and Individuality* – and point out that it requires the group to approach the discussions with a certain amount of maturity and sensitivity. Remind the group of the agreed expectations, particularly emphasizing confidentiality and the importance of treating one another with respect. Check that everyone is in agreement, looking for nods or verbal recognition that they're on the same page. Remind the group that if something comes up in the session that upsets them or makes them feel uncomfortable, they have permission to leave the room or find some space, and remind them of where they can go or who they can approach for support. Creating a safe environment is covered in more detail in the Introduction. Before starting, briefly set out what will be covered in the workshop.

Note: With this topic, it is particularly important to assume that there will be a handful of young people in your group who will be experiencing or exploring the issues covered in the exercises, and to ensure that you are facilitating the workshop sensitively, inclusively and with a curious, open mind.

Exercise 1: Stand Up If...

This exercise is about finding commonality and accepting differences. Encourage the group not to comment on each other's responses during the activity and just to notice instead.

1) Ask the group to cover their eyes or look to the floor.
2) Say 'Stand up if...' followed by one of the statements below. Once everyone has moved, invite the group to open their eyes and look around. Then instruct them to close their eyes again ready for the next statement. (Facilitators' note: If you are able to, this activity can be powerful conducted with the young people standing in a circle rather than sitting in their normal places. Adapt the wording to 'Step into the middle if...')

Example statements can include:

- You prefer cats to dogs.
- You have ever felt embarrassed.
- You have ever felt different.
- You have ever said something horrible about another person.
- You have ever felt not good enough.
- Someone has made a negative comment about you.
- You have ever felt judged.
- You've ever disliked something about yourself.
- You've ever teased someone about their appearance.
- You've ever felt pressure to fit in.
- You have ever worried about what other people think of you.
- You think everyone is unique.

3) Ask the group if anyone has their own (appropriate and on-topic) statement they want to try.

4) Lead a discussion around why the group think you've done this exercise. (Facilitators' note: This could include exploring things we have in common, realizing that we are not alone in some of our less comfortable feelings, taking responsibility for our behaviour, etc.)

Exercise 2: Exploring Values and Beliefs – Group Debate

Ask the group to imagine that there is a line across the room. Explain to the group that one side of the room is 'Agree' and the other side is 'Disagree' (you can put up signs to make this clear). Let them know that when you read out a statement they are invited to stand where they feel they are on the line in relation to the statement. If it isn't possible for the young people to move about in the room, you can ask them to put up a hand or stand up if they agree, or give out the green, amber and red cards to each participant representing 'agree', 'neither agree nor disagree' and 'disagree' in Resources and Handouts 1.1. Reassure the group that there are no right or wrong answers, that they can stand in the middle if they are unsure and that they are able to move at any time if their opinion has been swayed. Remind the group to remain respectful when listening to and debating views and opinions that differ from their own. If the group find it hard not to talk over each other, you can use an object to represent a 'talking piece' which allows the person holding it permission to speak, while everyone else needs to listen until their turn with the talking piece (see Appendix 5).

When the young people have moved to where they want to stand, facilitate a debate between individuals or sides. Feel free to contribute to the debate (there are some facilitators' notes below that may be helpful discussion points).

You don't need to go through all of the statements; pick those that seem most relevant to the group.

Once you have used a few statements, ask the group if they have any other ideas that they want to debate. It might help if the young people talk briefly in pairs to help them to come up with a statement.

- **Being gay is a choice.** (Facilitators' note: This is not the case, but it is a common myth – nearly a third of British people still believe that being gay is a choice and in some countries being gay is illegal based on the government believing that people have 'decided to be gay'.[2])
- **Bisexuals are individuals who can't make up their minds.** (Facilitators' note: Seeing bisexuals as 'indecisive', 'greedy' or 'in doubt' is both dismissive and an example of biphobia – bisexuals can even be on the receiving end of biphobic attitudes towards their sexuality from others in the LGBTQI+ community.)
- **There are more than just two genders.** (Facilitators' note: This is true – there are many ways that people can express their gender identity and we will explore this further in the workshop.)
- **All genders are equal.** (Facilitators' note: Treating people differently because of their sex, gender or gender identity is discrimination and increases the chances of hate crimes.)

Exercise 3: Difference and Diversity

Part 1

Ask the group to discuss with the person next to them what the word 'normal' means, and then ask the whole group for feedback. There is no right or wrong answer as 'normal' means different things to different people. Read out or show the group PowerPoint slide 2 for one example of how 'normal' is defined by the dictionary:

WHAT IS NORMAL?

Normal: Conforming to a standard; usual, typical or expected.

Synonyms include: common, conventional, customary, ordinary, familiar, predictable, unexceptional, predominant.

▲ **PowerPoint slide 2**

Part 2

Ask the group whether there is such a thing as 'normal' when it comes to humans. Again, there is no right or wrong answer, and this discussion is just to open up the minds and dialogue of young people about difference.

---

2   Smith, M. (2017) 'Nearly one in three Brits still think being gay is a choice.' YouGov. Accessed on 14/3/2020 at https://yougov.co.uk/topics/relationships/articles-reports/2017/02/22/nearly-one-three-brits-still-think-being-gay-choic; 'YouGov Survey Results.' Accessed on 14/3/2020 at https://d25d2506sfb94s.cloudfront.net/cumulus_uploads/document/waaljvz3ed/InternalResults_170217_Homosexuality_W.pdf

Part 3

Watch the video 'Everyone's Welcome' made by CBeebies:

www.bbc.co.uk/cbeebies/grownups/everyones-welcome (video length: 1 minute 58 seconds).

▲ **PowerPoint slide 3**

Following the video ask the group:

1) What message is this video conveying? (Facilitators' note: When it comes to difference, children see things differently.)
2) How does our view of 'difference' change as we get older?
3) What attitudes do we have towards people who are viewed as 'different'? (Facilitators' note: Whether differences are to do with appearance, sexual orientation, gender identity, race, mental health issues or disabilities, our brains are hardwired to seek out people who are similar to us, which is why accepting difference can be so difficult for some people and can lead them to try and label others or put people into boxes and categories.)
4) What does 'stigma' mean?

Part 4

After eliciting responses from the group show them PowerPoint slide 4 or read them the definition of 'stigma':

WHAT IS STIGMA?
Stigma: A mark of disgrace associated with a particular circumstance, quality or person.

Synonyms: Shame, disgrace, dishonour.

▲ **PowerPoint slide 4**

Ask the group: What could be the impact of being stigmatized? You could write the group's ideas on the board or a flipchart.

After you've elicited feedback, you can add any additional ideas by sharing the list below:

- increased mental health problems
- feeling like you don't 'fit in' or belong
- experiencing discrimination or hate crimes
- isolation and loneliness
- being disowned by your family
- feeling ashamed of who you are.

Read out or show the group PowerPoint slide 5 before moving on to the next section:

We live in a society that is becoming more tolerant, understanding and accepting of the diverse range of **sexual orientations** and **gender identities**. The more people understand about **difference** and **diversity**, the easier it becomes to act **inclusively** towards people who are different from ourselves.

We know that the more people can be themselves (**without fear** of being judged, stigmatized, harassed or abused), the **happier** and more **resilient** people are. But there is still some way to go before homophobia, biphobia and transphobia are non-existent. We are working towards a society that not only accepts, but **celebrates difference**.

▲ PowerPoint slide 5

Exercise 4: Exploring Gender and Sexuality as a Spectrum

Part 1

Remind the group about the difference between 'Sex' and 'Gender' that we covered in Workshop 14 (you can also read out or show them PowerPoint slide 6 to recap):

SEX, GENDER AND GENDER IDENTITY

Sex: The UK Government (ONS) defines sex as 'referring to the biological aspects of an individual as determined by their anatomy, which is produced by their chromosomes, hormones and their interactions; generally male or female; something that is defined at birth'.

Gender is more difficult to define. It often refers to the perceived 'roles' of a male or female in society (**gender role**) or to an individual's concept of themselves (**gender identity**).

Sex has a basis in science whereas gender is a socially constructed way for people to identify with their sex. People don't always identify with the sex they were born with (**gender incongruence**, or **gender dysphoria** if accompanied by discomfort or distress).

▲ PowerPoint slide 6

Part 2

Explain the difference between gender identity and sexuality, using PowerPoint slide 7:

GENDER IDENTITY AND SEXUALITY

Gender identity refers to the gender(s) we identify with, whereas **sexuality** refers to which gender, or gender identity, we are romantically and/or sexually attracted to.

You can't tell someone's gender identity or sexuality just by looking at them.

Gender identity and **sexuality** are only one element of people's character – not the whole person.

▲ PowerPoint slide 7

Part 3

Before moving on to explore the 'Genderbread Person', do a quick quiz to see if anyone in the group knows what LGBTQI+ stands for... (i.e. lesbian, gay, bisexual, transgender, queer and intersex). The + represents other sexual identities (e.g. pansexual and asexual) and also means that the term is inclusive of people who don't identify with any of the existing labels but still identify as part of the queer community (e.g. don't identify as 'straight' or 'cisgender').

Let the group know that although it is important to have awareness of the terminology, the boxes and labels we use to define people don't actually tell us anything about them. Introduce the Genderbread Person,[3] either on PowerPoint slide 8 or using the handout (Resources and Handouts 16.1).

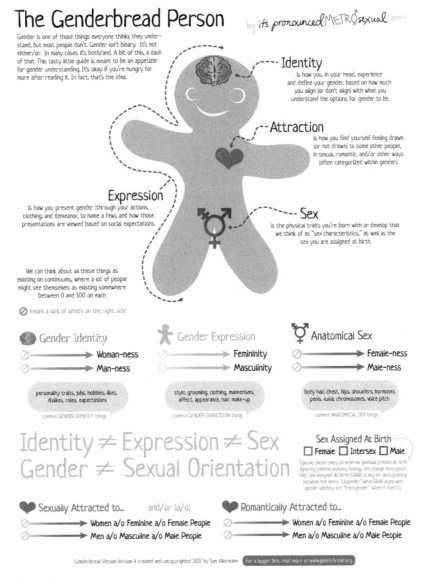

▲ **PowerPoint slide 8**

---

3   Created by Sam Killermann. www.itspronouncedmetrosexual.com
    Image reproduced courtesy of Sam Killermann.

Part 4

Go through each of the spectrums on the Genderbread Person, pointing out that each identity and expression is on a continuum – there are many grey areas rather just being black and white.

Ask the group if they have any questions about the Genderbread Person.

To reinforce the point that identity and expression go beyond male, female, gay or straight, move on to the terminology section exploring sexual orientation/ sexual attraction. Make the group aware that with definitions relating to identity, it's important to always trust the person's definition of themselves over anything else. The definitions they are sorting through are guidelines only as no description can perfectly and accurately reflect a label for everyone and boxing people in can limit rather than free people.

Part 5

In small groups, ask the young people to match the words with their definition (Resources and Handouts 16.2). (Facilitators' note: Terms and definitions quickly go out of date. Ensure that you are up to date, by checking with a respected source such as Stonewall.[4])

Facilitators' Answers[5]

Term	Definition
Ally	A (typically) straight and/or cis person who supports members of the LGBTQI+ community (an Upstander).
Bi/bisexual	An umbrella term used to describe a romantic and/or sexual orientation towards more than one gender.
Cis/cisgender	Someone whose gender identity is the same as the sex they were assigned at birth. Non-trans is also sometimes used.
Gay/homosexual	A term used to describe someone who has a romantic and/or sexual orientation towards someone of the same gender – some women define themselves as gay rather than lesbian.
Gender dysphoria	Used to describe when a person experiences discomfort or distress because there is a mismatch between their sex assigned at birth and their gender identity. This is also the clinical diagnosis for someone who doesn't feel comfortable with the sex they were assigned at birth.
Heterosexual/straight	Sexual or romantic attraction to people of the opposite sex.

---

4   Stonewall (n.d.) 'Glossary of terms.' Accessed on 5/2/2020 at www.stonewall.org.uk/help-advice/glossary-terms
5   Definitions reproduced with kind permission from Stonewall (n.d.) 'Glossary of terms.' Accessed on 5/2/2020 at www.stonewall.org.uk/help-advice/glossary-terms

Homophobia/ biphobia/lesbophobia	The fear or dislike of someone, based on prejudice or negative attitudes, beliefs or views about lesbian, gay or bi people, which may include bullying behaviour and discrimination.
Intersex	A term used to describe a person who may have the biological attributes of both sexes or whose biological attributes do not fit with societal assumptions about 'male' or 'female'. Intersex individuals may identify as male, female or non-binary.
Lesbian	Refers to a woman who has a romantic and/or sexual orientation towards women.
Non-binary	An umbrella term for people whose gender identity doesn't sit comfortably with simply 'man' or 'woman'.
Pan/pansexual	Refers to a person whose romantic and/or sexual attraction towards others is not limited by sex or gender.
Trans	An umbrella term to describe people whose gender is not the same as, or does not sit comfortably with, the sex they were assigned at birth. People may describe themselves using one or more of a wide variety of terms, including (but not limited to) transgender, transsexual, gender-queer (GQ), gender-fluid, non-binary, gender-variant, genderless, agender, nongender, third gender, bi-gender, trans man, trans woman, trans masculine, trans feminine and neutrois.

Part 6

At the end of the exercise, reveal the correct definition for each of the terms and ask the groups to score themselves out of 12. You can make this activity more competitive by giving the winning group a prize. Elicit feedback on how the group found the task and whether they have any questions. Remind the group again that gender identity/ expression and sexuality are part of people's character – not the whole person.

Exercise 5: The Equality Journey and Celebrating Difference

Part 1

Let the group know that Pride celebrated its 50-year anniversary in 2019. Pride is a celebration of the LGBTQI+ community and a platform for continuing the fight for equality.

Part 2

Show the group PowerPoint slide 9 or read out some of the key moments and milestones the LGBTQI+ community have experienced in their fight for equality, including many victories as well as many obstacles.

We've come a long way	There's a long way to go!
1969: LGBTQI+ people of colour lead the Stonewall Uprising in New York, where members of the community protested against continued oppression by the police and society in general.	**1940s–1960s:** LGBTQI+ individuals were regularly being arrested for violating what was called the 'three-piece-article rule' (a law which never actually existed), which required a person to wear at least three gender-appropriate articles of clothing to avoid being arrested for cross-dressing.
1972: The first official UK Gay Pride takes place in London to encourage the LGBTQI+ community to celebrate and embrace their identity.	**1952:** The American Psychiatric Association's *Diagnostic and Statistical Manual of Mental Disorders* includes homosexuality as a mental health problem/sociopathic personality disorder.
1978: Inspired by Harvey Milk to develop a symbol of pride and hope for the LGBTQI+ community, Gilbert Baker designs and stitches together the first rainbow flag.	**1953:** In the USA, President Eisenhower signs an executive order which bans people who are homosexual from working for the federal government, stating that they are a 'security risk'.
1987: Princess Diana opens the UK's first purpose-built unit for the treatment of patients with HIV. She helped destigmatize and myth-bust common misconceptions about HIV and AIDS by shaking the hands of patients without wearing gloves.	**Early 1980s:** London is hit by the AIDS crisis, with thousands diagnosed with HIV over the course of the next decade, causing more stigma and discrimination towards the LGBTQI+ community.
1988: Many protests were staged by lesbian activists against the planned enactment of Section 28, which stated that the government could not 'intentionally promote homosexuality or publish material with the intention of promoting homosexuality' or 'promote the teaching in any maintained school of the acceptability of homosexuality as a pretended family relationship'. Protests included invading the BBC's Six O'Clock News and abseiling into Parliament.	**1987:** Prime Minister Margaret Thatcher delivers an anti-gay speech at a Conservative Party Conference, seen by many as setting the foundations for Section 28 being passed, which includes her stating that she doesn't believe children should be taught that they have the right to be gay.
2000: Lesbian, gay and bisexual people are finally able to openly serve in the British Armed Forces, and the House of Lords finally passes a law that the age of consent is equal for homosexual and heterosexual couples in the UK.	**26 July 2017:** President Donald Trump tweets that 'The United States Government will not accept or allow Transgender Individuals to serve in any capacity in the US Military'.

2013: Same-sex couples can now legally marry in England and Wales (Scotland followed in 2014).	**2019:** Even after 50 years of Pride marches, homophobic, biphobic and transphobic protestors continue to hijack Pride celebrations all over the world and the number of attacks on trans individuals triples.
2016: There are 40 MPs in the UK Parliament who identify as LGBTQI+, which is more than there are anywhere else in the world.[6]	**The fight for equal rights continues…**

▲ **PowerPoint slide 9**

Part 3

Let the group know that despite many victories in the fight for equality for LGBTQI+ individuals and communities, there is still a long way to go, and these communities still face prejudice, discrimination, stigma and oppression in many parts of the world, including in Britain.

Read out or show the group PowerPoint slide 10, with statistics collated from Stonewall,[7] who campaign for 'Acceptance without Exception':

DID YOU KNOW…?

Changes in the law don't always translate into true equality, and there is still much progress and change to be made:

- **One in five** LGBTQI+ people have experienced a hate crime or incident due to their sexual orientation and/or their gender identity in the past year.
- **Two in five** trans people have experienced a hate crime or incident because of their gender identity in the past year. **81%** of these individuals did not report the incident to the police.
- **29%** of LGBTQI+ individuals avoid certain places because they don't feel safe, and **36%** don't feel comfortable walking down the street holding their partner's hand (this increases to **58%** for gay men).

▲ **PowerPoint slide 10**

Part 4

After eliciting any feedback on PowerPoint slide 10, watch the video of Pink sharing her opinions on gay marriage:

---

6   Hooper, M. (2016) 'The UK has more LGBT MPs than anywhere else in the world.' *Gay Times*. Accessed on 6/2/2020 at www.gaytimes. co.uk/community/28378/the-uk-has-more-lgbt-mps-than-anywhere-else-in-the-world

7   Bachmann, C.L. and Gooch, B. (n.d.) *LGBT in Britain: Hate Crime and Discrimination*. London: Stonewall. Accessed on 20/7/2020 at www.stonewall.org.uk/system/files/lgbt_in_britain_hate_crime.pdf

www.goalcast.com/2017/05/17/pink-its-all-about-love (video length: 1 minute 25 seconds).

▲ **PowerPoint slide 11**

Elicit feedback from the group about the video including:

1) What do you think about Pink's statement?
2) What are the obstacles to saying or hearing 'I'm gay' being as commonplace as saying 'I'm a Virgo'?

Exercise 6: Respecting, Accepting and Celebrating Difference

Part 1

Explain that this exercise is about exploring gender identity in society. Begin by eliciting a discussion using the following prompts:

1) Is society inclusive of people who don't identify as cisgender?
2) Is the media representative of all different gender identities, gender expressions and sexual orientations?

Part 2

Let the group know that being an advocate, ally and Upstander for individuals who identify as LGBTQI+ involves awareness of the privileges and benefits attached to being cisgender and/or heterosexual. Read out or show the group PowerPoint slide 12 and lead a discussion about it:

Being an advocate, ally or Upstander for others involves being aware of the **privileges** and **benefits** attached to being cisgender and/or heterosexual.

Imagine if...

1. You had to **come out** to your family as straight.
2. You had to **hide** your sexuality from other people for fear of their reaction/rejection.
3. People told you **not to** 'flaunt' or express your 'straightness' in public.
4. You were a **target** for verbal, physical and emotional violence based on your sexual orientation and/or gender identity/expression.
5. People **dismissed** your sexual identity by thinking your straightness was **'just a phase'**.
6. People **assumed** that there was 'something wrong with you' because of your sexual orientation and/or gender identity/expression.

7. People thought it was OK to ask what sort of genitals you had and how you have sex.
8. People **tokenized**, **fetishized** or **hypersexualized** your sexual orientation and/or gender identity/expression.
9. Your gender was **not an option** on a form.
10. You had to **explain** your sexual orientation and/or gender identity/expression to strangers.
11. You had to **defend** your rights as a human for **not fitting into** other people's views of 'normal'.

▲ **PowerPoint slide 12**

Part 3

Show the young people the 'Did you know...?' PowerPoint slides 13–16 exploring celebrities who advocate for diversity and are open about their non-conforming gender identities:

DID YOU KNOW...?

Conchita Wurst, who has been described as a 'Bearded Beyoncé'[8] and won the Eurovision Song Contest for Austria, uses masculine pronouns (he, him) when referring to himself, and feminine pronouns when he is referring to Conchita.

Conchita, aka Tom, is an ambassador for gender fluidity. Tom is also gay, so when he is Conchita, she is a trans straight woman (sexually and romantically attracted to males).

▲ **PowerPoint slide 13**[9]

---

8   Lees, P. (2014) 'Drag queen? Transgender? Conchita's an ambassador and that's what matters.' *The Guardian.* Accessed on 5/12/2020 at www.theguardian.com/commentisfree/2014/may/12/conchita-drag-queen-transgender-ambassador-eurovision-winner-trans-gender-diversity
9   Image courtesy of Shutterstock.

DID YOU KNOW...?

RuPaul identifies as a drag queen and is indifferent toward gender-specific pronouns used to address him – he tweeted: 'You can call me he. You can call me she. You can call me Regis and Kathie Lee; I don't care. Just as long as you call me.'[10]

RuPaul's Drag Race supports other drag artists on to the stage, but RuPaul has stated that he doesn't allow trans people who are or have transitioned on to his show as he doesn't see this counting as 'drag'. RuPaul also famously said, 'My hope is that my career will be a shining example to children everywhere that life is more meaningful when you are not afraid to see all the colours of the rainbow.'[11]

▲ **PowerPoint slide 14**[12]

DID YOU KNOW...?

Both Miley Cyrus and Ruby Rose identify as gender-fluid and bisexual.

▲ **PowerPoint slide 15**[13]

---

10   RuPaul's Drag Race @RuPaulsDragRace, 30 May 2013.
11   https://rupaulsdragrace.fandom.com/wiki/RuPaul
12   Image courtesy of Shutterstock.
13   Images courtesy of Shutterstock.

DID YOU KNOW...?
Sam Smith identifies as gender non-binary and gender-queer.

▲ **PowerPoint slide 16**[14]

Exercise 7: Inclusion

Part 1

Let the group know that the rules and laws of consent are true for everyone. Re-read the definition of consent or show PowerPoint slide 17. Ask the group: Is this definition of consent inclusive? (Facilitators' note: You could point out that the answer is no, because it states he/she.)

A person consents if he or she agrees by choice with the freedom and capacity to do so.
– Sexual Offences Act 2003

▲ **PowerPoint slide 17**

Part 2

Ask the group to rewrite the definition of consent so that is inclusive. (Facilitators' note: Examples include 'A person consents if *they* agree by choice, with the freedom and capacity to do so' or 'A person consents if *everyone* agrees by choice with the freedom and capacity to do so'.)

---

14   Image courtesy of Shutterstock.

Part 3

Ask the group how they think society can become more inclusive and accepting of diversity and individuality. (Facilitators' note: This could include increased media coverage and normalization of the LGBTQI+ community in the media, being a friend or an ally to LGBTQI+ individuals, being aware of the privileges and opportunities given to cisgender and heterosexual people.)

Part 4

Refer back to the Rights and Responsibilities activity in Workshop 2 (for every right we also have a responsibility to respect the rights of others). Let the group know that people who don't identify as cisgender or heterosexual have the same rights to dignity, respect and safety as everyone else, and ask them what their responsibility as individuals is to respect the rights of others (e.g. I have the responsibility to accept, respect, celebrate and include difference; I have the responsibility not to jeopardize other people's safety, not to make assumptions, not to treat others unfairly, etc.).

Read out or show the group PowerPoint slide 18:

Equal rights for others does not mean fewer rights for you.

It's not pie.

▲ PowerPoint slide 18

End the session with PowerPoint slide 19 and let the group know that there are many places they can go to get resources on this subject or seek support, and there are procedures in place for anonymous reporting. It is important for them to share any issues or concerns that they have about themselves or others related to this topic. Be mindful of the possible impacts and emotions that might be evoked for individuals from the discussion, and if a topic is emotive for someone, offer an opportunity to explore this outside the group, to ensure that they feel heard and safe.

SIGNPOSTING AND RESOURCES

If you are affected by the issues from today's workshop, help is available.

▷ **Stonewall** offers information and support for people who are LGBTQI+ and their allies. You can contact Stonewall's Information Service on Freephone 0800 0502020. Lines are open from 9.30am to 4.30pm, Monday to Friday.

▷ **Gendered Intelligence** is a not-for-profit organization which provides support for trans young people aged 8–25. Check out their website: www.genderedintelligence.co.uk

▲ PowerPoint slide 19

Ten Principles of PSHE Education

The PSHE Association has produced its ten principles for effective PSHE education:[1]

1) Start where children and young people are: find out what they already know, understand, are able to do and are able to say. For maximum impact involve them in the planning of your PSHE education programme.

2) Plan a 'spiral programme' which introduces new and more challenging learning, while building on what has gone before, which reflects and meets the personal developmental needs of the children and young people.

3) Take a positive approach which does not attempt to induce shock or guilt but focuses on what children and young people can do to keep themselves and others healthy and safe and to lead happy and fulfilling lives.

4) Offer a wide variety of teaching and learning styles within PSHE education, with an emphasis on interactive learning and the teacher as facilitator.

5) Provide information which is realistic and relevant and which reinforces positive social norms.

6) Encourage young people to reflect on their learning and the progress they have made, and to transfer what they have learned to say and to do from one school subject to another, and from school to their lives in the wider community.

7) Recognize that the PSHE education programme is just one part of what a school can do to help a child to develop the knowledge, skills, attitudes and understanding they need to fulfil their potential. Link the PSHE education programme to other whole school approaches, to pastoral support, and provide a setting where the responsible choice becomes the easy choice. Encourage staff, families and the wider community to get involved.

8) Embed PSHE education within other efforts to ensure children and young people have positive relationships with adults, feel valued and where those who are most vulnerable are identified and supported.

---

1   PSHE Association (2014) 'Ten principles of effective PSHE education.' Accessed on 6/2/2020 at www.pshe-association.org.uk/curriculum-and-resources/resources/ten-principles-effective-pshe-education

9) Provide opportunities for children and young people to make real decisions about their lives, to take part in activities which simulate adult choices and where they can demonstrate their ability to take responsibility for their decisions.

10) Provide a safe and supportive learning environment where children and young people can develop the confidence to ask questions, challenge the information they are offered, draw on their own experience, express their views and opinions and put what they have learned into practice in their own lives.

Information about RSE

It is important for anyone delivering RSE to stay up to date with government guidance and Ofsted requirements. The following documents provide helpful guidance on the teaching of RSE.

Sex and Relationship Education Guidance (2000)

Guidance for head teachers, teachers and school governors.
https://assets.publishing.service.gov.uk/government/uploads/system/uploads/attachment_data/file/283599/sex_and_relationship_education_guidance.pdf

Relationships education, relationships and sex education (RSE) and health education: FAQs

Information from the Department for Education about the introduction of compulsory relationships education and RSE from September 2020.
www.gov.uk/government/news/relationships-education-relationships-and-sex-education-rse-and-health-education-faqs

Working Together to Safeguard Children (DfE 2018)

A guide to inter-agency working to safeguard and promote the welfare of children.
www.gov.uk/government/publications/working-together-to-safeguard-children--2

The Equality Act 2010 and schools

Advice for schools; guidance to help schools understand how the Equality Act affects them and how to fulfil their duties under the Act.
https://assets.publishing.service.gov.uk/government/uploads/system/uploads/attachment_data/file/315587/Equality_Act_Advice_Final.pdf

Key Organizations

There is lots of support out there, including up-to-date CPD and training available.

PSHE Association

Guidance, resources and training on every aspect of PSHE.
www.pshe-association.org.uk

Brook

A national charity offering resources, training, clinical sexual health and education and wellbeing services for young people.
www.brook.org.uk

Sex Education Forum

Resources, training and support to help schools achieve quality RSE.
www.sexeducationforum.org.uk

Childnet International

PSHE resources, guidance, reporting tools and helplines to support professionals in helping to keep children and young people safe online.
www.childnet.com

Online Times Educational Supplement

Includes resources and PSHE lesson plans.
www.tes.com/resources/search/?&q=rse

Protective Behaviours Consortium

Training courses, resources and information about protective behaviours.
www.protectivebehavioursconsortium.co.uk

Transforming Conflict

Training and consultancy in the field of restorative approaches in schools, residential care and other youth settings.
https://transformingconflict.org

Stonewall

Best practice guidance, toolkits and resources to support schools and other organizations in creating inclusive and accepting cultures for LGBTQI+ young people.
www.stonewall.org.uk/about-us/our-mission-and-priorities

Gendered Intelligence

A charity that works to support the trans community by delivering trans youth programmes, providing support for parents/carers, and offering professional development and trans awareness training for schools, colleges, universities and other educational settings.
http://genderedintelligence.co.uk

Unicef Rights Respecting Schools Award

Unicef's Rights Respecting Schools Award recognizes a school's achievement in putting the United Nations Convention on the Rights of the Child into practice within the school and beyond.
www.unicef.org.uk/rights-respecting-schools

Resources Out There[1]

There are loads of resources on RSE out there, some with the PSHE Quality Mark. Here is a small selection.

PSHE Association

The PSHE Association has lots of guidance for adults delivering RSE, including 'Handling Sensitive or Controversial Issues'.
www.ghll.org.uk/sensitive%20issues%20pshe%20Association.pdf

NSPCC

The NSPCC offers guidance on handling disclosures by children and young people.
www.nspcc.org.uk/keeping-children-safe/reporting-abuse/what-to-do-child-reveals-abuse

They also give guidance for talking about difficult topics, and ideas for parents about how to broach difficult topics with their children.
www.nspcc.org.uk/keeping-children-safe/support-for-parents/talking-about-difficult-topics

There is also guidance for parents on keeping their children safe online.
www.nspcc.org.uk/keeping-children-safe/online-safety/talking-child-online-safety

Childline

Childline is a counselling service provided by the NSPCC for children and young people up to 18 in the United Kingdom. Most children will be aware of Childline and they can be encouraged to remember the helpline number and signposted to the website. The Childline website also has links to support for professionals and parents, and offers

---

1   The authors cannot accept responsibility for the appropriateness or quality of these resources. Facilitators are advised to check the suitability of all resources before using them or recommending them to students and/or parents and carers.

resources including posters and credit-card-sized cards with the Childline number that can be given out to children and young people.
www.childline.org.uk/about/about-childline

Brook

Brook has developed a traffic light tool with examples of presenting sexual behaviours, to help professionals respond appropriately.
www.brook.org.uk/our-work/the-sexual-behaviours-traffic-light-tool

SAFE! Support for young people affected by crime

The charity SAFE! has developed a series of videos created by teenagers for teenagers exploring issues such as sexting, online gambling and online abuse.
www.safestories.org

NWG Network

The NWG Network provides information to professionals about child sexual exploitation.
www.nwgnetwork.org/agency-structure-abused-consent-relation-young-peoples-decision-making

Thinkuknow

NCA-CEOP offers an education programme called Thinkuknow, with resources exploring the risks children and young people face online, including a film that addresses sexting issues called 'First to a Million'.
www.thinkuknow.co.uk
www.thinkuknow.co.uk/professionals/resources/first-to-a-million

The Grid

The Grid have put together a useful booklet on sexting in schools:
'Sexting' in schools: advice and support around self-generated images – What to do and how to handle it.
http://www.thegrid.org.uk/info/welfare/child_protection/documents/sexting-booklet.pdf

Sex Education Forum

The Sex Education Forum has produced an e-magazine on teaching about pornography.
www.sexeducationforum.org.uk/resources/sex-educational-supplement.aspx

Farrer & Co

Farrer & Co have created a peer-on-peer abuse toolkit in collaboration with Dr Carlene Firmin which offers practical guidance for schools on how to prevent, identify early and respond appropriately to peer-on-peer abuse.
www.farrer.co.uk/news-and-insights/peer-on-peer-abuse-toolkit

Media Smart

Media Smart has developed a set of teachers' notes and a lesson plan on body image, which introduces the connection between the media and young people's perceptions of body image.
https://mediasmart.uk.com

Raisingchildren.net.au

Australian parenting site Raisingchildren.net.au has some interesting ideas on media and its influences.
www.raisingchildren.net.au

Young Minds

Young Minds has created a Parents' Guide to supporting young people with low self-esteem.
https://youngminds.org.uk/find-help/for-parents/parents-guide-to-support-a-z/parents-guide-to-support-self-esteem

Council for Disabled Children

The Council for Disabled Children has produced a booklet for parents of children and young people with disabilities in relation to sex education.
https://councilfordisabledchildren.org.uk/sites/default/files/uploads/documents/import/growing-up-sex-and-relationships.pdf

Books

What Does Consent Really Mean? by Pete Wallis and Thalia Wallis (Jessica Kingsley Publishers, 2018)
  A graphic novel about a group of teenagers chatting about consent on their way home from school.
Fault Line by Crista Desir (Simon Pulse, 2013)
  Written from the perspective of the boyfriend of a rape victim.
Some Boys by Patty Blount (Sourcebooks Fire, 2014)
  Written from the point of view of both a victim and a friend of the perpetrator.

Unslut by Emily Lindin (Zest Books, 2015)

> The diary of a middle-school girl who was 'slut-shamed' after going to 'third base' with her boyfriend. It is annotated by the author as an adult, who provides context and perspective.

Asking For It by Kate Harding (Da Capo Lifelong Books, 2015)

> Addresses rape culture, with ideas and suggestions for how we as a culture can take rape much more seriously without compromising the rights of the accused.

May I Kiss You? A Candid Look at Dating, Communication, Respect, and Sexual Assault Awareness by Michael J. Domitrz (Awareness Publications, 2003)

> A friendly, collaborative approach to the topic of express consent.

We Need to Talk about Pornography: A Resource to Educate Young People about the Potential Impact of Pornography and Sexualised Images on Relationships, Body Image and Self-Esteem by Vanessa Rogers (Jessica Kingsley Publishers, 2016)

> A resource book for teachers which covers issues including pornography, sexting, revenge porn and the law, for delivery to young people aged 11–19.

Working in a Circle

It can help to create a safe and open atmosphere if you are able to arrange the room with the chairs in a circle (recognizing that this may be impracticable if you are delivering an assembly in a lecture theatre or working in a classroom with regimented tables and chairs). There are many benefits to circle work, which is inclusive, non-hierarchical and encourages accountability and participation. You may wish to introduce a 'talking piece' (such as a juggling ball), which ensures that everyone has an opportunity to speak and feel heard, and can help in creating a respectful atmosphere. Here are some thoughts on using the talking piece:

- Explain the rules of using the talking piece:
  - The ball will be passed round the circle – not thrown across it!
  - Only the person holding the talking piece may speak (although you as facilitator are allowed to intervene and direct the conversation or ask clarifying questions).
  - It is fine to say 'pass' if you don't wish to speak.
  - Once the ball has gone around the circle, the facilitator will check in with anyone who didn't speak, to see if they wish to do so now.
- You can start the conversation yourself, and then pass the ball in a chosen direction, or ask if anyone would like to start. If you have a volunteer, ask them in which direction they wish to pass the ball once they have finished sharing.

Popcorn vs Creeping Death

The downside of passing a talking piece round the circle is that it creates a 'creeping death', with people seeing the ball coming closer to them, and feeling pressure to speak. It may be helpful to be aware of this, and mix up your activities. If you choose to do the 'popcorn' version where young people can throw the ball across the circle, ensure you instruct the group to use underarm throws and make eye contact or use the name of the young person they intend to receive the ball. This means that people can share when they are inspired to speak rather than feeling that they have to add something to the circle.

Eliciting Ground Rules

This exercise was created by Belinda Hopkins, drawing on the understanding of the importance of needs developed by Marshall Rosenburg (who developed the non-violent communication (NVC) approach). It is reproduced here with grateful thanks.

Creating a safe atmosphere is vital before initiating conversations about relationships and consent. This is a collaborative exercise for establishing ground rules.

You may want to start off with your own rules for the session or programme. These may include confidentiality, asking the young people not to share their own personal stories or talk about others in the group.

1) Write on a flipchart/whiteboard: 'What I need from others [in the class or group] to work at my best' (in a large group, you may need more than one flipchart sheet).

2) Give each participant three Post-its.

3) Invite everyone to write three things that they need from the others in the room to work at their best in today's session(s).

4) Ask each participant to stick their Post-its on the flipchart/whiteboard, and then sit down again. As they do so, start clustering the Post-its into themes. It is helpful to have 'respect' represented, and you and your co-facilitator may wish to join in the exercise, adding your own needs.

5) Give each participant a flipchart pen (or three sticky coloured spots). Explain that they now have three votes. When they come up to the flipchart/whiteboard, they can draw/stick a spot on their top three needs. They can choose their own Post-it, vote for someone else's if they prefer it, and use more than one vote on one Post-it if it is very important to them.

6) Quickly count the votes and present the result (this might be best done by your co-facilitator while you keep the group focus). You should now have a mutual agreement for the group, prioritized by importance, which you can write up on a fresh flipchart. Check that everyone is willing to sign up to the agreement. This can be displayed on a wall. You can refer back to it if people need reminding of the agreement, and you can check that everyone feels it is being adhered to, to ensure that all needs are being met.

Tip: The process of people queueing to place their Post-its on the flipchart or board and placing their votes can become a bit chaotic in a big group, and the exercise may need adapting – for example, by only giving everyone a single Post-it and voting from their seats.

Example Ground Rules

These example ground rules are reproduced with kind permission from the PSHE Association's resource 'Handling complex issues safely in the PSHE education classroom and creating a safe learning environment'.[1]

- **Openness:** We will be open and honest, but not discuss directly our own or others' personal/private lives. We will discuss examples but will not use names or descriptions which could identify anyone.
- **Keep the conversation in the room:** We feel safe discussing issues and we know that our teacher will not repeat what is said in the classroom unless they are concerned we are at risk, in which case they will follow the school's safeguarding policy.
- **Non-judgemental approach:** It is OK for us to disagree with another person's point of view but we will not judge, make fun of, or put anybody down. We will 'challenge the opinion, not the person'.
- **Right to pass:** Taking part is important. However, we have the right to pass on answering a question or participating in an activity and we will not put anyone 'on the spot'.
- **Make no assumptions:** We will not make assumptions about people's values, attitudes, behaviours, identity, life experiences or feelings. We will listen to the other person's point of view respectfully and expect to be listened to ourselves.
- **Using appropriate language:** We will use correct terms rather than slang terms, as they can be offensive. If we are not sure what the correct term is, we will ask our teacher.
- **Asking questions:** We are encouraged to ask questions and they are valued by our teacher. However, we do not ask personal questions or anything intended to deliberately try to embarrass someone.
- **Seeking help and advice:** If we need further help or advice, we know how and where to seek it – both in school and in the community. We will encourage friends to seek help if we think they need it.

---

1   www.pshe-association.org.uk/curriculum-and-resources/resources/handling-complex-issues-safely-pshe-education

The Body Scan: A Grounding/ Ending Exercise

At the end of a session, it may be helpful to bring the group back to the present with a grounding exercise, before sending them off to another lesson, particularly if the subject matter has been potentially distressing for the young people. Here is an example of a mindfulness exercise that can be safely used with young people.

1) Sit up in your chair on the middle of your sitting bones, with an alert posture. Feel your feet touching the floor. Now close your eyes. Become aware of your breath. Imagine your breath is saturated with kindness as you breathe in, and with acceptance as you breathe out. It is normal for your mind to go off into criticizing your body, which happens to most of us, but know that the breath is full of kindness and acceptance. You can choose to believe the breath rather than the mind.

2) Imagine your head is like a balloon. As you breathe in, it fills and swells with the breath. As you breathe out, it softens a little. Do that for a few breaths.

3) Now bring your awareness to your neck. Imagine that your neck is like a balloon. You can feel your breath in your neck and throat as the air goes in and out.

4) Do the same for the arms, imagining them like balloons filling with kindness and emptying with acceptance as you breathe.

5) Now move your awareness of the breath to your chest. Feel it expanding and softening like a balloon. You might notice how the breath moves your back and sides as well as the front.

6) Then you move your awareness to the belly. Notice your belly rising and falling as you breathe in a more relaxed way. You might notice how the breath moves your back and sides as well as your belly.

7) Do the same for the legs, imagining them like balloons filling and emptying as you breathe.

8) End by feeling your feet on the floor, and your whole body full of kindness and acceptance.

Discuss the role of kindness and acceptance in our relationships.

Games and Safe Place Visualization

Ultimate Rock, Paper, Scissors

Instructions

Ask the group to get into pairs for the first round of Rock, Paper, Scissors (if there is an odd number, you can invite someone to volunteer as the referee, or have a quick three-player knock-out round to determine which pair will take part in the rest of the tournament).

Round 1

Instruct each pair to play three games of Rock, Paper, Scissors. The person who wins two of these games is through to the next round.

Round 2

Ask each of the winners to find a new (also winning) partner for round 2.

Encourage everyone who is knocked out to be the cheerleader for the person who beat them in round 1.

Instruct each pair to play three games of Rock, Paper, Scissors. The person who wins two of these games is through to round 3. And so on until there are only two ultimate champions left.

People who have been knocked out are encouraged to continue cheerleading for others in the tournament, so when there are two ultimate champions left, there will be a group of people cheering each side on.

The last person standing is the winner, which means they will not have lost any of the previous rounds before the final.

Count 21

Instructions

The aim of this game is for the group to collectively count from 1 to 21 with each number spoken by a different person, and only one person at a time. There should be no prior agreement as to who says what or when, and no 'shotgunning' or assigning numbers to particular students.

Ask all the students to look down or to close their eyes. This game is about mind-reading so discourage eye contact or whispering.

Anyone can start the round by saying 1, and the game continues with people shouting out the next number, trying to reach 21. If two or more people shout a number at the same time, you go back to 1 and start again.

Note: If 21 seems too ambitious, you can start with a lower number (e.g. 11).

Facilitators' tip: If the group are enjoying this game and you have time, you can add in a new rule which says that the person who says '21' (or whatever number you are aiming for) can add a new rule for the next round – for example, instead of saying 4, we now say 'banana'. If someone then shouts 4 instead of 'banana', you go back to 1.

Safe Place – Facilitator-Guided Visualization

Using relaxation and visualization techniques can be helpful in grounding young people back into the present moment after a potentially triggering or distressing exercise. This can build coping skills and boost confidence to respond to a variety of situations calmly and rationally, and provide an internal safe space to help people regulate their emotions.

It certainly does not guarantee safety, but it may support people in being able to take risks that may be necessary for their development and enjoyment of life without being paralysed by fear or incapacitated by their survival brain.

Instructions

Ask the group to make themselves comfortable either on a chair or lying down on the floor – whatever feels most comfortable and safe for them and is most practical in the space you have available.

Suggest that they might find it helpful to close their eyes or alternatively concentrate on a fixed point in the room or their hands. Remind them that they don't have to take part in the exercise and that they have a choice, but invite them to be mindful not to disrupt the participation of their peers if they choose not to engage.

Read gently through the suggested script.

Script

Take three deep breaths. With each breath, fill your stomach and lungs with air, in through your nose so you can feel the air ballooning your belly. As you breathe out through your mouth, allow the air to flow out like water from a glass and empty your lungs and stomach.

Now just breathe normally and rhythmically, in and out.

Close your eyes or focus on a fixed point in the room such as your hands, letting the focus of your eyes go soft. Allow yourself to just become aware of your breath and your heartbeat.

In a moment I am going to ask you to remember, or imagine, a special place – somewhere you can feel or have felt safe. It's OK if you can't think of or remember a safe place; this could be an opportunity to start imagining one. Take a few deep breaths...

Breathe out the tension in your body.

Breathe in relaxation.

Breathe out the tension.

Breathe in relaxation.

When you are relaxed, imagine yourself moving towards this place that feels very special and safe to you. You are encouraged by those who know and love you to visit this wonderful place and experience the feelings of safety. The temperature is just right for you... You feel relaxed and comfortable... You have control.

Imagine yourself in this safe place, moving around it if you like, exploring and noticing what's around you [silently and slowly count to 20]...

See the colours [silently and slowly count to 10]...

Smell the smells in this safe place [count to 10 again]...

Listen to the sounds [count to 10]...

Taste the tastes [count to 10]...

What can you touch? [count to 10]...

Be aware of how you feel in this safe place [count to 10]... Do you notice any sensations in your body?

If your eyes are closed, keep them closed and, when you are ready, come back into this room, just with your ears, and notice a sound you hadn't heard before...

Now go back to your safe place [count to 10]...

Notice how you feel when you return [count to 10]...

See the colours [count to 10]...

Smell the smells [count to 10]...

Listen to the sounds [count to 10]...

Taste the tastes [count to 10]...

Now choose one of these images to remind you of your safe place. It may be a colour, a sound, a smell or a taste. Associate this image with feeling safe. With practice, you could return to this safe place any time you want... Now, when you are ready, come back into this room again just with your ears, hear the sounds... Then wriggle your toes and feel your feet on the floor.

Now think again of the image you have chosen as your safe place and quickly go back there, to that place where you feel safe and comfortable, where you can make decisions calmly. Enjoy this feeling for a few moments... [count to 20]

Now come back again into this room, first with your ears, and when you are ready, open your eyes if they have been closed and make a big smile.

Acknowledgements

Jamie Peto, Marguerite Wallis, Russell Jefferies, Jo Brown, Rupert Allison, Dan Charrington, Betty Martin, Iman Haji, Emily Wallis, Jessica Taylor, Sian Rowland, Alice Henley, the Schools Consent Project, The Training Effect, Safer London, Alison Brookman, the PSHA Consortium, Belinda Hopkins, Ben Lovatt, Mat Lister, Lisa Ward, Celeste Stevens, Sylwia Kieran and OSAAC, John White, Kiki Kingsland, Kristie Waller, Rachel Fitzsimmons, Maria Huffer and the Protective Behaviours Consortium, Carmen Chan, Joseph Wilkins, Chloe Purcell and everyone at SAFE!, Hollie Williams; pupils and students who have provided feedback on the materials including John Mason school, Faringdon Community College, Henry Box School, King Alfred's School, Ruskin College and Brookes University; Lisa Clark, James Cherry, Simeon Hance, Hannah Snetsinger and everyone at JKP.